COMPUTERS *and the* LAW

COMPUTERS
and the
LAW

SECOND
EDITION

DANA VAN DER MERWE
BJuris (UPE) LLB LLD (Unisa)

JUTA & CO, LTD

First published 1986
Second edition 2000

Juta & Co, Ltd
P O Box 14373, Kenwyn 7790

ISBN 0 7021 5087 8

Cover design by Joy Wrench

Typesetting by THE DESIGN HOUSE

Printed in the Republic of South Africa by Creda Communications, Eppindust, Cape Town

CONTENTS

INTRODUCTION

We have entered a stage of development where many traditional concepts have changed.

INTRODUCTION

(1) Progress

Thirteen years have elapsed since publication of the previous edition of *Computers and the Law*, at the time a pioneering work in South Africa, but now sadly outdated. At that time developments such as the Internet and electronic commerce were as yet unthought of. None the less, the computer still lies at the heart of most of these new technological wonders. The present work strives to bring the reader up to date with these developments. It also attempts to gauge the law's reaction, or lack of it. Another factor which has to be borne in mind is the fact that South Africa now has a Constitution[1] (with teeth) against which legislation can be tested.

The introduction to the first edition drew a distinction between informatics law (the problems which the use of computers pose to the law) and legal informatics (the ways in which computers assist the law). Except for this brief mention, legal informatics did not feature in that book. This omission will be rectified in the final chapter in the present edition, especially since the role of legal informatics has expanded dramatically and many law practices will begin to experience great difficulty in trying to carry on their work without the aid of computers. As a legal academic, I am also aware of the great potential that technology presents for legal research and teaching.

Most readers should be familiar with the concept of the Internet, the so-called 'network of networks', but perhaps a few words of explanation to our 'non-techie' readers will be in order. Originally developed by the US Department of Defence as a highly decentralized network that could not be knocked out by nuclear strikes, it has become the worldwide means of communication. The term 'Internet' describes the network itself, whereas the 'World Wide Web' describes the added layer of multimedia (graphics, animations, digitized sound and video). One therefore speaks of a 'Web site' which may contain 'Web pages' and is run by a 'webmaster'. The Internet's present 'killer application'[2] is probably electronic communication in the shape of electronic mail (e-mail) and, to a lesser extent, mailing lists[3] and Internet relay chat (IRC).[4] It has also been used for voice telephony, competing directly with established telephone services. The Internet spans the globe, connected by all kinds of communications technology: from

1 Act 108 of 1996.

2 The one application that makes a commercial success of the entire medium.

3 A type of subject-specific electronic debating society.

4 A communication system on the Internet where two or more users are logged on simultaneously and what is typed by one immediately appears on the screen of the other so that a 'dialogue' (or chat) is possible in real time.

satellite (expensive but fast), through cellular and microwave transmission and including plain old copper telephone cabling (inexpensive).

One of the buzzwords which will occur frequently in this work and therefore had better be explained immediately is 'electronic commerce' (hereinafter referred to as 'e-commerce'). E-commerce[5] roughly boils down to selling things 'electronically' by means of the Internet. Since there are no paper-based contracts and whole transactions are carried out electronically, this phenomenon has obvious implications for the law of contract and the law of evidence, to mention but two areas. The matter is also treated below in chapter 7 Mercantile Law Issues.

Another buzzword is the so-called 'convergence' of technologies. This has been defined as 'the merging of telephone, broadcasting and computing technologies, industries and cultures'.[6] Traditionally, a technology such as broadcasting, first on radio[7] and then on television, enabled communication between one party (the broadcaster) and any number of passive receivers within range of the broadcast. The whole regime could be governed in a legal sense by a 'Broadcasting Act',[8] which took into account the nature of the medium, its content, its technological restraints and possibilities and so on, and imposed a government monopoly. The same type of regime applies to telecommunications, which differs from broadcasting in that it deals more with interactive communication between two parties by means of telephone or two-way radio. Its governance is currently embodied in a 'Telecommunications Act'.[9] In its previous format, a 'Post Office Act'[10] and a 'Telegraph Messages Act'[11] took care of asynchronous[12] two-way communication. Content regulation applicable to traditional media such as films and books (as provided for by the Films and Publications Act[13]) seemed also to be adequate to deal with broadcasting and telecommunications.

---

5 Some people speak of a wider concept of 'e-business', which would include electronic commerce (e-commerce). See also (1999) 61 *THRHR* at 226ff.

6 In the Advanced Postgraduate Certificate Programme in Telecommunications and Information Policy (1997) offered by Unisa's Department of Communication, the School of Law, Macquarie University (Sydney) and the Communications Law Centre, University of New South Wales (Sydney) 74.

7 cf the old Radio Act 3 of 1952.

8 Act 73 of 1976, in itself a 'convergence' of the media of radio and television.

9 Act 103 of 1996. Although this Act is of comparatively recent vintage, it does not seem to take any cognizance of the existence of the Internet.

10 Act 44 of 1958.

11 Act 44 of 1963.

12 This means the message is not sent and received at (almost) the same time. A telegram was much more rapid than a letter, of course, but the telegram strips still had to pasted on to a sheet of paper, inserted into the famous orange envelope and delivered by bicycle to your home or office.

13 Act 65 of 1996. This seems to indicate that even publishing has become part of the stream of convergence on the Internet.

It is interesting to note that most of these media were regulated as independent state monopolies, being operated in the common interest but with a vague profit motive. Even in an Act of as recent a vintage as the Telecommunications Act,[14] s 3 specifically excludes broadcasting from its ambit:

> 'This Act shall not apply in relation to broadcasting, broadcasting signal distribution or broadcasting services frequency bands, except as provided in sections 28(3) and 127 to 129.'

(The exclusions refer to a joint liaison committee with the Independent Broadcasting Authority and to the amendment of certain sections in the Independent Broadcasting Authority Act.[15])

The Internet has changed all this. A user sitting at his or her desk is able to 'broadcast' his or her thoughts to the whole world in a simple and inexpensive way. Internet service providers are starting to compete with traditional telecommunication authorities in that they can provide alternative telephony services, usually at much lower rates. When two Internet users are involved in a 'realtime'[16] conversation on an Internet 'chatline', this takes the place of what would have been a telephone call. Great savings may be made in the cost of international communication, since one's Internet connections are made at local telephone rates.[17] Electronic mail (e-mail) is starting rapidly to replace the aptly named alternative: 'snail mail.' Since computers are only part of this new convergence of technologies, I seriously considered naming the present book something like 'High Technology Law'. Nevertheless, computers still form the very heart of the Internet and I therefore decided to retain the name *Computers and the Law* for reasons of brand loyalty as well as the fact that I did not have the space or time to deal with the administrative law which is really at the heart of these parastatal organizations. The remarks in the next paragraph will have to suffice in this regard.

(2) LEGAL CONVERGENCE?

A pertinent question for lawyers is whether technological convergence will also lead to legal convergence. Internationally one hears of previously nationalized telecoms being privatized and being run for profit. In South Africa, this has given rise to a dispute about control of the Internet between Telkom and the Internet

14 103 of 1996.

15 153 of 1993.

16 The opposite to 'asynchronous'. Here the message is sent and received at (almost) the same time.

17 This is probably the reason why Telkom South Africa is bringing down the cost of international calls, while hiking up the price of local calls. If, however, your nearest Internet service provider is a long-distance call away, you will pay that call charge in order to connect to the Internet.

Service Provider Association (ISPA), the latter consisting mostly of members of the private sector. Telkom itself has been 'privatized' and sold to a consortium of whom the major partners are Malaysia Telekom and Sprint (an American telecom service). According to the new Telecommunications Act,[18] Telkom has an exclusive right for five years to supply basic telecommunications services such as public switched telecommunications services,[19] national long- distance telecommunication services,[20] local access telecommunication services and public pay-telephone services.[21] ISPA disputes that the Internet is such a basic service and maintains that it is a value-added network service.[22] The matter came before the South African Telecommunication Regulatory Authority (SATRA) in October 1997 for a ruling and SATRA ruled in favour of ISPA. Telkom appealed this decision to the Transvaal High Court and yet again ISPA won its case. Telkom then appealed the case once more and at the time of writing the matter is still unresolved. Behind-the-scenes efforts to come to some kind of settlement have reportedly failed. Apparently one of the reasons for this breakdown in negotiations has been the use of Internet telephony, which Telkom argues is in contravention of s 40(3) of the Telecommunications Act:

> 'No person who provides a value-added network service shall permit that service to be used for the carrying of voice until a date to be fixed by the Minister by notice in the *Gazette*.'

Perhaps one way of dealing at the question of legal convergence is to have a look at the underlying values and philosophies brought to the fore by the Internet. Harley Wright, in an article entitled 'Law, Convergence and Communicative Values on the Net'[23] mentions the fact that technical convergence has led to calls for legal convergence. As stated above, 'convergence' has been defined as 'the merging of telephone, broadcasting and computing technologies, industries and cultures'. As also stated above, the most outstanding example of this convergence would be the Internet—the so-called 'network of networks' which runs on a personal computer, is connected by a piece of apparatus called a modem to the telephone network and enables a user to send text, images and even video to any other people connected to the Internet.

Wright mentions that there are two schools of thought with regard to the legal consequences of the technical convergence of media. The first group, led by Pool,[24]

18 103 of 1996.

19 Section 36.

20 Section 38.

21 Section 39.

22 Section 40.

23 (1996) 7 (1) *Journal of Law and Information Science* 54.

24 Ithiel de Sola Pool *Technologies of Freedom* (Belknap Press 1983) 8.

argue that technological convergence should lead to legal convergence. In other words, the relative freedom of speech that exists with regard to print media should be extended to the Internet, rather than trying to regulate the Internet on the same basis as broadcasting or telecommunications.[25] Pool fears that freedom of speech will be compromised with the increasing displacement of print by the electronic media.

The second group (which includes Wright himself) is led by Ethan Katsh.[26] He argues that all media should be regulated in terms of the communicative values involved, such as user control, access and privacy. This applies not only to the different technologies but even to different uses of the same technology such as the Internet:

> 'In a private Email conversation privacy is paramount; if downloading information (or entertainment) then user control is likely to be paramount.'[27]

This indicates that the physical form of technology employed is no longer as important as the use to which the technology is being put. Wright argues that in the case of political discussion, whether it be from a milk crate or on the Internet, few, if any, legal restrictions should be imposed on freedom of expression.

A strong argument may therefore be made out that regulation has to be imposed in terms of communicative values such as user control, access and privacy. Are these the only values involved with regard to information technology, however? What about the strong commercial value which has come to be attached to information in the 20th century?[28] And can communicative values be reconciled with legal values?

(3) WHAT ARE INFORMATION AND THE 'INFORMATION SOCIETY'?

This issue has already been broached in the previous edition of *Computers and the Law*, in the form of an inquiry into the legal status of information. At the time of writing the present edition, this matter has still not been resolved. In the previous edition I argued that information was probably the most valuable asset in the present-day commercial world, and yet our law is structured around physical goods:

---

25 This does seem to be a limited view of 'convergence' however, limiting it to convergence between print media and the Internet and excluding telecommunications and broadcasting.

26 Ethan M Katsh *Law in a Digital World* (Oxford University Press 1995).

27 Harley Wright (1996) 7 (1) *Journal of Law and Information Science* 63.

28 This matter is explored further in the following section.

> 'In my opinion it is exactly this lack of appreciation of the value of information which bedevils our present goods-based law and which has been exposed by the appearance of computers upon the scene. For instance, the only thing that may be stolen, according to even the current definitions of theft, is a movable corporeal object. This means that not only information but even the twentieth-century concept of money lacks protection by the criminal law!'[29]

This ticklish issue has also been researched by Tertius Geldenhuys for his doctoral thesis 'Die Regsbeskerming van Inligting'.[30] He follows the doctrine of subjective rights and their accompanying competencies first popularized in South Africa by W A Joubert[31] and applies this to the protection of information. This long-held foundation of all legal debate from the Afrikaans universities has been challenged recently, specifically because of its insistence that the law of things ('sakereg') confine its attention to material, movable things, thus leaving all immaterial things, from electricity to information, to be handled by the law of immaterial property. The first such challenge came from the present writer in an article entitled 'Diefstal van Onliggaamlike Sake met Spesifieke Verwysing na Rekenaars'.[32] Here I argued that the problem of 'theft of information' was not really a problem of criminal law, but that it had originated from the failure of private law, notably the law of things, to deal adequately with immaterial things. This was followed by Duard Kleyn's contribution to the 1992 edition of *Silberberg and Schoeman's The Law of Property*[33] as well as L C Coetzee's 'Die Rol van die Onstoflike Saak in die Sakereg'[34] and, finally, an article by Kleyn entitled 'Dogmatiese probleme rakende die rol van onstoflike sake in die sakereg'.[35] Kleyn argues that the concept of 'thing' should be extended to 'anything whether corporeal or incorporeal that is of use and of value to man and which is regarded as *in commercio*'.

At any rate, I wish to confine the debate, at the present stage,[36] to the concepts defined by Geldenhuys relating to information. He did this in Afrikaans, which might make the following discussion a bit tricky, since something might be lost

---

29 Dana van der Merwe *Computers and the Law* 1 ed (Juta 1986) viii.

30 Translated as 'The Protection of Information by Law' (unpublished LLD thesis, Unisa 1993).

31 See his articles in (1958) 21 *THRHR* at 12ff and 98ff.

32 Translated as 'Theft of Immaterial Goods with Specific Reference to Computers' (1985) 9 SACC 129.

33 D G Kleyn & Boraine *Silberberg and Schoeman's The Law of Property* 3 ed (Butterworths 1992) chapter 2.

34 Translated as 'The Role of the Immaterial Thing in the Law of Things' (unpublished LLB thesis, University of Pretoria 1992).

35 Translated as 'Dogmatical problems with regard to the role of immaterial things in the law of Things' in (1993) vol 26 *De Jure* 1ff.

36 The matter is discussed further in chapter 4 Private Law below.

in my translations. His definition of 'inligting' (information) is rather long and runs (freely translated) as follows:

> 'Information is any representation (... "voorstelling") of facts relating to any subject or object, which representation
>
> (1) is perceptible by the senses or can be converted into a form perceptible by the senses;
>
> (2) carries on a virtual ("onstoflike") and distinct existence, separate from that to which the facts which it represents, relate;
>
> (3) has the potential to apprize ("op die hoogte te stel") a person who perceives it with his senses, of the facts which it represents, even though that to which the facts relate is not perceptible to the senses of the person, either not at all, or not at that moment;
>
> (4) has the potential to be duplicated an infinite number of times, either by copying the same representation or by compiling other representations of the same facts, and by supplying such representations to one or more persons, enabling such persons to be apprized ("op die hoogte te kom") of the facts which are represented thereby, without the person supplying, relinquishing ("daarvan afstand doen") through the process of supplying, any knowledge ("kennis") concerning the facts represented by such representation;
>
> (5) in the case of a mental representation ("geestesvoorstelling"), cannot be removed from a person, without a serious infringement of the physical or mental integrity of the person in whose mind the representation took place.' [37]

He then distinguishes information from certain related concepts, such as fact ('feit'), knowledge ('kennis') and data (he also distinguishes between 'gegewens' and 'data'[38]). Facts are distinguished from information in that many facts have been and gone without ever having been represented to human perception. Because these facts are now gone forever, they are no longer even capable of such representation and can therefore never qualify as information in terms of the definition above. (One assumes that facts which have so been represented may then carry on a simultaneous existence with the 'information' they have given rise to.)[39] Knowledge comes right at the end of the feeding chain, according to Geldenhuys, since it presupposes a person to whom the representation actually has been made, this process thus converting the information into knowledge. Information may therefore be conceptually separated from knowledge in that it represents facts

---

37 Geldenhuys op cit 59.

38 See below.

39 Because they have the potential still to become somebody else's information.

which have not yet come to the perception of anyone, but still has the potential to do so.[40] (Again one assumes that facts which have come to the notice of someone may then carry on a simultaneous existence with both 'information' and 'knowledge'.) Geldenhuys then distinguishes 'gegewens' from 'data' in that 'gegewens', like knowledge, presupposes actual perception by someone. (Unperceived 'data' would then presumably be exactly the same thing as unperceived 'facts' in that it may also vanish from all possibility of human perception and therefore never amount to 'information'.) Human perceptibility seems to play a major role in the Geldenhuys hierarchy.

An interesting counterpoint to the above is a speech by Tony Twine (of Econometrix) at a conference on *Knowledge Management—overcoming the information overload*.[41] He arranges the concepts we have been discussing thus far in an ascending order of 'data', 'information', 'knowledge' and 'wisdom'. The concept of 'intelligence' works as a catalyst on the other four, transforming, say, data to information, information to knowledge and knowledge to wisdom. He then argues that among the four factors of production resources, namely land, capital, labour and entrepreneurship, only the last factor possesses the intelligence to 'process' the other factors: 'He who owns the Intelligence is king!'. This intriguing argument echoes the distinctions made by Alvin Toffler[42] with regard to land being the main commodity of the Agricultural Revolution (the so-called 'First Wave'), capital and labour being the main commodities of the Industrial Revolution (the 'Second Wave') and information being the main commodity of the Information Revolution (the 'Third Wave').

Personally, I have found it very instructive simply to consult the *Concise Oxford Dictionary*[43] for clarity on these confusing and often overlapping concepts.[44] It defines 'datum'[45] as 'facts or information, especially as a basis for inference; quantities or characters operated on by computers'. (It is worrying that two of the other concepts we are concerned to distinguish from 'data', namely 'facts' and 'information', are used, in fact, to define data itself.)

The *Concise Oxford Dictionary* further defines 'fact' as a 'thing *certainly* known to have occurred or be true; datum of *experience*, thing used as a basis for inference.[46] This brings to light an interesting contrast to the Geldenhuys definition above.

---

40 If the potential were lacking, it would no longer be 'information', but mere 'facts'.

41 Held at Kyalami, Gauteng on 5 August 1998.

42 Alvin Toffler *The Third Wave* (Pan Books 1980).

43 Seventh edition 1983.

44 Note that the full published definition, in all its senses, is not used, but only those parts relevant to the present discussion.

45 'Datum' is simply the Latin singular form for 'data'.

46 My emphasis.

Instead of focusing on the potential 'knowability' by man (or woman), the distinguishing feature of 'fact' seems to be its reliability, the fact that it can be vouched for by experience.

'Knowledge' is defined as 'knowing, familiarity gained by experience; person's range of information'. This seems to presuppose a broader category of 'information', which becomes 'knowledge' when it becomes part of a particular individual's 'range of information', often by experience. (Perhaps it could also be argued that every person has some knowledge which he knows to be reliable, since he has had personal experience of it—but also has some knowledge which has only been reported to him and is therefore untested?)

'Information' is defined as 'knowledge, (desired) items of knowledge, news;' Read with the definition of 'knowledge' it would again seem to be centered around a specific person's spectrum of knowledge (range of information), but to go further than that by including desired items of knowledge. Information therefore implies a potential marketability, which will be reverted to below when the so-called 'commodification of information' is dealt with.

'Wisdom' is defined as '(possession of) experience and knowledge together with the power of applying them critically or practically, sagacity, prudence, common sense'. Again it is interesting to note the association between experience and knowledge, but even more significant is the distinguishing characteristic of wisdom, namely the power to apply these 'critically or practically'. This almost sounds like the 'intelligence' which Twine spoke of above, as a factor enhancing the others. It also brings to mind the quote from Kahlil Gibran: 'A little knowledge that acts is worth infinitely more than much knowledge that is idle.'

The *Concise Oxford Dictionary* defines 'intelligence' as 'intellect, understanding, quickness of understanding, sagacity; information (especially of military value)'. Taking the last meaning of 'intelligence', namely in its military sense, it would again seem to indicate that information usually has the characteristic of being desired by, and of potential use to, someone. Taking the first meaning of 'intelligence' it becomes clear that Twine should perhaps rather have used the term 'wisdom' instead of 'intelligence' as the catalyst in his scheme. Understanding something cognitively does not necessarily bring with it the conative ability to also act upon it critically or practically. This interpretation also fits in well with the pecking order in Bloom's *Taxonomy of Educational Objectives*,[47] in which evaluation is rated as one of the highest skills and mere understanding as one of the lowest. In Werner Gitt's *In the Beginning was Information*,[48] the author progresses from a mere signal to an understandable code (syntax), to meaning

47 B S Bloom *Taxonomy of Educational Objectives: the Classification of Educational Goals* (Longmans 1984).

48 Werner Gitt *In the Beginning was Information* (CLV Publishers 1997) 111.

(semantics), to pragmatics (action) to apobetics (achieved result). Thus, acting effectively with critical insight is the ideal end-result of information.

To recap, this book will deal with the following definition of information: '(desired) items of knowledge, news.' In order to understand this definition we shall also have to standardize on a definition of knowledge, namely as: 'a (personal) range of information.' Reading the two definitions together, we find that information (or news) is something that is desired and which can be collected by, and fall within the range of, a particular person.

A further perspective on the precise meaning of 'information' as well as of the so-called 'information society' is given in an unpublished lecture by Sandra Braman entitled 'New Information Technologies and the Making, Interpretation and Implementation of the Law'.[49] She mentions that 'information' is being used in four senses these days, namely as a resource, as a commodity, as perceptual patterns and as a constitutive force in society. Perceptual patterns probably have to do with the cognitive aspects of understanding and societal aspects have to do with the Information Society to which we shall presently come. The word 'commodity' is also of great import because of a phrase which the speaker explains further in one of her written works, namely the 'commodification of information'.[50] According to Braman, the first stage[51] began in the middle of the 19th century and consisted of the electrification of communication. The second began in the late 20th century and has been characterized by the convergence of technologies and the awareness of the centrality of information to society. As the title indicates, the third stage consists of the harmonization of systems:

> '[C]ommunication systems with each other (eg linkage of broadcasting systems with telecommunications systems), national communication systems with those across borders (eg linkage of broadcasting systems internationally through shared ownership, production, and/or regional or global distribution) and communication systems with other social systems (eg the transformation of finance into a system of international information flows, or the dependence of just-in-time manufacturing, production, and distribution upon the telecommunications network). Harmonization has been dependent on the increased capacity, speed and ubiquity of the global information infrastructure, on the mobility of its intelligence, and on its geodesic (nonhierarchical) nature.'[52]

---

49 Delivered at the University of South Africa on 10 February 1998.

50 'Harmonization of Systems: The Third Stage of the Information Society' Summer 1993 *Journal of Communication*.

51 This classification forms an interesting counterpoint to the three 'waves' of Alvin Toffler—see above.

52 P Huber *The Geodesic Network: 1987 Report on Competition in the Telephone Industry* (United States Department of Justice 1987), as cited in Braman's article.

This harmonization (especially internationally) will prove to be a recurring theme through the remainder of the present work. Also interesting in Braman's article, however, is the fact that commodification of information already started in the first phase of the Information Society. According to Braman this commodification was the result of changes in organizational form brought about by the electrification of communications and by news agency treatment of news[53] as property. During the second stage (convergence) 'economists began to see information as the driving force of a new stage of societal development, following agricultural and industrial eras'.[54] Also, 'many ... argued and argue that economics must be rethought in order to deal with the intangibility of information'.[55]

To sum up, it seems to me that we have entered upon a stage of development (whether we call it an 'information society', or not) where many traditional concepts have changed. When we speak of a 'commodification of information', the *Concise Oxford Dictionary's* definition of both those terms should be kept in mind. A 'commodity' is 'a useful thing, article of trade, 'product' as opposed to 'service'. Thus we are now trading in information). We have considered above the *Concise Oxford Dictionary's* definition of 'information' and it seems to me, in the end, to be a concept distinguished by the fact that it has potential marketability.

Our law is, at present, not geared towards meeting this development. Private law (in the shape of the law of things) seems to have abdicated all its responsibilities with regard to 'information' and other intangibles to the law of intellectual property. This could lead to a withering away not only of the law of things, but also of criminal law, which is dependent upon the former for an idea of the 'things' which may be stolen.

One should also try to find out in what legal sense the word 'information' is being used. In the United Kingdom's section under Trade Secrets below, a distinction is made between personal information (involving privacy issues), government information (involving security issues) and trade secrets (which involve commercial issues.) The last field is likely to drive legal development the fastest. However, privacy issues and commercial issues may often be in conflict with each other and the law will have to reconcile the constituents behind these two types of information. In South Africa privacy issues may seem likely to come out on top because of the protection of individual's right to privacy in the Constitution,[56] but another

---

53 Remember that news has been defined as part of 'information' above. Braman's statement might thus be translated into a declaration that information may be seen as property.

54 Op cit 135. See, for instance, the views of Toffler discussed above (although he is more of a futurologist than an economist!).

55 Ibid.

56 Section 14 of Act 108 of 1996, which includes 'privacy of communications'.

section protects the right to a 'trade, occupation or profession'.[57] In the end, the Constitutional Court may have to be called in to resolve this issue. It is also worth noting that s 32 provides for a right of access to information as against the government and that legislation has to be passed to give effect to this right. A so-called 'Freedom of Information Act' has been drafted but at the time of writing has not yet become law.

Partly as a result of this lack of appreciation of immaterial goods by the law and partly as a result of a lack of the necessary technological insight on the part of magistrates and judges, many civil matters are hived off to methods of alternative dispute resolution, such as mediation and arbitration. At least the parties can contract for a technologically literate person to conduct the arbitration and they may therefore also hope for the necessary insight into the exact nature of their problem. The problem again is that this alternative is not available in criminal matters. Also, because of the legality principle, courts are unlikely to extend analogically crimes such as theft, malicious injury to property and even trespassing to encompass criminal threats to information. For many activities which have been criminalized overseas, such as hacking and the planting of a computer virus, the possibilities of a successful prosecution in South Africa are uncertain.[58]

Finally, the phrase 'Information Society' should also be treated with care. In the first place, information has become a valuable commodity which is being traded to an increasing extent. Secondly, the market-place is becoming virtual[59] and thereby international. This means that legal solutions will have to become internationally viable. Thirdly, the currency we are using to trade with has long ago dematerialized. It has simply taken these latest, extreme developments to show us that this has, in fact, happened, again with serious repercussions for the law of things, as well as for criminal law. These matters will be further explored in the relevant chapters below.

(4) Y2K—THE MILLENNIUM BUG

One of the most serious threats presented to the Information Society may be constituted in the so-called Y2K problem,[60] also known as the millennium bug (since it will first show itself on 1 January 2000).[61] Owing to the scarcity of memory during

57 Section 22.

58 The South African Law Commission has recently published an Issue Paper with regard to possible legislation against computer crime: see www.lawcomm.co.za.

59 For instance, by means of the Internet.

60 'Y' stands for year and 'K' for a thousand—therefore the 'Year two thousand' problem.

61 Although some people feared that it might start showing its effects even earlier, owing to year-long periods starting in 1999, and expressed as '99/00', being read as 1999/1900.

the early days of computers the first two digits of a year were hard-coded as '191', so that only the last two digits could be changed to read 1956, 1957, etc.

Human nature being what it is, most people who had a grasp of the full implications of Y2K have left fixing the problem very late and it is being increasingly predicted that not everything will be fixed in time. There are only a limited number of computer professionals available to work on the problem, which is a worldwide phenomenon. In South Africa, a book has been devoted to the legal situation surrounding the Y2K problem, namely Lance Michalson's *South Africa and the Millennium Time Bomb*.[62] Reference will be made to this work in the appropriate chapters below.

Unfortunately, the Y2K problem may prove to have much more than just legal implications. In *Time Bomb 2000*[63] (which is much more factual than the title may sound) the authors analyse the possibilities not only of computers breaking down on 1 January 2000 but also our losing (at least temporarily) many of life's other necessities: because of the impact on municipal services ('utilities'), our electricity and water may be cut off; because of the embedded microchips many pieces of equipment which seem totally unrelated to computers (such as motor cars, lifts, alarm systems and medical pacemakers) may cease to function reliably. The authors analyse scenarios in which these services are interrupted for two days, one month, one year and ten years respectively. Although this field lies beyond computer law and touches more upon civil defence, the matter is mentioned here as a reminder to readers to take reasonable precautions, physically and legally.

In *Computerrecht*[64] the valid point is made that trade secret and copyright protection actually hinder a solution to the Y2K problem, because the licence agreements of most software packages prohibit licensees from altering the source code of the program. Even worse, in many cases the source code is not available. In a later issue, Jos Du Mortier and Wendi Hoeben analyse the whole Y2K phenomenon thoroughly.[65] At the moment many anxious businesses are asking their suppliers to provide them with written statements of Y2K compliance. The suppliers, on the other hand, are hesitant to do this—both because they are not very compliant yet and/or because such guarantees might lead to contractual and delictual liability if they proved to be hollow. Again, these attitudes do not contribute much towards a solution. Du Mortier & Hoeben remark upon the fact that people are more intent on avoiding possible legal liability for Y2K than on finding a solution to the actual problem itself.

---

62 Lance Michalson *South Africa and the Millenium Time Bomb: a Guide to the Legal Issues* (Franklin 1998)—just in time to warn us!

63 E Yourdon & J Yourdon *Time Bomb 2000* (Prentice Hall 1998).

64 (1998) 6 *Computerrecht* 261.

65 (1999) *Computerrecht* 22.

In this regard, cognizance should be taken of the American Year 2000 Information Readiness Act,[66] an example of 'Good Samaritan legislation' encouraging people to exchange information about their Y2K readiness by extinguishing any liability which might have been incurred by such statements. This means that South African users of American software should not rely too much on possible legal recourse arising out of assurances from their suppliers, since these might possibly be brought under the protection of the American Act.

The whole matter will be touched upon further in chapter 3 Private Law below, where Michalson's views will also be discussed.

66 Passed on 19 October 1998.

CHAPTER ONE

PATENT

It stems from an era where everything was technical and tangible and money could be made from later manufacture.

1 PATENT

This is the first part of an entire division of the law—the law of intellectual property. Others are the law of copyright, trade mark law, design law, competition law and the law of trade secrets. As will be shown, each has its own strong and weak points with regard to the protection of computer hardware and software. Traditionally, patent is supposed to protect ideas (provided that they are original), as against copyright, which protects only the concrete expression of ideas. As will be shown below, the law of trade secrets is probably even more effective than patent in protecting ideas, at least over a long period of time. The secret formulas of Coca-Cola and Chartreuse liquor are still bringing in profit, whereas a patent in either would have expired long ago.

If the law could have developed in such a way that all protection of goods by means of the criminal and private law had not been focused upon tangible goods, the law of intellectual property might not even have been necessary. Nevertheless, the latter field has coped manfully with the problems the law faces in protecting so-called 'intellectual' or intangible property. Coped, that is, until the advent of the computer and the Information Age. The fact that the law of intellectual property is the only legal protection for what has grown to be one of the most valuable assets of the century, namely information,[1] has placed some strain on the system.

1.1 THE RELATIONSHIP BETWEEN PATENT AND THE OTHER FIELDS OF INTELLECTUAL PROPERTY

After the pioneering South African decision of *Northern Office Micro Computers v Rosenstein*,[2] Coenraad Visser contrasted the protection offered by patent, copyright and trade secret with regard to software:

> 'Each has its advantages and its disadvantages, its strengths and its weaknesses, each proceeds upon its own conceptual and jurisprudential basis rendering its governance under each head more or less appropriate and more or less desirable. At present the protection offered by patent law is at best very uncertain, and currently greater reliance tends to be placed upon copyright in situations where it is proposed to market a program to the general computer-using public, and upon trade secrets when the program can be kept secret or, failing that, divulged upon a confidential basis to a very few.'[3]

1 The question also arises whether 'information' can be the conceptual hold-all that enables the law to cope with the dematerialization of goods.

2 1981 (4) SA 123 (C).

3 *Computerweek* 23 November 1985 at 10.

This quotation was borrowed from the first edition of the classic British work on computer law by Tapper.[4] In the most recent version of his work[5] Tapper elaborates further upon the relationship between the law of intellectual property (in its various branches) and computers:

> 'Computers pose special problems to the law of intellectual property because they are not, like other machines, merely the product of human intellect, but in addition mimic its functions.'

Tapper states further that the diversification of parties in present-day commerce has made the law of contract less useful in overcoming some of the uncertainties associated with computers and law. To this, one might add that e-commerce is specifically meant to be a storefront 'open to the world', where little opportunity exists for one-on-one bargaining before the deal is struck electronically. Accordingly, there is very little chance of negotiating an intricate contract with lots of legal niceties, except on a 'take it or leave it' basis.

Even worse, the fact that many magistrates and judges are not computer literate also makes the result of any litigation flowing from disregard of contractual provisions uncertain, to say the least.[6] These contractual problems are addressed in more detail in chapter 4 Private Law below.

Be that as it may, it seems clear that the law has put almost all its eggs in one basket as far as the protection of intangibles is concerned. That basket is the law of intellectual property.

In the latest version of his work, Tapper makes the following apposite remarks on the precise relationship between patent and copyright in computer context:

> 'A major complicating factor is the increased importance of software in the market place which creates serious conceptual problems for the two major planks of the law of intellectual property, patent and copyright. In brief and crude terms the law of patent has traditionally protected the inventor by granting him a limited monopoly over the exploitation of his invention; and the law of copyright has traditionally protected the writer, by granting him an exclusive right to reproduce his work.'[7]

The author follows this up with a more 'negative' test for distinguishing between the different application areas of patent and copyright with regard to computer programs:

---

4 Colin Tapper *Computer Law* 1 ed (Longman 1978) xxiii.

5 Colin Tapper *Computer Law* 4 ed (Longman 1989) 1.

6 One way out of this specific problem is to contract for alternative dispute-resolution, as explained in the Introduction to the present work.

7 Tapper op cit 2.

> 'On the one hand the law of patent may be said to be inappropriate to protect such sets of instructions which seem in principle more akin to literary works; and on the other the law of copyright may be said to be inappropriate to cater for the means of controlling machines.'[8]

Later on, Tapper also distinguishes the fields of trade secret, breach of confidence (which in the United Kingdom is almost, but not quite, the same thing) and the law of competition. Amongst these, Tapper differentiates between the fields of trade secret and competition in that trade secrets have a more proprietary nature, whereas the law of competition is based more on delict. There is much overlapping, however:

> 'For all of these reasons the law in this area defies simple conceptual characterization. It cannot be explained or understood solely in terms of contract, property or confidence.'[9]

Differentiating these fields from patent and copyright, Tapper finds the role of legislation 'muted' in the case of trade secret, breach of confidence and competition. With other factors, this gives the area more flexibility and room for innovation which might help make it more suitable for dealing with a new field such as computers and law.

Distinguishing between extreme cases of patent and copyright is easy, as the following example illustrates:

> 'A document setting out a novel chemical process would attract copyright protection, but that protection would protect the document against copying not the process from being carried out. A patent for the process would prevent it from being carried out but not from being written about or broadcast.'[10]

This fits in with Tapper's equation above of patent with processes or machines and of copyright with artistic works. The problem with computer programs and with information in general, however, is that it does not fit easily into either the categories of machine or artistic work. This difficult fit will become apparent from some of the case law discussed below. By focusing so hard on physical industrial machines and processes[11] (patent) and on artistic creations (copyright), these two fields now find it hard to regulate the general trade in intangible goods and information and electronic commerce which has been entrusted to them.

8 Ibid.

9 Op cit 78.

10 Chris Reed (ed) *Computer Law* (Blackstone Press 1996) 192.

11 Typical assets from the Industrial Revolution. Alvin Toffler in *The Third Wave* (Pan Books 1981) contrasts this (as the 'Second Wave') with the Information Revolution, which he calls the 'Third Wave'.

Armed with this (very basic) background on the law of intellectual property, the reader should be able to follow the arguments and notice the overlaps when dealing with the next few headings.

1.2 PATENTING COMPUTER HARDWARE[12]

We have seen above (in the comparison between patent and copyright) that copyright is deemed to be inappropriate to cater for 'the means of controlling machines' and therefore, by implication, that patent is the proper vehicle to achieve this purpose. This inference is borne out by experience. Patent, with its 'limited monopoly', has proven to be one of the most effective ways legally to protect computer hardware.

In fact, ENIAC[13] (the very first computer) was patented, but all kinds of problems arose from that patent.[14] The first proper computer was really invented by a professor John Vincent Atanasoff of Iowa State University, who had developed a prototype electronic[15] computer in 1938 in co-operation with a graduate student, Clifford Berry. It was later named the Atanasoff Berry Computer (ABC). From 13 to 18 June 1941 a rival scientist, John W Mauchly, visited Atanasoff, exchanged ideas and started work on his own computer. In 1946 Mauchly and J Presper Eckert Jr, a colleague at the University of Pennsylvania, started their own commercial computer enterprise, the Electronic Control Company, which was later incorporated as the Eckert-Mauchly Computer Corporation. They filed patents in ENIAC in 1947. In 1950 Remington Rand acquired Eckert-Mauchly and the rights to the ENIAC patent, which eventually passed to Sperry Rand as a result of a merger between Sperry and Remington Rand.

---

12 Although it seems less likely than with the first edition of this book, 13 years ago, there may still be some lawyers around who are baffled by the distinction between 'hardware' and 'software'. Perhaps the closest analogy might be found in the distinction between a CD-player and the music on a compact disk. The computer, its keyboard, disk drives, printer, etc may be seen as the machinery (or 'hardware') in the shape of the CD-player which plays the compact disk. The disk itself contains the 'software' in the form of musical data. This is the equivalent of computer software which when inserted into the computer, transforms it into a wordprocessor or workstation (or play station). It should be borne in mind that the instructions to the computer contained on the disk form the true software and not the container or receptacle (the physical disk) by means of which it is introduced into the computer.

13 Acronym for 'electronic numeral integrator and calculator'.

14 The following piece of computer patent history comes from the Internet itself (the world's biggest library) at http://www.cbi.umn.edu/inv/sperry72.html.

15 Atanasoff's electronic 'pulse' principle (eg '01 101 101', representing electronic digital on-off switches within the computer) should be distinguished from the 'differential analyzer' built by Vannevar Bush at MIT (Massachusetts Institute for Technology). The latter worked on 'analog' or mechanical principles.

In co-operation with Atanasoff, the Honeywell company instituted action against Sperry Rand in 1971 in what was to be the very first computer-law case.[16] It lasted for nearly five years—-one of the longest cases in the history of the federal courts in the United States. At the trial, Mauchly abandoned his previous position—-that he had only seen Atanasoff's machine in 1941 'in a very poor light and with the cover on'. The court found that during his visit he had witnessed operations of the ABC, had read Atanasoff's 35-page manuscript on the construction and the operation of the ABC, immediately after his visit had written letters to a friend[17] and to Atanasoff expressing enthusiasm about the ABC and had taken a crash course in electronics at the University of Pennsylvania immediately afterwards. Atanasoff himself testified that he had explained to Mauchly:

> 'the base-two number system, the process of solving linear simultaneous equations, the timing mechanisms and synchronization of the ABC, the capacitor memories and readers, a one-cycle switch, the circuits and devices for automatic operation, and the subject of ring counter and racheting and the logic circuits.'[18]

The case finally ended on 13 March 1972. Larson J ruled that Mauchly's ideas were not original but derived from Atanasoff. In an interesting sideshow, the judge also ruled that a 1956 agreement between Sperry Rand and IBM was a 'conspiracy in restraint of trade'—an unlawful monopoly on this side of the Atlantic. (This seems to be almost a foreshadow of the proceedings which the Department of Justice is undertaking against Microsoft for allegedly the same kind of thing.) In emotive language the Internet reporter sums up his view of the proceedings:

> 'Judge Larson had ruled that John Vincent Atanasoff and Clifford Berry had constructed the first electronic digital computer at Iowa State College in the 1939—1942 period. He had also ruled that John Mauchly and J Presper Eckert, who had for more than twenty-five years been fêted, trumpeted, and honored as the co-inventors of the first electronic digital computer, were not entitled to the patent upon which that honor was based. Furthermore, Judge Larson had ruled that Mauchly had pirated

---

16 *Honeywell v Sperry Rand and Illinois Scientific Instruments* (Minnesota District, 4th Div, 4-67-Civ 138).

17 Although the Sperry Rand lawyer objected to the friend's letter as hearsay, it was obviously tendered circumstantially (to prove that it was actually written, leaving the court to make its own deductions concerning this fact) and not testimonially (to prove the truth of the contents). The latter would have been hearsay evidence, and therefore inadmissible.

18 Again from the Internet at http://www.scl.ameslab.gov/ABC/Trial.html.

> Atanasoff's ideas, and for more than thirty years had palmed those ideas off on the world as the product of his own genius.'[19]

Notwithstanding the fate of the ENIAC patent (which was invalid since the invention was not original), the law of patent does seem to be the best way of protecting computer hardware. Major computer manufacturers such as IBM[20] and Compaq make extensive use of the law of patent to protect their research and development in computer hardware. The conventional distinction between patent and copyright is that patent protects the idea, whereas copyright protects the expression of that idea. For the moment, this may be accepted, but the arguments underlying this statement will be re-examined when copyright is dealt with. Another distinction is that patent provides a monopoly for a limited period in return for publication of the idea (after which it falls into the common domain), whereas copyright lasts much longer than the life of the author, but is far from providing a monopoly (or even watertight protection).

The above distinction is well illustrated by the following quotations from two United States decisions. *Brown Instruments v Warren*[21] gave rise to the following statement: 'Both law and policy forbid monopolizing a machine except within the comparatively narrow limits of the patent system.' From *Brief English Systems Inc v Owen*[22] comes: 'The way to obtain the exclusive property right to an art, as distinguished from a description of the art, is by letter patent and not by copyright.'

Of course, there are certain procedural drawbacks in obtaining a patent. It takes time and money to register a patent with the Registrar of Patents in Pretoria and the applicant has to disclose many particulars concerning his or her brainchild. The disclosure means that he or she will no longer be able to make use of the law of trade secrets, since the product specifications have to be published in the monthly *Patent Journal* as part of the process.[23]

Furthermore, a patentable invention also has to comply with the two requirements of novelty and non-obviousness. Briefly, novelty[24] means that the product should not form part of the state of the art in the sense that it has been made available to the public before, whether in the Republic of South Africa or elsewhere. This entails a search through the patent journals of other countries,

---

19 Ibid.

20 IBM was granted the most US patents for the sixth consecutive year in 1998. With 2 682 patents, the company topped its 1997 numbers by about 40%. The No 2 receiver of US patents was Canon Inc of Japan (*Los Angeles Times* 11 January 1999).

21 161 F 2d 910 (DC Cir 1947).

22 48 F 2d 555 (2d Cir 1931).

23 Section 14 of the Patents Act 57 of 1978.

24 Section 25(1) of the South African Patents Act 57 of 1978 speaks of 'any new invention'. The corresponding factor in the United States sank Mauchly's abortive patent in the computer, as described above.

a process which used to be lengthy and expensive, but which may now be speeded up by virtue of the fact that computer searches are becoming available.

Non-obviousness[25] means that there had to be an 'inventive step' on the part of the applicant—the new product should not have been so obvious that a person skilled in the art would naturally have tried that solution. Once these intrinsic hurdles have been passed, another extrinsic hurdle remains—the product must be 'useful' or capable of being applied in trade, industry or agriculture.[26]

In the final analysis, the monopoly granted by patent does provide strong protection to hardware which you have invented. It means that even a competitor who had arrived at the same solution quite independently would be precluded from manufacturing his product without your licence, provided that your product had been registered earlier.

1.3 PATENTING FIRMWARE AND SOFTWARE

1.3.1 Firmware

Most of the considerations mentioned with regard to hardware above apply also to 'firmware'. The latter basically comes down to a program, or series of instructions to a computer, which is not conveyed to the computer by means of tape, disk or serial port, but is built in to a semi-conductor chip which usually forms part of the computer. The startup sequence of a computer is usually built into its ROM (read-only memory) chips and the computer can therefore do its boot-up sequence without accessing its disk drives. When this is finished, it then loads the operating system, usually from the hard disk where it was stored during primary installation. One main distinction between 'firmware' and software is that firmware is usually 'hard-wired', that is, the program cannot be changed or erased as it would have been as software.[27]

This combination of program and processor is built into a great number of 'smart' machines and appliances. Users are usually blissfully unaware that their machinery is operating by courtesy of a computer until something unpleasant such as the 'Y2K problem' comes along. This is computer shorthand for the 'Year 2000 problem', which is set to strike many computers on 1 January 2000. The point has been mentioned above in the introduction and the legal implications are discussed more fully below in chapter 4 Private Law. For present purposes it may be noted that one of the major areas which is considered to be particularly vulnerable is that of 'embedded software', in other words, firmware.

---

25 Section 25(1) of Act 57 of 1978.

26 Section 25(1) of Act 57 of 1978.

27 With the exception of PROM 'programmable read-only memory') and EPROM ('erasable programmable read-only memory') chips.

In the United States, a patent claim for a piece of firmware was submitted to the Supreme Court in *Diamond v Bradley*[28] and a prior grant of the application by the CCPA (Court of Copyright and Patent Appeals). According to Hilary Pearson, this could give rise to problems further down the line:

> 'One possible problem that could arise if a piece of firmware is patented on the basis of what it does rather that how it does it is whether such a patent could be infringed by use of functionally equivalent software, even though expressed differently and in a different medium, eg on a disc.[29]

The United States has solved the problem with the Semiconductorchip Protection Act of 1984. This type of protection amalgamates design and patent and actually focuses on something called the 'mask', or rather a 'mask work', since this embodies the design which is later transferred onto the microchip by means of a masking process. Provision is made for a system of registration without inspection, which gives the registrant a rebuttable presumption in favour of the validity of his registration, which may only be overcome by evidence. In South Africa, this type of protection has specifically been provided for by means of the Designs Act,[30] as will be seen below.

1.3.2 Software

(1) Patenting of software in the United States

The United States seems to have taken the lead with regard to the patenting of computer programs. This might be an indication of the tremendous commercial importance which is attached to software in that country, but less reverent observers ascribe it to the notorious litigiousness of the Americans! Keeping in mind the typical application area for copyright (artistic creative work) and for patent ('controlling machines') respectively, it does sound unwarranted for something more analogous to writing to be patentable.

The idea behind the patent system is, according to the Constitution of the United States of America:

> 'To promote the Progress of Science and useful Arts, by securing for limited Times for Authors and Inventors the exclusive Right to their respective Writings and Discoveries.'[31]

The original Patent Act of 1793 was authored by Thomas Jefferson. Although he did not like monopolies, he supported the grant of temporary monopoly power to inventors of useful products and processes. The Constitution entrusts this matter

28 Quoted in Hilary E Pearson *Computer Contracts* (Financial Training 1984) 284.

29 Ibid.

30 Act 195 of 1993.

31 Constitution of the United States of America, art 1 s 8 cl 8.

to the Patent Act,[32] which provides that, for an invention to be patentable, it has to fall within at least one of the statutory categories. These include machines, new and useful processes, manufactures, compositions of matter and improvements to any of the above. The courts have, besides these statutory criteria, excluded from patentable subject-matter categories such as the laws of nature, physical phenomena and abstract ideas.

These principles have been worked out by American courts in a series of important, if sometimes confusing, decisions. In 1964 the Patent and Trademark Office Board of Appeals decided in *Ex parte King*[33] that a computer program could be patented on the basis that it combined with a computer to form a novel and unique machine (or apparatus). However, in line with a 1966 report by the President's Commission on the Patent System, the Patent Office became opposed to the patenting of computer programs, whether defined as an apparatus or not.

This in turn led to the Board often being upset on appeal by the Court of Customs and Patent Appeals (CCPA). The CCPA has been more favourably disposed towards patenting software but has used a number of different steps in supporting its decisions. One of these is the so-called 'mental steps' doctrine, which roughly boils down to an argument that steps which can be performed only in the mind belong to the realm of ideas, and should therefore not be patentable. This test was later abandoned in favour of the 'technological arts' doctrine. According to the latter, a process was patentable if it fell within 'the technological or useful arts'.

The Supreme Court first had its say on this topic in the case of *Gottschalk v Benson*.[34] The claim involved a method of converting binary coded decimal notation to pure binary code. Reference was made in the claim to something called a 're-entrant shift register', but the claim was also for the pure method alone without the need of any apparatus other than a piece of paper and a pencil. The court felt that the basis of this method was something called an algorithm, which was nothing else than an idea, and therefore not patentable.

The concept of an 'algorithm' often becomes relevant with regard to patent registrations. The *Concise Oxford Dictionary*[35] defines it as 'process or rules for (esp machine) calculation etc'. *Webster's New Collegiate Dictionary* defines it as 'a procedure for solving mathematical problems ... in a finite number of steps that frequently involves repetition of an operation'. The latter definition is particularly

---

32 35 USC 101 (1972).

33 This and some of the following sources have been extracted from the excellent article by L N Flewellyn, 'An anomaly in the Patent System. The Uncertain status of computer software', Vol 8 1980 – 1 1981 *Rutgers Computer and Technology Law Journal* 273.

34 409 US 63 (1972).

35 Seventh edition.

important because the courts have, in interpreting the *Benson* case amongst others, differentiated between two concepts of 'algorithm'. In *Paine Webber etc v Merrill Lynch* etc[36] the judge differentiated as follows:

> 'Unfortunately the term 'algorithm' has been a source of confusion which stems from different uses of the term in the related, but distinct, fields of mathematics and computer science. In mathematics, the word algorithm has attained the meaning of recursive computational language, defining a computational course of events which is self contained, for example [$a^2 + b^2 = c^2$]. In contrast, the computer algorithm is a procedure consisting of operation [sic] to combine data, mathematical principles and equipment for the purpose of interpreting and/or acting upon certain data input.'

Further on he states that, whereas the mathematical model is self-contained, the computer model has to have some outside application. The latter has in fact been used to describe 'nearly any step by step procedure', according to author Richard H Baker.[37] According to Baker, '[b]y that definition all computer programs are algorithms.'[38] From this one may deduce that whereas the mathematical model is more within the realm of ideas, and therefore unpatentable, the computational model may well be patentable, especially since it is always coupled to some outside application, such as a computer program.

The judge in *Benson* made it quite clear that the court wanted to avoid giving a patent over the algorithm incorporated in the invention:

> 'What we come down to in a nutshell is the following .... The mathematical formula involved here has no substantial practical application except in connection with a digital computer, which means that if the judgment below (granting patent protection) is affirmed, the patent would wholly pre-empt the mathematical formula and in practical effect would be a patent on the algorithm itself.'[39]

The court also rejected the reasoning of the CCPA (the court *a quo*) that, because of the practical application of the idea in the re-entrant shift register, or in digital computers generally, the claim did not cover the field exhaustively (and should therefore be patentable). The Supreme Court felt that the claimed patent was broad enough to apply for use with any existing or future machine. The main drift of the objection seems to be that the claim was formulated too widely and that the claimed procedure did not form part of a specific process, or the workings of a specific machine, with which concepts patent courts seem happier.

---

36 564 F Supp 1358.

37 Richard H Baker *Scuttle the Computer Pirates* (Tab Books 1984) 54.

38 Ibid.

39 Benson (supra) 71.

The possible applications of an invention also played an important role in the next decision of the Supreme Court on this point. In *Parker v Flook*[40] the claim involved a method of updating alarm limits, by continuously measuring a variable in a process involving the catalytic chemical conversion of hydrocarbons. Flook's claim transformed the traditional method by means of an algorithm embodied in a computer program. The CCPA had held that the claim did not pre-empt the incorporated algorithm but the Supreme Court disagreed again, holding that 'post-solution activity' could not transform an unpatentable principle of nature into a patentable process. That would amount to letting the form of the application override the substance of the claim itself. A dissenting minority, however, distinguished *Flook* from *Benson* in that the use of the algorithm should have been patentable in the present case (a decision which the present author supports).

Flewellen is also critical of this decision, and points out that because the algorithm of Flook was claimed in the context of a specific application, other uses of the algorithm would not have been precluded had a patent been issued. The court had also ignored constitutional policy vis-à-vis the patent system, namely to 'promote the progress of Science and the Useful Arts' by creating an incentive to future inventors in the field.[41]

The later view of the Supreme Court on this topic is reflected in *Diamond v Diehr*.[42] Here the claim was for a process of curing synthetic rubber in a mould. A computer program was used to monitor the temperature inside the mould, previously considered to be an uncontrollable variable. The CCPA again granted patent on the grounds that the basis of the claim was for a process incorporating an algorithm and not for the algorithm itself. On appeal, the minority view in the *Flook* decision now became a bare (five to four) majority in the Supreme Court. Since only the use of the particular algorithm in context with all the other steps of Diehr's rubber moulding process would be patented, there was no danger that the algorithm itself would be withdrawn from the public domain by the grant of patent to the process.

After the *Diamond* case, a so-called 'means plus function' (also known as a 'means for') test was developed in the case of *Re Abele*.[43] In the first part of the test it is determined whether an algorithm was involved. In the second part it is determined whether the algorithm is *applied* to physical elements or process steps. The algorithm represents the 'means' (unpatentable) which enables a certain 'function' to be carried out (an application of the algorithm and therefore

---

40 (1978) 437 US 584.

41 Flewellen op cit 295.

42 450 US 175 (1981). The test became known as the *Freeman-Walter-Abele* test, because of two prior cases which had taken the same view.

43 (1982) 684 F 2d 902.

patentable). Finally, a test is carried out to determine whether the algorithm is 'circumscribed' in the sense that its use is limited to that particular application, otherwise a patent would have been granted in the algorithm itself. The application should also be circumscribed by more than 'a field of use limitation or non-essential post-solution activity'. *In casu*, the patent was granted in a system of tomography (CAT scanning). With regard to the present as well as the *Diamond* cases the court held that the improvement (on the basic algorithm) 'resides in the *application*[44] of a mathematical formula within the context of a process, which encompasses significantly more than the algorithm alone'.

In *Re Iwahashi*[45] patent was granted in an 'autocorrelation unit' for use in pattern recognition. A broad interpretation was given to the 'means for' test in that a large number of 'means' elements (algorithms) could be 'applied' by merely programming a general-purpose computer. What might have saved the claim was reference to certain specific hardware elements (ROM and RAM chips) in which the programs were stored. (Patent courts are usually happy to grant patent in some visible form of 'machinery' which represents the practical application of the idea. In actual fact, the programs may as well have been loaded from a disk or from a network!)

Re Alappat[46] could be seen 'in part as a return to the *Diamond v Diehr*-test'.[47] The claim was for a patent in an anti-aliasing system which smoothed the display of waveforms on an oscilloscope. Rich J, in a majority opinion, came to the conclusion that using calculations to transform digitized waveforms into anti-aliased pixel data was 'concrete' enough. Section 101 of the US Patents Act should be given its broadest interpretation and it would be sufficient if a machine produced a 'useful, concrete and tangible result'. Furthermore, a general-purpose computer amounted to a 'machine' when programmed in a particular way and would be patentable if the other requirements for patentability were met. According to Reed,[48] this case actually reversed the *Abele* rule on claim interpretation:

> 'The accent has shifted back to looking at the claim as a whole to see whether it is for a patentable thing (machine, manufacture, process etc) rather than on searching out algorithms in the claim and then seeing if the claim goes beyond that (the *Freeman-Walter-Abele* approach).'[49]

---

44 My emphasis.

45 888 F 2d 1370 (1989).

46 33 F 3d 1526 (1994).

47 Reed *Computer Law* 178.

48 Op cit 179.

49 Ibid.

The claims in two further cases were specifically drafted to avoid the *Freeman-Walter-Abele* approach, and were successful in doing so. In *Re Lowry*[50] patent was granted in a computer memory organized in a particular way, namely an 'attributive data model'. In *Re Warmerdam*[51] a technique of collision avoidance by robotic machines, grounded in a 'bubble hierarchy', was also granted patent. In an as yet unreported case, the US Supreme Court has now apparently let stand a lower court ruling that mathematical algorithms used in a computer program may be given intellectual property right (IPR) protection provided they produce 'a useful, concrete and tangible result'.[52]

The USPTO[53] has issued some guidelines to patent examiners in the present regard. In its preamble a distinction is made, inter alia, between 'functional and non-functional descriptive material'. Reed[54] makes use of this distinction to illustrate that the patentable material in the *Lowry* and *Warmerdam* cases was 'functional' in that it influenced computing processes, whereas plain text or music data files would not have been. He also notes that this 'neatly sidesteps' the often arbitrary distinction between what is considered a 'program' and what is considered 'data'. (This question will again be addressed later on in the present work.)

Reed comes to the conclusion that 'US law has now adopted a very liberal position on the patentability of computer-related and other inventions whose subject matter is essentially the manipulation of numbers ...' and '[c]laims to any new and useful machine or article will be allowed protection regardless of any fears that an algorithm is being patented by the back door'.[55] This may explain the infamous *Compton's Multimedia Encyclopaedia* case, where Comptons were granted an abortive patent in 'a computer search system for retrieving information, comprising means for storing interrelated textual information and graphical information'. This amounted to giving to one firm a monopoly on the system of hypertext and hypermedia used in the retrieval system, which system is, however, also the *lingua franca* of the entire Internet. After a storm of protest and some fiery debates on the Internet, the American patent office retracted the patent and is reexamining the claim.[56]

---

50 32 F 3d 1579 (1994).

51 33 F 3d 136 (1994).

52 *New York Times* 12 January 1999.

53 Acronym for United States Patent Office.

54 Op cit 182–3.

55 Op cit 183.

56 See W A Joubert (ed) 'Computer Law' *LAWSA* Vol 5(3) (Butterworths first reissue 1998). Although the patent filing date was October 1989, the grant became generally known only when Comptons started pressing its rivals for licensing fees. The debate took place during the last half of 1993 and the first half of 1994.

Reed also detects a 'lack of zeal on the part of US examiners and judges, when compared to their European counterparts, for digging for the essence of an invention in order to find that it addresses non-patentable matter'.[57] This leads us to examine the situation in Europe.

(2) Patenting software in Europe

Before the recommendations of the Banks Commission[58] led to the 1977 Patents Act in the United Kingdom, a trend towards granting patent in software had been set by the United Kingdom courts. In *Slee & Harris Applications*[59] computer software was held patentable because of the form in which the claim had been framed. No application was made for a patent in the software by itself, but for a 'computer as programmed'. In *Burrough's Corporation (Perkin's) Application*,[60] the patent claim was for a 'method of transmitting data over a communication link between a central processor and designatable ones of a plurality of addressable remote data terminals couples via said communication link to said data processor'. Graham J dismissed attempts to draw distinctions on the basis of formulation as mere casuistry and found that apparatus programmed to operate in a new way was patentable, as were computer programs embodied in a physical form which had the effect of controlling a computer (firmware).

The Patents Act of 1977 was passed to enable the United Kingdom to comply with its obligations in terms of the EPC[61] to which it was a signatory with most other European countries. The EPC had been set up to provide for harmonization of the domestic patent legislation of the signatory countries and also to provide for the EPO[62] which would deal with the granting of European patents. Section 1(2) of the Patents Act excluded the possibility of patenting computer programs. Nevertheless, in *International Business Machines Corporation's Application*[63] the court stuck to the line taken in the *Burrough's Corporation* case. Although the court's reasoning (in the IBM Application) has been described as 'undoubtedly weak' by R August,[64] he thought that it might establish a precedent for granting patents in software where the program is permanently affixed in some medium (*in casu* it consisted of holes punched in a card which could be read by the computer). That case had also been decided in terms of the old 1949 Patents Act, which did not refer to computers at all, whereas the new Act only excludes patent protection for programs 'as such'. The latter phrase has been interpreted to allow the patenting

57 Op cit 181.

58 Which sat in 1977.

59 1966 RPC 194.

60 1974 RPC 147.

61 Acronym for European Patent Convention.

62 Acronym for European Patent Office.

63 1980 FSR 564.

64 March/April 1985 *Computer Law and Practice* 117.

of 'a computer as programmed'. Although at first the 'Guidelines for Examiners in the EPO' (with regard to the EPO provision which excludes patenting computers) seem also to exclude computers 'as programmed',[65] a later amendment in the instructions seems more positive:

> 'If, on the other hand, a computer program claimed in connection with the computer it is designed to control, causes the computer to operate in a different way from a technical point of view, the combination might be patentable.'[66]

The further history of patenting of computer programs in Europe (as well as the later United Kingdom cases) can only be understood in the light of the EPO cases which have followed. The tone was set by *Vicom/Computer-related invention*,[67] where the claims were for a general method and apparatus for processing digitized images within a computer in certain ways. A mathematical formula altered the digital image in certain ways, smoothing out the edges, for instance (anti-aliasing). The patent was granted, apparently because manipulating an image was held to be an 'industrial process'. The crux of the decision was that images were useful in the field of industrial design.

This desperate search for something 'industrial' or 'technical' to link the claim to characterizes most of the following EPO cases. In the German case of *Koch and Sterzel/X-ray apparatus*[68] the claim was in respect of ordinary X-ray apparatus which was linked to and controlled by a computer. Opponents to the claim argued that the 'technical effect' kicked in only after the computer had performed its function and that the *Vicom* case was decided too broadly, in that it allowed patent in any computer 'when programmed'. The Technical Board of Appeal held that it was not relevant when a technical effect[69] occurred, as long as it did occur. It also decided that if an invention 'uses technical means', it would not constitute a claim to a computer program 'as such', notwithstanding the fact that it may also contain non-patentable matter such as computer programs. Finally, it held that an invention was patentable, whether or not the apparatus, without the program, formed part of the state of the art[70] (which an ordinary X-ray machine obviously would, since it lacked novelty). Another German case was *Siemens/Character form*,[71] which claimed patent in a process for displaying on a VDU[72] screen characters

---

65 See (1983) 100 *SALJ* 755–6.

66 October 1985 *EIPR* 279ff.

67 [1987] EPOR 74.

68 [1988] EPOR 72.

69 In the present case, the operation of the X-ray apparatus.

70 If something is 'state of the art' it lacks novelty and is therefore unpatentable.

71 [1992] EPOR 69.

72 Acronym for 'visual display unit' (for instance, an ordinary computer monitor).

which assumed different forms depending upon whether they were used at the beginning, end or in the middle of words. The Technical Board of Appeal rejected the invention since they felt that the invention lacked technical content. The *Koch* case was distinguished on the grounds that although no technical means were used there either, the 'effect was technical'!

A number of claims followed from IBM, one of the major computer manufacturers. In *IBM/Data processor network*[73] the claim was for the arrangement of a number of data processors as nodes for a communications network. The Technical Board of Appeal held that 'the co-ordination and control of the internal communication between programs and data files held at different processors in a data processing system … is to be regarded as solving a problem which is essentially technical'. In *IBM/Computer-related invention*[74] the claim was for a method of displaying one of a set of predetermined messages in response to certain computer events. The Technical Board of Appeal had no problem:

> 'Generally the Board takes the view that giving visual indications automatically about conditions prevailing in an apparatus or system is basically a technical problem.'[75]

On the other hand, the patent was refused in *IBM/Document abstracting and retrieving*,[76] where the claim was for a system automatically making and storing abstracts. It was held that the claims could not be patented by reason of a lack of technical character and also for falling within the category of schemes, rules and methods for performing mental acts. Strangely enough, the court held that there were no changes to the documents themselves as 'technical entities', but only changes in the electrical signals representing the information stored. By contrast, in the *Vicom* case there had been a change in the image.

(This seems a curiously illiterate statement in the light of the fact that any computer data, whether documents, images or even music, are stored and restored by 'changes in the electrical signals'!) Patent was also refused in *IBM/Text clarity processing*,[77] which claimed a patent in a method of identifying expressions in a text processing system, measuring which expressions fell below a certain level of understandability[78] and then replacing them with more understandable expressions. It was held that this kind of evaluation came down to a mental act and that this mental act could then be translated to a computer by any programmer. The only novelty was therefore not in the technical field.

---

73 [1990] EPOR 91.

74 [1990] EPOR 107.

75 Ibid.

76 [1990] EPOR 99.

77 [1990] EPOR 607.

78 Probably some kind of 'FOG index', identifying words with too many syllables.

In summary, one has to agree with Reed that European examiners do try to find underlying general principles in coming to a decision, instead of deciding cases by case as the Americans do. Unfortunately, the overriding principle seems to be to look for something 'technical'. This test also governs cases before the Royal Patent Court (RPC), such as *Merrill Lynch's Application*.[79] Here the claim was for a computerized method of setting up a trading market in securities. Although the court held that the system must be looked at as a whole and not excluded simply because a computer was involved, the patent was still not granted since improved business methods were not considered to be technical advances. In *Gale's Application*[80] the Court of Appeal held that differences in the physical structures holding the program (a ROM[81] chip, in the present case) were not material and that the program was not novel. This is in contrast with the *Iwahashi*-case in the United States, discussed above. There the fact that the program had been encased in ROM and RAM[82] chips made all the difference. Finally, in *Wang Laboratories Inc's Application*[83] Aldous J pointed out that the EPO's use of the term 'technical' was not clear at all. He therefore tried to avoid reliance on this concept in his judgment:

> 'The machine, the computer, remains the same even when programmed. The computer and the program do not combine together to produce a new computer. They remain separate and amount to a collocation rather than a combination making a different whole. The contribution is, to my mind, made by the program and nothing more.'[84]

According to Reed, this test of 'a new computer' is not much more useful than 'a technical alteration of behaviour'. He feels that '[t]he problem is to distinguish those aspects of computer configuration (whether permanent or temporary 'hardware' or 'software') in which developments are deemed patentable from those that are not.'[85] Unfortunately Reed's summation also seems to beg the question. The main question IMHO[86] is whether a system of patent law which has developed around physical, technical inventions can really protect ideas adequately in the intangible world of information and computer programs.

79 [1989] RPC 561.

80 [1991] RPC 305.

81 Acronym for 'read-only memory'.

82 Acronym for 'random-access memory'.

83 [1992] RPC 463.

84 As quoted in Reed op cit 172.

85 Op cit 173.

86 Acronym for 'in my humble opinion' (a shorthand often found in Internet debates).

(3) Patenting of software internationally

The Paris Convention[87] provides that patents belonging to a national from one of the convention countries will be protected in all the other convention countries. The Patent Cooperation Treaty provides for 'international applications' to be made at a 'receiving office', which could be within the applicant's own country. The receiving office can also carry out international searches upon request. This gives a one year 'option' to the applicant to decide whether he or she wants to make the claim permanent, by pursuing it further in the other countries (or supranational groupings such as the EPO).[88] Good news is that South Africa has recently joined the Patent Cooperation Treaty by means of amendments brought about by Chapter V of the Intellectual Property Amendment Act.[89]

Outside of the European Union it is instructive to look at Japanese and Canadian patent law. According to Jerrard,[90] it is not easy to make computer programs comply with art 2 of the Japanese Patent Law, which defines patentable inventions as technical ideas using the laws of nature. The Japanese Patent Office sees programs as mere mathematical algorithms (and therefore unpatentable), but the position is still open as far as programs inseparably incorporated into hardware is concerned (firmware).

In Canada, the case of *Schlumberger Canada Ltd v Commissioner of Patents*[91] illustrates that the Canadian court used to take a restrictive line where patents on computer programs are concerned. It was held that a grant for a process of securing information from seismic testing apparatus[92] by means of a computer would amount to patenting a set of calculations, and the claim was therefore rejected. According to Tapper[93] later decisions such as *McDonald's Application* (1983), which dealt with modulating tests of jet engines, were more favourable toward patenting programs. In the latter case patent was allowed notwithstanding the inclusion of a novel computer program which helped achieve the desired effect.

(4) Patenting of hardware and software in Africa, particularly South Africa

In Africa, an African Intellectual Property Organization (AIPO) has been in place since 1962, with its headquarters in Yaoundé in the United Republic of

87 The International Convention for the Protection of Industrial Property. We shall return to this convention when dealing with trade marks and designs below.

88 See Reed op cit 156.

89 Act 38 of 1997. For more detail about the time frames, see *The South African Institute of Intellectual Property Law Newsletter* 59 (9 of 1998). See also E du Plessis in 'News' (May 1999) *De Rebus* 12.

90 *Computer Law and Practice* (September–October 1984) 3.

91 (1981) 38 NR 299.

92 In connection with oil wells.

93 *Computer Law* 13.

Cameroon. The agreement is limited mainly to French-speaking countries in Africa,[94] whose intellectual property laws are equivalent to those of France. The 1962 Libreville agreement which created the organization also administers the examination, grant and publication of patent and utility models. The agreement excludes computer programs from the list of patentable inventions.

Nevertheless, many countries in the SADEC region, such as Zambia, Zimbabwe and Malawi, do not belong to AIPO but have formed a similar organization for English-speaking Africa. This is called the African Regional Industrial Property Organization (ARIPO).[95] Its headquarters are at present in Harare, Zimbabwe, having moved there in 1985. Alan J S Dunlop[96] discusses South Africa's options in a recent article—-either to join ARIPO or to try to form its own group with the SADEC countries (Namibia, Angola and Mocambique are not part of ARIPO). Dunlop rejects arguments that ARIPO does not legally comply with the requirements of TRIPS[97] and that it is in a 'parlous financial state'. At a recent council meeting in Lesotho, ARIPO passed an amendment of the Harare Protocol[98] which should meet the requirements of art 62 part 5 of TRIPS, namely that administrative procedures should be subject to judicial or quasi-judicial review. As far as the finances are concerned, South Africa's economy, with its high rate of patent and design registrations, may help to make ARIPO viable.

Creel & Wintringham recommend regional co-operation to overcome the lack of finance and experienced manpower which currently hampers uniform patent practices and is causing the lack of the necessary search and examination systems in the Third World.[99]

To come even closer to home, the South African Patents Act is modelled on the British Patents Act and British case law will therefore be considered to be persuasive authority.[100] South Africa is also a signatory to the Paris Convention. In South Africa no formal bar exists to the patenting of computer hardware, but in practice it is unlikely that there would be many original applications. It seems

---

94 Members consist of the Malagasy Republic, Benin, Burkina Faso, the Ivory Coast, Senegal, Niger, the Central African Republic, Togo, Gabon, Mauritania, Chad, Mali, Guinea and the Republic of Djibouti.

95 SADEC's members include South Africa, Namibia, Malawi, Botswana, Lesotho, Swaziland, Zimbabwe, Democratic Republic of Congo and Mozambique. ARIPO's membership consists of Ghana, Kenya, Malawi, Mauritius, Uganda, Zambia, Sudan, The Gambia, Zimbabwe, Botswana, Lesotho and Swaziland.

96 *The South African Institute of Intellectual Property Law Newsletter* 58 (4 of 1998).

97 Acronym for 'trade-related intellectual property rights'.

98 Document ARIPO/AC/XXI/8.

99 1984 *Rutgers Computer and Technology Law Journal* 255.

100 Alain S Gutterman & Bentley J Anderson *Intellectual Property in Global Markets* (Kluwer 1997) 414. See also *Tolima (Pty) Ltd v Cugacius Motor Accessories (Pty) Ltd* 1983 (3) SA 504 (E).

that most computer hardware is nowadays sourced from the United States or from the Far East, where countries such as Taiwan, Malaysia, Singapore and Thailand have flourishing hardware industries. Overseas firms are, of course, interested in obtaining adequate protection for their products marketed in South Africa and the rest of Africa.

As far as computer software is concerned, the Patents Act[101] specifically excludes a computer program from being treated as a patentable invention. This is not the end of the matter, however. Section 25(3) also provides that the prohibition relates only to the thing *as such*. In *LAWSA*[102] it is pointed out that some guidance might be obtained from the views expressed on the interpretation of the corresponding provisions in the European Patent Convention. As is clear from the discussion above, the situation has been affected by pan-European considerations and, even so, some disparity still exists with regard to the patentability of computer programs. It is still not clear whether South Africa will follow a European, American, Asian or African lead. Even South Africa academics disagree on the precise import of the term 'as such' in the limitation to the prohibition mentioned above.[103]

The South African Patents Act also poses two substantive requirements for all inventions, namely 'novelty' and 'inventive step'. With regard to inventive step regard may be had to overseas authorities on the topic of obviousness. The test is that the new idea should not have been obvious to a person skilled in the area in which the patent application is submitted.[104]

With regard to novelty, the inventions should not have been part of the 'state of the art' at the time the application was submitted. This 'state of the art' includes anything which has been available to the public at the time of application, including pending applications with earlier priority dates. If the item had been used at all in South Africa prior to the patent application, it is considered to be 'state of the art'.

Specifically with regard to computer programs, novelty could be a difficult requirement to meet, since very few computer programs are really original.

Although the factual background remains vague, one South African case has been reported where a computer program, or at least an algorithm seems to be involved. In *Meter Patent Development (Pty) Ltd v Ash Electronic Industries & another*[105] the latter party (formerly Altec) had assigned a patent to the former party (formerly Spescom) in something called 'a credit supply system', which involved the

101 Act 57 of 1978.

102 Volume 20 'Patents Inventions and Heraldry' (1984) § 6.

103 See the correspondence in this regard in (1983) 100 *SALJ* 755–6.

104 Section 3 of Act 57 of 1978.

105 1995 *Burrell's Patent Law Reports* 185.

encryption and matching of codes. The assignment had been registered at the patent office but Meter now applied for an amendment in the patent to address the problem of novelty, in the light of overseas patents by Schlumberger and Sloan. Ash had applied for revocation of the patent but this matter was held over until the amendment had been dealt with. Under the circumstances, Van Dijkhorst J granted the amendment.[106]

1.4 CONCLUSION

There seems to be general agreement that patent is the best way to protect computer hardware, notwithstanding the fact that the application procedure is lengthy and that many patents have been thrown out by the courts. Some of these include the patent on ENIAC,[107] the original computer!

On the other hand, obtaining a patent is an uncertain, time-consuming and expensive process as far as software is concerned. It is especially difficult to meet the novelty requirement and by making public the contents of his or her program, the inventor also loses all protection which the law of trade secrets might have provided (see below). Patenting of software should be attempted only if it forms part of a greater process, preferably having to do with something 'technical' and with hardware. Framing the application narrowly is also important. For instance, Samuel Morse was denied a patent in the use of electromagnetic force for making or printing intelligible characters at a distance, whereas Alexander Graham Bell obtained a patent on the telephone by not framing his claim so widely and by concentrating on the specific application.

In the end, one is left with an uneasy feeling that patent law feels itself much more comfortable with inventions from the Industrial Revolution, clanking and puffing away and emitting clouds of steam. It stems from an era where everything was technical and tangible and money could be made from later manufacture. This does not really apply to information technology, or even to the world of immaterial assets typical of the Information Revolution.[108] Would one of the other branches of the law of intellectual property be more suitable in this regard? This possibility will be explored later in this section on Intellectual Property Rights (IPR).

106 The report does not state what transpired with the application for revocation.

107 Acronym for 'electronic numeral integrator and calculator'. See the interesting history of this machine related earlier in this chapter.

108 Although it does manage to cope better with the products of modern biology, such as plant and animal breeders' rights, which may extend even to the DNA strands obtained.

CHAPTER TWO

COPYRIGHT

The relationship between copyright and computers and computer-related products is claiming an increasing share of attention, necessitating a rethink of the whole field of copyright and resulting in new legislation both locally and overseas.

2 COPYRIGHT

Before embarking on the following section, the reader should be warned not to expect a lengthy exposition on copyright as a topic in itself. Being part of a book on computers and the law, only those aspects of copyright that are directly relevant to computers will be treated. That said, it must be conceded that the relationship between copyright and computers and computer-related products (the whole referred to below as 'digital copyright')[1] is claiming an increasing share of attention, necessitating a rethink of the whole field of copyright and resulting in new legislation both locally and overseas.

Since the field of digital copyright contains a number of disparate problems and sub-topics, it is difficult to treat the subject systematically. Nevertheless, an attempt has been made and the following subheadings are used:

2.1 the relationship between copyright and the larger field of intellectual property;

2.2 the subsistence of digital copyright (including the protection of ideas or their expression);

2.3 the scope of digital copyright protection (including the question of substantial taking);

2.4 the evolving information technologies and their relationship with digital copyright; and

2.5 alternative means of protection.

After this, some special problems arising with regard to the Internet, databases, multimedia and video games, government information and libraries are treated, in that sequence. Finally, following on the more general section, some countries (including South Africa) will be examined for specific legislation and case law with regard to digital copyright, roughly following the same sequence used in dealing with patent above. Finally, a brief conclusion is attempted.

As was pointed out in chapter 1 Patent, as well as in the case of *Tolima (Pty) Ltd v Cugacius Motor Accessories (Pty) Ltd*,[2] the South African fields of copyright and patent have been modelled on those of England and this is not an area where the common law of South Africa has any particular relevance. Comparative law is therefore of greater interest than historical research into the Roman-Dutch law.

1 For an explanation of 'digital' see section 2.4 below.

2 1983 (3) SA 504 (E).

2.1 THE RELATIONSHIP BETWEEN COPYRIGHT AND INTELLECTUAL PROPERTY

Some space was devoted in the previous chapter to distinguishing the type of protection which patent law can uniquely provide. Although patent has many advantages, it does not adequately cover the need for authors, artists, computer programmers, etc to prevent unauthorized copying of their work, and here the field of copyright comes into play.

Hilary E Pearson[3] also feels that patent is not the most suitable field of law for protecting computer software. She mentions that it is expensive to obtain and even more expensive to protect, especially since the outcome of patent litigation concerning software is very difficult to predict. Copyright, on the other hand, requires a much lower degree of originality than the degree of novelty required for patent protection. As long as the work has not been directly copied from some other source, and some degree of intellectual effort has gone into it, this should be sufficient to found copyright. In Pearson's view: 'The main reason for this difference between patent and copyright is that copyright does not confer a true monopoly as a patent does; it merely provides protection from piracy.'[4] She does concede that if only identical copying infringed copyright the latter's protection would almost be worthless; but she maintains that although copyright goes further than this, it was never meant to protect the author's *ideas*. These distinctions introduce the difficult distinction between an idea and its expression: 'The difficulty is to determine the dividing line between copying sufficient of the author's expression to infringe his copyright, and merely using his ideas, which may inevitably require expression in similar language.'[5] Both these problems are dealt with under the next heading.

In a contribution entitled 'A Review of Suggested Systems for the Protection of Computer Software'[6] Manfred Kindermann emphasizes the 'book-like nature of a licensable software package', which suggests to him that copyright might provide the most suitable protection. The personal efforts of the programmer to make the program more 'user-friendly', together with and the supporting documentation, add to the book analogy. Kindermann emphasizes that the whole software package needs protection and that the protection should not 'be restricted to inventive data-processing concepts implemented in a small minority of highly advanced programs.' He reviews various protection schemes put forward by MITI[7] and WIPO,[8] amongst

---

3 Hilary E Pearson *Computer Contracts* (Financial Training 1984) 190.

4 Op cit 205.

5 Op cit 208.

6 In H Brett & L Perry (eds) *The Legal Protection of Computer Software* (ESC Publishers 1981) 140ff.

7 Acronym for (Japanese) Ministry of Industry and Technology.

8 Acronym for World Intellectual Property Organization.

others, but in the end comes to the conclusion that the normal principles of copyright, with a few modifications, are still superior to any of the other schemes put forward. The fact that underlying ideas or concepts are not protected by copyright does not worry him overmuch. Because so much of the development time of a new software package is spent on debugging[9] the program, it is the exact copying of the much more valuable, debugged program which worries him, and copyright does prohibit this. Kindermann's remarks about the length of time spent debugging are borne out by experience in trying to fix the Y2K problem, mentioned in the introduction. It has been found that even experienced programmers cannot complete more than 20 to 30 lines of fully debugged and tested code per day.

Daniel Remer[10] also prefers copyright to patent protection as far as software is concerned. He stresses that one cannot obtain a patent on an algorithm,[11] which would have given protection to the underlying idea, but that a resort to trade-secret law would be necessary. With patent one cannot ignore petty infringers without fear of losing the patent. Copyright does not present the same problem. Infringers of a patented program will claim that the program was obvious and not novel or that of the many technicalities for registration had not been complied with:

> 'You can see how expensive and bothersome this whole process can become. Since most programmers only want to protect the *expression*[12] of their ideas, copyright law normally will meet this goal more cheaply and easily than patent law.'[13]

Remer's point concerning the importance of trade-secret law is well made. As will be seen below, this is often the only effective form of legal protection in the Information Age.

In his book *Legal Protection of Computer Programs*[14] Bryan Niblett also points out the vast difference in commercial value between a first prototype and a program which has been thoroughly tested and proved. Even though he finds a patent a 'highly desirable form of intellectual property', he is also aware that copyright is much easier to obtain: 'Cases show that the standard of originality is not high and bears no correspondence to the requirement of novelty in a patent for an invention.'[15] Copyright is also not dependent on the laborious system of patent registration but is an 'example of on-line and line by line[16] creation of intellectual property'.

---

9 ie rendering it error-free.

10 Daniel Remer *Legal Care for your Software* (Gower 1984) 138.

11 See chapter 1 Patent above.

12 My emphasis, to contrast it with the protection of the idea itself.

13 Remer op cit 138.

14 Bryan Niblett *Legal Protection of Computer Programs* (Oyez 1980).

15 Op cit 43.

16 The way in which one writes computer programs, ie line by line.

This procedural advantage which copyright enjoys over patent is not limited to registration, but extends also to the litigation process. Because of procedural advantages, the copyright litigant enjoys a higher success rate than the enforcer of patent—one need only refer back to the failure of the patent on ENIAC (the first computer) discussed in the previous chapter.

Besides these formal differences, some authors are of the opinion that there is a substantive, qualitative gap between patent and copyright. This notwithstanding, many of them still find it difficult to categorize computer programs as pertaining to one or the other. In the view of Perry[17] the programs are too much of pure science to belong to patent, yet also too applied to belong to copyright! In a contribution to the same work,[18] Le Stanc points out that an author like Troller wants to reserve copyright to works which are deserving of aesthetic appreciation. A similar point was made in the minority report of Commissioner Hersey, a dissenting member of the National Commission on New Technological Uses of Copyrighted Works (CONTU). According to this point of view, computer programs are too 'technical' to deserve the same protection as works of art. Eugen Ulmer shows the fallacy of this argument:

> 'Der Gründ fur den Urheberrechtschutz liegt in dem Schutz der individuellen geistigen Arbeit, die sich in dem Werk manifestiert, nicht in dem aesthethischen Genuss, den das Werk vermittelt.'[19]

According to Le Stanc, Germany, Italy and France have made clear their support for this broader view by including the adjective 'scientific' in the phrase 'literary, artistic and scientific works' in their copyright legislation.[20]

Much of the lack of interest in the protection of computer programs by copyright possibly stems from the pat phrase that copyright protects the expression of ideas, but never the ideas themselves. The next rubric deals with this topic in more detail.

It should also be borne in mind that not only computer programs themselves present copyright problems,[21] but also the output of those programs. This would apply particularly if the output is also stored in digital format, which means that computers are needed to access and utilize these products. Examples are digital databases and so-called 'video-games' which are created and accessed by means of computer but

---

17 Brett & Perry op cit 173.

18 Brett & Perry op cit 93.

19 'The object of copyright protection is the individual's mental labour, as manifested in his work, not the aesthetic pleasure which the work conveys' (freely translated). From Eugen Ulmer *Der Urheberschutz wissenschaftlicher Werke unter besonderer Berücksichtigung der Programme elektronischer Rechenanlagen* (Bayerische Akademie der Wissenschaften 1967) 13.

20 Brett & Perry op cit 93–94.

21 Although the bulk of this chapter deals with this problem.

do not qualify as computer programs themselves. The growing commercial importance of these digital products has expressed itself in increased litigation and necessitates that some clarity be brought to this twilight zone of the law.

2.2 The subsistence of digital copyright (including the protection of ideas or their expression)

With the coming of the digital age, copyright has had to look anew at its own development and adaptability. Not only did computer programs and products fall into a difficult niche between copyright and patent (as should be clear from the aforegoing), but most objects of traditional copyright such as music, drawings and writing were digitized and became accessible and capable of manipulation by computer. The Internet has become an unexpectedly popular medium of distribution of copyrightable content, leading to increasing fears among traditional publishers. Most of the early development of digital copyright law took place in the area of computer programs and most of the text that follows therefore deals with this topic. Specific problems with regard to databases, video games and the Internet are dealt with under those respective headings later in this chapter.

In order to deal properly with this topic it is important to have some understanding of the technical phrases applicable to computer programs. 'Algorithm' has already been defined while dealing with patent, and the analogy to a CD-player and the compact disks themselves has been used to explain 'hardware' and 'software'. The 1976 American Copyright[22] requires that the copyrightable work be fixed in a 'tangible means of expression', which medium may be one 'now known or later developed', which seems to make provision for recent technological developments.

In answering the question 'what is a program?' Gemignan[23] states that a program begins as a problem to be solved and ends as a pattern of switch settings inside a computer. The programmer expresses the precise way of solving the problem in something called a flow chart. This is a schematic representation, usually on paper, of the logical steps required to solve the problem. Though it may not mean very much to an outsider, it is readily understood by fellow programmers who may use the idea embodied in the flow chart to write their own program. Gemignani calls the flow chart 'a graphic way of portraying the algorithm'. It is therefore important for copyright purposes as the first concrete manifestation of the idea which its author is seeking to protect. The next step is to encode the solution presented in the flow chart into a series of instructions,

---

22 The Act which, according to R P Merdes, P S Menell, M A Lemley & T M Jorde *Intellectual Property in the New Technological Age* (Aspen Law and Business Publications 1997) 323, 'governs most works today'.

23 M C Gemignani 'Legal Protection for Computer Software: The View from '79' (1980) 7 *Rutgers Journal of Computers Technology and the Law* 269ff.

making use of a higher- or lower-level computer language.[24] Once this series of instructions is complete, we have a computer program. The program, when fed into the machine, causes a series of switches to be thrown inside the computer which, one would hope, enables it to perform the operations which the programmer had in mind.

Gemignani warns against confusing the program with its algorithm, or underlying idea, and accuses the court in *Gottschalk v Benson* of equating the two.[25] Perry[26] has pointed out that the proposals of WIPO were aimed at protecting computer programs but not the concepts on which the programs are based. (The reference is slightly dated and WIPO has done a lot of further development work, as will be seen below.) Reference has already been made above to Remer,[27] who states that programmers would have to resort to trade-secret law for the protection of ideas but that copyright is quite adequate if they are interested only in protecting the expression of those ideas.

If this is true, should copyright protection be limited to exact copying? Does this mean that changing a few lines of code will remove the copyright protection (since the expression is not identical)? Courts in both the United Kingdom and the United States have struggled with this problem of differentiating between 'an idea expressed' (no copyright possible) and 'the expression of an idea' (copyright possible).

American courts made it clear quite early on that the idea underlying an application cannot be copyrighted. The classic case, decided in 1930, was that of *Nichols v Universal Picture Corp.*[28] Learned Hand J decided the case by making use of the 'abstractions test':

> 'Upon any work ... a great number of patterns of increasing generality will fit increasingly well, as more and more of the incident is left out. The last may perhaps be no more than the most general statement of what the play is about, and at times may consist only of its title; but there is a point in this series of abstractions where they are no longer protected; since otherwise the playwright could prevent the use of his ideas to which, apart from their expression, his property is never extended.[29]

24 The higher-level language, known as the source code, is more readily understandable by a knowledgeable human, but it has to be compiled into the low-level machine language, known as the object code, before it can activate the computer. The compilation is done by yet another program, usually built into the computer's firmware.

25 Op cit 276n37.

26 Brett & Perry op cit 177.

27 See the text accompanying note 10 above.

28 45 F 2d 119 (2nd Cir 1930).

29 At 121.

In casu, the idea was contained in the premise of a Jewish and an Irish family becoming involved with each other, as is illustrated by the titles of the two plays involved—*The Cohens and the Kellys* allegedly copied the idea behind *Abie's Irish Rose*. Nevertheless, it should be borne in mind that the structure, sequence and organization of the original work is protected and a newcomer may not simply paraphrase the text to get around copyright protection. Otherwise, as Hand J put it: 'a plagiarist would escape liability by immaterial variations of the work.'[30]

In 1954 the court in *Mazer v Stein* decided that 'protection is only given to the expression of the idea—not the idea itself'.[31] The court applied the above principles to computer programs in *Synercom Technology, Inc v University Computing Co*.[32] A competitor of the copyright holder constructed a preprocessor program by making use of descriptions contained in the plaintiff's instruction manual. The program made use of a certain sequence of formats obtained from the plaintiff's material. The court held that this was 'ideas expressed' and not the 'expression of an idea' and that therefore the program itself was not entitled to copyright protection. However, because the defendant's accompanying material contained too much from the plaintiff's manual, the court was still able to protect the plaintiff.

In the United Kingdom the courts dealt with an analogous issue in the case of *Elanco v Mandops*.[33] The defendants had copied the plaintiff's instruction leaflet for a weedkiller and, when forced to withdraw it, issued a revised version in different style but making use of the same data. In a 1979 decision the judge held the copied information to be 'raw experimental data', being in fact 'ideas or information in which no copyright existed'.[34] On appeal, however, the court upheld copyright because the defendants were not entitled to utilize the skill and judgment which the plaintiff had exercised in accumulating the data.

The distinction between 'ideas expressed' and the 'expression of an idea' remains subtle and the 'abstractions test' proposed by Hand J in the *Nichols* case is not much clearer. To my mind a more workable test is that expressed by Ulmer.[35] He argues that copyright does not protect the core ('*Kern*') of scientific works but the related rights surrounding it ('*das Gewebe*').[36] He rejects the distinction which Fichte & Kohler made between form and substance (with only the former being entitled to copyright protection). With regard to literary works

30 Ibid.

31 347 US 201 (1954) at 217. This case also confirmed that copyright and patent protection may exist in the same object at the same time.

32 462 F Supp 1003.

33 28 1980 RPC 213.

34 (1979) 29 FSR 46.

35 See note 19 above.

36 Literally 'the Web'—quite prophetic with regard to the Internet!

such as poems he shows that a fable, such as the Faust legend, is common property ('*Gemeingut*'), and therefore not subject to copyright. On the other hand, a fable created by the imagination of the poet himself should be protected: 'Die *Grenze, die wir zu ziehen haben, verläuft demnach nicht zwischen Inhalt und Form, sondern zwischen dem, was vorgegeben ist, und dem was der Dichter geschaffen hat*.'[37] The emphasis should therefore be placed on the mental labour and creativity of the poet (the '*Gewebe*') rather than on the basic idea which was his starting point (the '*Kern*'). This seems to be a more productive distinction to use than that between content and form.

Applying this to scientific works, Ulmer again emphasizes that it is not merely the giving of form which is protected but also the '*Gewebe*' surrounding that activity. By '*Gewebe*' he means the mental labour attendant on the form-giving, for example conjuring up examples, thinking on the different ways of arranging the form or of solving the problem, etc. He does not think, however, that the central idea underlying the whole project should be copyrightable. To distinguish between the central idea and the '*Gewebe*' he suggests the test of '*Freihaltungbedürfnis*'[38]. If an application does not leave open the possibility of individualized alternatives in which the personal style of each creator can be seen, it should not be protected by copyright. To illustrate: a plot in which an Irish and a Jewish family become involved with each other should not be copyrighted, because it leaves no room for a second author to deal with the same theme, although with a completely different style, with unique characterization, etc. This example, taken from the *Nichols* case, shows that Hand J's 'abstractions test' leads to the same result, although I consider the latter criterion to be more difficult to apply.

In using this 'keeping the idea free' test, the original idea or inspiration is not protected because it is too wide. As soon as the creator starts particularizing and individualizing it, however, he receives copyright protection because his variation on the idea is unique and leaves the field free for other renditions and variations. Applying this to computer programs, Ulmer remarks that the programmer might find it paradoxical that his greatest achievement, the original solution, does not attract copyright protection, but that the secondary steps of implementing the solution in the detailed steps of the program are protected.

---

37 'The dividing line has to be drawn, not between content and form, but between that which is known and that which the poet has created' (freely translated). It is interesting to note that the literal translation of the phrase '*dem, was vorgegeben ist*' is 'that which has been given before'. Compare this with the 'raw data' mentioned in the *Mandops* case—the Latin translation of *data* also means 'that which has been given'. If copyright exists only in mental creations and not in mere (given) data, then the protection of accumulations of data by copyright is problematical—see the section on databases below.

38 Literally 'the need to keep free or clear'.

He feels, however, that the need for keeping ideas free sets limits to the subsistence of copyright protection.[39]

In an interesting article entitled 'Copyright in Ideas?'[40] A J C Copeling argues that copyright does protect ideas. From the examples given it seems that what he really has in mind, however, is the mental labour (exercising skill and judgment) following upon the original inspiration:

> 'Yet "skill" and "judgement" are qualities of the mind and devoid of any physical attribute. Indeed, in the context in which they are referred to by the courts, they are simply complementary parts of the literary concept or idea which gives rise to and later becomes embodied in the eventual compilation.'[41]

In so far as he does argue that the basic concept may be copyrighted, I cannot agree for the reasons set out by Ulmer above. Copeling's article is valuable, however, in rejecting the cliché that only form may be copyrighted and indicating that it is the product of mental labour and creativity which is the true object of copyright. One should add the warning, however, that Copeling might have the Continental rather than the common-law view of copyright in mind.[42]

Another fallacy which should also be exposed at this stage is that a mere idea may be patented. The law of patent is as concerned as copyright to prevent a monopoly being given to anything as sweepingly wide as an original idea, rule of calculation or law of nature. That is why patent applies only to the concrete application of an idea in the form of an apparatus, process, etc. Only in that specific manifestation has the idea been particularized enough to leave the field free for other interpretations. Patent does go further than copyright in the second stage, however, where once it has been settled that an idea in itself is not at stake, copyright has to struggle to establish whether substantial copying has taken place. Here patent protects even against an independent arrival at the same solution and the following maxim applies: *Qui prior est in tempore potior est in jure*.[43] The holder of the patent simply has to prove that his invention was earlier in time, something which is easily done thanks to the system of registration obtaining to patent. The whole question of substantial copying is addressed below under the next heading relating to the scope of protection.

---

39 Seeing that patent may also not protect the original algorithm, criminal law may be the only remedy against the theft of ideas embodied in mass-marketed software. The problem is that, according to the law of things, only material matter may be owned and stolen. For individually sold software, protection by trade secret may be contracted for.

40 (1965) 28 *THRHR* 3ff.

41 Copeling op cit 10.

42 See the text accompanying note 77 below.

43 'He who is earlier in time is stronger in law.'

If copyright does subsist, in whom does it subsist? Although I do not like the term 'ownership',[44] who is the 'owner' of the intellectual property? According to s 21(1)*(a)* of the South African Copyright Act,[45] the ownership of any work vests in the author. Before exploring who the author is defined to be, contract programmers should carefully note the provisions of s 21(1)*(d)*:

> 'Where in a case not falling within either *(b)* or *(c)*[46] a work is made in the course of the author's employment by another person under a contract of service or apprenticeship, that other person shall be the owner of any copyright subsisting in the work by virtue of section 3 or 4.'

The 'author' of a computer program is defined by s 1(i) of the Act to be 'the person who exercised control over the making of the computer program'. Section 1*(h)* introduces another interesting category of work, namely 'a literary, dramatic, musical or artistic work or computer program which is computer-generated' and defines the author as 'the person by whom the arrangements necessary for the creation of the work were undertaken'. (Would this, for instance, include a video game or a computer game?)[47]

2.3 The scope of digital copyright (including the question of substantial taking)

2.3.1 General

In the words of Coenraad Visser:

> 'the problems experienced in determining the scope of copyright protection in the present context, would make those experienced in relation to the subsistence of copyright in software, look pale in comparison.'[48]

One does find some guidance in the South African Copyright Act,[49] which first provides generally as follows:

> **'23. Infringement.**
>
> Copyright shall be infringed by any person, not being the owner of the copyright, who, without the licence of such owner, does or causes any other

44 The term really belongs to the law of things, but is used in the Copyright Act itself.

45 Act 98 of 1978.

46 Both relating to non-computer works.

47 Although purists may shudder at the idea of a video game or computer game being a literary, dramatic, musical or artistic work, a recent game release entitled *The Ring* features the music of Wagner directed by George Solti!

48 (1984) *CILSA* 32.

49 Act 98 of 1978.

> person to do, in the Republic, any act which the owner has the exclusive rights to do or to authorize.'[50]

In subsec 2, importation, sale, letting and distribution of infringing articles are prohibited. Section 12 provides general exceptions in the case of use for purposes of research or private study, personal or private use, criticism or review or reportage. These exceptions are sometimes categorized overseas as the fair use exceptions and are further explored when dealing with the copyright problems of libraries below. As far as computer programs are concerned, however, s 19B of the Act does not extend the reasonable and private uses which literary works enjoy to computer programs. Since most overseas countries protect computer programs as literary works, this means that the South African copyright regime is stricter than most.

Section 2*(a)* of Chapter 1 of the Copyright Regulations[51] permits reproduction of a work in terms of s 13 of the Act 'if not more than one copy of a reasonable portion of the work is made, having regard to the totality and meaning of the work', while s 2*(b)* adds the proviso that the cumulative effect of the reproductions should not 'conflict with the normal exploitation of the work to the unreasonable prejudice of the legal interest and residuary rights of the author'. The latter sounds somewhat repetitive in the light of s 13 of the main Act:

> 'In addition to reproductions permitted in terms of this Act reproduction of a work shall also be permitted as prescribed by regulation, but in such a manner that the reproduction is not in conflict with a normal exploitation of the work and is not unreasonably prejudicial to the legitimate interests of the owner of the copyright.'

The mention of 'a reasonable portion of the work' in s 2*(a)* constitutes the legislative foundation for the doctrine of substantial copying (which is not permitted, since it would be more than a 'reasonable portion', of course).

2.3.2 Ideas

The question remains: what actions may the owner of the copyright authorize? The obvious answer seems to be 'copying'! Yet we have seen that only substantial copying is prohibited and that certain general exceptions are provided for. Also, the whole question presupposes the subsistence of copyright, in other words, that the author is not striving to protect an idea *per se*,[52] as we have seen in the previous section. Still, according to Alastair Wilson,[53] the latter question hardly

---

50 The latest version substituted by s 20*(a)* of Act 125 of 1992.

51 Contained in GN R2530 published in *GG* 6252 of 22 December 1978.

52 Meaning in or by itself.

53 'The Protection of Computer Programs under Common Law-Procedural Aspects' and 'UK Copyright Law and Trade Secrets' in Brett & Perry op cit 85.

ever engages the attention of the courts: 'It is fair to say that there are few decided UK cases in which a plaintiff has failed on the ground that only ideas have been taken.' If such a problem does arise, in the opinion of this author Ulmer's test, described above, should be applied. More difficult to apply in practice is the question of substantial copying of something in which copyright does exist (the expression and not the idea) and this is treated in the next section. After that some problems pertaining to the scope of protection for specifically computer software are discussed, namely the thorny issues of use, and of programs co-operating.

2.3.3 Adaptations and translations ('substantial taking')

It should be borne in mind throughout that the fact that copyright may subsist in an adaptation will not have any bearing on the question whether copyright in the original (first generation) is infringed by that adaption.[54] In turn, the reproduction or publication (third generation) of any adaptation of a computer program would also constitute an infringement if done without authority.[55]

Cornish[56] draws attention to the fact that the new CDPA[57] has specifically set the requirement, in s 16(3)*(a)*, that the taking with regard to an adaptation has to be 'substantial'. He couples this with the 'imprecision of any line between idea and expression' (discussed above) and asks why such a vague test should retain international acceptability. The answer (according to Cornish) is that 'there seems to be no better indicator of the judgment called for'.[58] Even though it may offer only general guidance, decisions in particular cases will have to rely on the 'tribunal's innate sense of fairness'. Under the section for specific countries below, we shall see what means have been used to distinguish between the expression and the idea.

The question of taking of a 'substantial' portion remains a difficult matter, as appears from the case of *Ladbrooke (Football) Ltd v William Hill (Football) Ltd*,[59] where the court considered a quotation which stated: 'What is worth copying is *prima facie* worth protecting.' In the end it laid down its own test: '[T]he question whether the defendant has copied a substantial part depends much more on the quality than the quantity of what he has taken.'[60]

An issue closely related to the above is the question whether translation into another computer language would infringe the original copyright. One of the

---

54 See Alan Smith *Copyright Compansion* (Butterworths 1995) 51.

55 Smith op cit 83.

56 W R Cornish *Intellectual Property* (Sweet & Maxwell 1996) 362ff.

57 Acronym for Copyright Design and Patents Act (1988).

58 Op cit 363.

59 1964 (1) WLR 273 at 291.

60 At 293.

normal rights bestowed by statute to the owner of copyright in a literary work is, of course, the right of translation, and a United States court has spoken on this precise point in *Synercom Technology, Inc v University Computing Co*.[61]

The question now seems to have been provisionally settled, in England at least, by a later version of the British Copyright Act, amended towards the end of 1985. This specifically reserves to the copyright owner the right to translate a computer program into a different computer language.

This right to adaptation has been placed firmly in the hands of the 'rightholder' by the European Directive on the Legal Protection of Computer Programs[62] by giving him or her the exclusive right to:

> 'the translation, adaptation, arrangement and any other alteration of a computer program and the reproduction of the results thereof, without prejudice to the rights of the person who alters the program;'.[63]

A new angle upon the whole adaptation debate arises from the need for interoperability between different computer programs. Article 6 of the European Software Directive intended to give guidance on what degree of decompilation[64] of an existing program was permitted, in order to make sure that new programs (being written by the decompiler) would be compatible with the existing program. The United Kingdom actually inserted s 50B into the CDPA which authorizes decompilation of programs for 'permitted objectives' and renders void any contractual terms which would prohibit such decompilation. The United States with its DMCA[65] introduced a similar provision, enabling reverse engineering to ensure interoperability.

In his proposals for amendment of the old South African Copyright Act, Piet Burger[66] suggested that the term 'adaptation' should include translation and that it should be reserved for the copyright owner. Burger also suggested that a program created by the interaction of two programs be included in the term 'adaptation'. In the event the actual amendment did include the translation into another (computer) language under 'adaption', but did not address the interaction issue. Section 1 of the amended South African Copyright Act now determines that an 'adaptation' of a computer program includes—

---

61 462 F Supp 1003 (ND Texas 1978).

62 Article 4b of 91/250/EEC of 14 May 1991. For further discussion see section 7.2.3 below.

63 Ibid.

64 Stripping a computer program down from its object code (the final form in which it is sold) to gain access to its source code (its more easily recognizable and understandable beginnings).

65 Acronym for Digital Millennium Copyright Act (1998).

66 Address to the Computer Society of South Africa, 1 October 1985, Johannesburg, Gauteng Province.

'(i) a version of the program in a programming language, code or notation different from that of the program; or

(ii) a fixation of the program in or on a medium different from the medium of fixation of the program;'.[67]

Section 11B*(c)* of the amended Act[68] now expressly vests in the copyright holder the exclusive right to reproduce or publish an adaptation of the program.

2.3.4 Use (transient reproduction)

To understand fully the problems of use of a computer program, a brief technical explanation is again necessary—with apologies to the computer literate! The concept of a program (the software or 'compact disk'), has already been explained above. Upon loading a program into a computer by means of a floppy disk or from the hard drive, the instructions are loaded into a number of RAM[69] microchips inside the computer, which then have an identical copy of the instructions on the disk. In fact, in many cases the disk can be removed entirely and the computer will operate on the copy in its own memory. This memory is usually volatile, however, which means that as soon as the computer is switched off, the working copy vanishes from its memory and before the computer can perform those particular functions again, the program will have to be loaded once more from the disk which contains the original. In a sense, therefore, a copy or reproduction is made of a program every time it is used. This is quite normal, however, and it is often the only way in which the computer can operate. The problem is whether a statute should in addition prohibit the unauthorized *use* of a program, in the light of the fact that unauthorized 'copying' (which is already prohibited) takes place any time the program is so used, in any event.

As will be seen in the section on the Internet below, every access of another Web site entails making a copy in one's own computer. Should this necessary reproduction of, say, a picture (merely to see it) need specific authorization from the original artist (or even from the relevant webmaster), it would slow down traffic on the Internet even more. In other words, merely by using the Internet, one is continually making (unauthorized) copies.

One finds an amazing variance of opinion on this point. In the United Kingdom, the Whitford Committee wanted any new legislation to prohibit specifically the unauthorized use of a program, rather than leave it to be inferred from the prohibition on reproduction. In a Green Paper[70] the government took the

---

67 Section 1(1) 'adaptation'.

68 Amended by Act 125 of 1992.

69 Random access memory. Some programs are stored permanently in ROM chips (read-only memory), but the situation is not so germane to the present discussion.

70 Cmnd 8302 of July 1983.

view that the creator should have control over the reproduction involved in first loading the program into the machine, but that any further restrictions on use should be left to licensing agreements. Burger has suggested that copying 'includes recordal of the program in the volatile and non-volatile memory of a computer.[71] Apparently *ex abundanti cautela* he then further provided for an exclusive right of use for the proprietor. In Great Britain, the 1985 amendment to the Copyright Act provided specifically that reproduction implicit in the use of a computer amounts to 'reproduction in a material form', which would therefore be an infringement if done without permission. This development was confirmed by s 17(6) of the CPDA, which makes it clear that even 'transient' copies or copies 'incidental to some other use of the work' are prohibited unless authorized. This would then seem to make a specific-use right superfluous, since each occasion of use would also represent a reproduction.

The 1980 amendment to the United States Copyright Act is enigmatic in this regard, since it changed the CONTU recommendation to give this right of 'use-reproduction' to the rightful possessor and instead, limited it to the owner. This result does not take the matter much further, since most lawful users are licensees and/or possessors and not owners. Reed[72] contrasts the American approach with the British view in this regard:

> 'Hence, United Kingdom copyright law appears to give indirect protection to the ideas underlying a program by making the literal copying inherent in simple use of the program an infringing act ... It is interesting to note, by way of comparison, that under the United States copyright law the owner of a copy of a program does not need a license to make or authorize the making of another copy or adaptation if doing so is "an essential step in the utilization of the computer program in conjunction with a machine".'

(Note, however, that the latter would apply only where title to the physical copy of the software program did pass legally to the user. The rights to 'incidental copying' are probably seen as a necessary corollary to the ownership of the software. Would these incidental rights of use be covered by the owner's prohibition on unauthorized copying?

A clear exposition of transient copies becomes even more necessary if one bears in mind that the statutory exemptions contained in s 19B(2) of the South African Copyright Act do not really take the matter much further:

> '(2) The copyright in a computer program shall not be infringed by a person who is in lawful possession of that computer program, or an authorized copy thereof, if—

71 Address to the Computer Society of South Africa, 1 October 1985, Johannesburg, Gauteng Province.

72 Reed *Computer Law* 130.

(a) he makes copies thereof to the extent reasonably necessary for back-up purposes;

(b) a copy so made is intended exclusively for personal or private purposes; ...'

Although the terms used are probably wide enough to cover the transient 'copy' implied in any *use* of that program, it seems obvious that the legislature has not specifically addressed this issue.

This has now been done by a European Union (EU) Software Directive,[73] which provides in art 5.1 that copying and adaptation 'shall not require authorisation by the rightholder where they are necessary for the use of the computer program by the rightful acquirer in accordance with its intended purpose, including for error correction'. According to Reed,[74] the words 'in the absence of specific contractual provisions' imply that the parties can exclude this permission by contract.

This lead by the EU with regard to transient copies was, however, not expressly followed by the 1996 WIPO Directive. The whole matter is further discussed below under section 2.7.3.

2.3.5 Co-operation of programs

A related copyright problem unique to software is the fact that two programs often co-operate. To give one example, a businessman may be creating a client list using a word processing program created by Corel, a software house. Does authorship of the final list reside in the businessman or the software house? The obvious answer would be the businessman, yet he used the program and 'reproduced' it in his computer's memory. Even though such use or reproduction has been licensed by Corel Products, it could be argued that the latter co-authored the work as an independent contractor and that the businessman and the software house are therefore co-owners of the copyright in the client list. To complicate matters further, the computer is using a high-level interpreter program (popularly known as 'the operating system') to translate the source code, in which Corel has written its program, into object code, a lower-level language which may be understood by the machine. This interpreter program has been created by a second software house, Microsoft. In the third place, the BIOS operating system[75] of the computer consists of another program, probably embedded in its ROM chips, created by a third software house, Digital Research Inc. Do they all share copyright in the client list?

---

73 Directive 91/250/EEC.

74 Op cit 130.

75 The program which activates the computer's memory, manages the disk drive and performs other 'housekeeping' functions before looking around for the Microsoft interpreter.

In my opinion the problem shows that 'reproduction' should be interpreted restrictively and that the rights of use should be spelled out clearly in any amending copyright legislation. In the United Kingdom, at any rate, the legislature has decided that the 'copying' into memory, which use of the program necessarily entails, does amount to a reproduction. This matter was supposed to have been resolved by the 1996 Geneva Convention, but after some heated debate, the matter was left open. See the further discussion under section 2.7.3 below.

2.4 THE RAPID DEVELOPMENT OF TECHNOLOGY—IMPLICATIONS FOR COPYRIGHT[76]

In olden times copying a book was a process undertaken by monks and usually took about half a lifetime. Copyright was obviously not a problem since no means of mass copying existed and one felt that if so much time and energy had been expended the copier had earned the right to his own copy. As long as penmanship remained the only means of copying, the law had no need to interfere.

All this changed with the invention of movable type and the printing press, by Gutenberg and Caxton respectively. These enabled multiple copies to be made and original authors found that other people were making money from their writings. In England the first copyright legislation was adopted with the Statute of Anne in 1709. As copyright was introduced throughout the world, it became clear that there were two ways of looking at copyright:

> 'Two traditions existed side by side: the Anglo-American tradition based on the Common law concept of Copyright as an economic right and so could be bought and sold, and the European mainland Civil Law concept of an ideological natural right of authors to control the intellectual fruits of their labours out of which developed a system of moral rights, and the belief that copyright should encourage creativity and the development of knowledge. So the Common Law countries were more concerned to protect the economic rights allied to the work whereas Civil Law countries put the right of the author first.'[77]

This distinction may still be seen in South Africa in the different philosophies behind the Afrikaans term 'outeursreg' (literally 'author's right'), which emphasizes the link between the creation and the creator, and the English term 'copyright', which emphasizes the actual process followed in multiplication. South Africa has traditionally followed the common-law rather than the civil-law

---

76 Part of this section is based on my article entitled 'Copyright and Computers with Special Reference to the Internet: "From Penmanship to Peepshow"' (1998) 115 *SALJ* 180ff.

77 Helge M Sonneland. 'Introduction to Copyright', Paper read at The IFLA Pre-Conference Seminar, Tianjin, China, August 1996.

approach with regard to copyright, but may now land in the same problems as other common-law countries which focus on the actual process of infringement followed with regard to certain specified categories of intellectual property.

Nevertheless, s 20 of the present Copyright Act does take heed of the moral rights of the author and prevents any 'distortion, mutilation or other modification of the work where such action is or would be prejudicial to the honour or reputation of the author'.

The problem is basically that intellectual property is rapidly changing from an 'analogue' to a 'digital' format, prompting sceptical remarks by commentators such as Negroponte and Barlow as to whether copyright will be able to keep up. The photocopier and microfilm were the more recent manifestations of analogue technology and the fact that copyright was able to cope (more or less) with these types of copies, perhaps lulled copyright lawyers into a false sense of security that their field was flexible enough to cope with all new technologies.

With 'digital', everything is different. It is the difference between the old gramophone record and a shiny silver compact disk. It is the difference between the well-known old brown magnetic recording tape and DAT[78] tapes. It is the difference between the ASTRASAT technology to transmit television, which the SABC is having difficulty selling to customers, despite a price advantage,[79] and digital transmission. As far as television receivers are concerned, it will be the difference between the fairly low-focused image that we are seeing at the moment and the pin-sharp image of HDTV,[80] which will soon be available. It is the difference between magnetic videotape jumping around on soon to be obsolete videotape players and the crystal-like clarity of DVD discs[81] that are now moving onto the market. The coming of the digital world has also led to products that would have been impossible before, such as the personal computer and the Internet.

What does 'digital' mean, exactly? It means that books, paintings, music, film, databases, documents and many other kinds of intellectual property may be reduced to binary digits,[82] which represent a series of 'on and off switches' comprehensible to a computer only. By means of the computer the original work may then be stored, modified, reproduced or even broadcast on, for instance, the

78 The acronym for 'digital audio tape'.

79 From an in-house brochure, called *Intercom*, analogue was claimed to be more 'user-friendly with regard to coast', whereas 'Digital technology, on the other hand, is still in its infancy'.

80 The acronym for 'high-definition television', which is digital.

81 The acronym for 'digital video disk'.

82 For instance, the composite signal '11001101' means 'on,on,off,off,on,on,off,on' and might represent the letter 'B' to a specific computer. Each of the individual '1' or '0' signals represents a 'bit' or 'binary digit'. Eight bits combine to form a 'byte', usually representing a single letter, numeral or icon.

Internet. It makes nonsense of the different categories of intellectual property still adhered to in copyright legislation, since in digital form the different works may be integrated with each other to form a so-called 'multimedia' product, which combines text, pictures, sound and video (see the separate heading below).

Suffice it to say that the copyright with regard to multimedia products is precarious, with so-called 'legal clearing houses' having to trace the original creator of each collection of bytes to ask whether he or she would be willing to licence its use as part of the main multimedia program.

The old emphasis of the term 'copyright' on the actual procedure of copying is fast losing its meaning, since the mere act of switching on a computer and taking a tour of the Internet (commonly known as 'surfing the Net') involves the making of hundreds of ephemeral 'copies', mostly unbeknown to the user.[83] Gazing at the colourful images moving across his computer screen, the new 'copier' is now using a 'peepshow' instead of a pen.

Even if the viewing of these fleeting images is seen to be 'copying' by zealous copyright lawyers, enforcement becomes a nightmare. The Internet was actually designed by the United States military to be a means of communication which would be unstoppable even in the event of a cataclysmic nuclear war. It has proven to be unstoppable even by governments attempting to impose some kind of censorship,[84] such as the Communications Decency Act introduced by President Clinton and passed by the American Congress in 1996. This Act would have made it a crime in the United States to broadcast on-line any 'indecent word or image'. The result has been constitutional challenges to obstructing free speech and has led to a Supreme Court case which has declared the Act to be unconstitutional.[85] Even if this Act were to pass muster, the international nature of the Internet would still make it almost impossible to enforce, short of cutting all overseas communications lines or stopping the supply of electricity to citizens. In the end, the international nature of the problem might lead to a solution via international public law and some treaties in this regard will be discussed later on. Even so, in such treaties governments may be undertaking international duties which are impossible to perform.

A possible solution has been suggested by Coenraad Visser in an address at a 'Current Commercial Law Workshop'[86] entitled 'Choice of Law in Internet Copyright Dispute' [sic]. According to Visser, any copyright holder who permits

83 See section 2.3.4 Use (transient reproduction) above.

84 According to 'cyberlibertarian' John Gilmore, '[t]he Internet treats censorship as damage, and routes around it' (*Time* magazine 17 March 1997 at 19).

85 See *Reno v The American Civil Liberties Union* (SC 26 June 1997, affirming 929 F Supp 824).

86 Held at Midrand on 11 March 1999. This has subsequently been published in the (1999) 11 *SA Mercantile Law Journal* at 268ff.

his or her work to be placed on the Internet has given a tacit licence for the user to make a temporary copy in order to view it. Saving it to disk or printing it out would constitute infringement, however.

To close this part, another high-tech example which might create particular difficulties for copyright, is put up for consideration. Many Internet users are now creating databases by means of software 'agents'. These are programs which cruise all over the Internet, armed with information which enables them to 'recognize' snippets of information that might interest their masters. These are automatically 'copied'[87] and when the master turns on his computer he finds a usefully augmented database. Who is the infringing copier: The author of the program? The webmaster who made it available to the end-user? The end-user for sending it on its expedition, without even knowing whether it will find anything? Is the latter 'owner' of the new database created by his or her agents? (See the section on databases below.)

2.5 ALTERNATIVE MEANS OF PROTECTION

Conventional wisdom holds that copyright protection is vitally necessary to protect the software industry. This view is well argued by D Ladd in an article entitled 'Securing the future of copyright: a humanist endeavour'.[88] Ladd review the explosion of knowledge in the technological field and feels cause for optimism as well as dread: 'Dread because if copyright is not provided for—creatively, thoughtfully and effectively—copyright can be grievously hurt.'[89] The recent trend towards 'consumer politics' means that the consumer wants the widest possible access to all copyright material at the lowest possible cost and, in many cases, free. This view is taken by the majority of voters and a comparatively small number of voters, who are copyright owners, are on the other side of the argument. According to Ladd, the latter are the 'good guys':

> 'The counter-argument, as you well know, is that without copyright, the liberty of the subject, including the liberty of speech and the freedom of expression in literature and the arts, would be in danger and ultimately some of the values of Western civilisation would be at risk. But this counter-argument is not as obvious as the popularist argument of cheap access to copyright works by the general public.[90]

---

87 It would be overstating the procedure to call it 'copying'. The agent merely makes a cross-reference to the Web Page or other form of on-line information where the relevant item was found, which its master may then access by means of a mouse-click.

88 Published in March/April 1985 *Computer Law and Practice* 114.

89 Op cit 115.

90 Ibid.

In the previous edition of this book the then chairman of FAST (Federation Against Software Theft), D Maclean, was quoted as stating that program piracy has reached 'desperate levels' and that some, formerly successful, firms producing computer games were going bankrupt because of copying. But according to a contemporary article,[91] piracy costs were not bad enough to warrant the pursuit by senior staff of those infringing.

> 'Like the reports of his own death that Mark Twain read in the paper one morning, the losses suffered by the software industry through piracy are greatly exaggerated.'

More up-to-date statistics can be obtained from the Internet (the biggest library in the world'). According to the home page of the BSA[92] worldwide software piracy losses are estimated at R11,4 billion for 1997. An interesting breakdown by country of piracy losses is also available at the same site. In ranking order the top ten countries are the United States, China, Japan, Korea, Germany, France, Brazil, Italy, Canada and the United Kingdom. Total losses for these countries are $7,8 billion, or 68% of worldwide losses. It is interesting to note that piracy rates in South Africa have actually steadily decreased over the last three years: 1995—58%; 1996—49% and 1997—48%; with corresponding retail piracy losses of R88 323, $43 783 and $69 833 (the last increase probably due to price increases and/or a falling rand/dollar exchange rate).

Is copyright really the only, or the best, vehicle for the protection of computer software? S Breyer is less than convinced. In an article in the *Harvard Law Review*[93] entitled 'The uneasy case for copyright', he undertakes empirical research to test the claims of the exponents of the view that greater copyright protection is necessary. When dealing with published works, he points to the valuable lead time which the original publisher obtains in the market. This lessens the force of many arguments based on a comparison between the original publishing costs and the costs of copying. According to Breyer, copyright should not be resorted to without looking at factors such as the possibility of subsidies and other ways of rewarding authors. He does concede, however, that the need for copyright may vary from one type of writing to another.

Specifically with regard to computer software, he points out that many program developers are able to recoup their development costs by selling copies at fairly high prices to a small number of buyers. The need for copyright protection therefore arises only in the case of generally usable programs, produced by independent software companies selling 'off the shelf', at low prices, to large numbers

91 (1986) *P C and Office Automation*.

92 Business Software Alliance, to be found at www.bsa.org.

93 1970 at 281ff.

of widely dispersed buyers.[94] He is also realistic about the efficacy of copyright protection. Because it is so difficult to prove that one program is a copy of the other ('statements of programs can be so easily altered without changing their function or efficacy'), courts could find it almost impossible to provide effective copyright protection. Furthermore, copyright may have monopolistic effects in an industry where one manufacturer[95] would have copyright in a large percentage of the software available.

Even though Beyer makes some valuable points concerning alternative ways of rewarding creators by, for instance, subsidies, his article is slightly dated in the light of the growth of the commercial importance of mass-marketed software. Also, there are procedural cures for the problems of proof. These are discussed in chapter 6 Evidence below. Finally, he does not seem to grasp the fundamental importance of the international reciprocity of protection that copyright provides: 'I have found no clear explanation presented of the advantages of uniformity *per se*'.[96]

Is copyright necessary in the light of the technical copy protection which may be built into the hardware or software itself? In the previous edition of the present work, the state of the art was reflected by a form of protection called 'Copylock', which seemed to embody some kind of encryption. Even today, encryption does play a major role in the protection of software and communication. 'Copylock' was probably embodied in a 'dongle', a piece of hardware—the program remaining disabled until the required 'dongle' is inserted into the serial or parallel port in the back of the computer. Since this piece of hardware is provided only with a licensed copy of the software, it should prevent a lot of unauthorized use. Unfortunately it also sometimes prevents authorized use. Daniel Remer[97] mentions the irritation of legal users who are unable to make legal backup copies of their software. Even worse is the situation where even use of the basic program itself is impaired because the computer decides, one day, not to recognize its own dongle. For this reason, this form of hardware protection has been abandoned by most software houses.[98]

The use of the dongle involves a form of hardware encryption. The latter process really comes into its own in the field of telecommunication, however. Spurred by the commercial need in this regard, cryptography has made great strides. If the Internet is ever to be a commercial success, certain data will have to be marketable. It is virtually impossible to prevent copying and to protect the marketability of certain data, unless use is made of cryptography.

---

94 In other words, typical 'mass marketed' software.

95 In the previous edition I used the example of IBM. In 1998 it would have to be Microsoft.

96 Op cit at 328.

97 Remer *Legal Care for your Software* 9.

98 Some expensive graphics packages still holding out.

Another form of 'technical protection' is to make popular programs, such as games software, available on CD-ROM. Certain parts of the program may be copied to one's hard disk to speed up use of the system, but usually the entire system cannot be copied.[99] It is also much more stable and reliable than when stored on the magnetic medium of floppy or 'stiffy' disks. Pistorius & Visser make the point that the South African Copyright Act's permission to make back-up copies probably does not apply in the case of CD-ROM disks, since these are subject to physical destruction only.[100]

A similar form of technical protection in the highly threatened world of games software is that used by the manufacturers of 'TV-Games' (such as Nintendo and Sega) who sell a little black box or console from which the game program cannot be copied.

The very latest manifestation of technical protection is a 'Musicbot', belonging to BMI, the music licensing agency that represents some 180 000 songwriters and music publishers. Musicbot is a so-called software 'agent' (a form of program which permanently roams the Internet) which is able to identify sites that use music, count the number of people that visit them and see that licensing conditions are complied with.

Another new development is the so-called 'digital watermark', which has been proclaimed by some to be 'the best way to protect intellectual property from illicit copying'.[101] In the same Internet article (by Dr Jian Zhao) the system is briefly described as follows:

> 'In contrast to a traditional watermark on an invoice, for example, a digital watermark can be detected only by appropriate software. Rather than ensuring the authenticity or integrity of documents, as a digital signature or a digital seal does, a digital watermark aims to identify the origin, author, owner, usage rights, distributor, or authorized user of an image, video clip, or audio clip, even if the image or clip has been processed and distorted (via analog-to-digital conversion, low-pass filtering, resampling, lossy compression, cropping or rotation).'

Being digital, the watermark is quite invisible and should serve to help bring the freebooters of digital content to book.[102] Apparently Adobe and IBM are two firms already making use of this technology in their software. Recently the assurance given by this new form of technological protection evaporated when

---

99 With the growth in popularity of 'burning' one's own CD-ROM, however, the copying of these is now also increasing. In terms of volume of copyrighted material contained per unit, this far transcends the former copying of floppy disks, which makes it even more of a threat.

100 (1992) 4 *SA Mercantile Law Journal* 346 at 358.

101 Picked up on the Internet at http://www.byte.com/art9701/sec18/art1.html.

102 Do *you* perhaps have a skeleton in the cupboard too?

a 'cracker' claimed to have defeated a watermark used by Digimarc Corporation. Word was spread on the Web concerning a software patch created by 'Frogs_Print' that supposedly can remove Digimarc digital watermarks. However, the technological war never ceases—version 1.51 of 'PictureMarc', Digimarc's basic watermarking program, includes revisions that specifically address the Frogs_Print patch, amongst other improvements.[103]

2.6 COPYRIGHT PROBLEMS IN CERTAIN SPECIFIC APPLICATION AREAS

The categories set out below are by no means a *numerus clausus* of problematical digital copyright areas. One could mention just one additional field as an example, namely that of DIP (Document Image Processing). Here, documents are no longer stored and processed physically, but only in digital format. This has tremendous workflow advantages and it will enhance commerce. It also has tremendous evidential implications, however, and these are discussed in chapter 6 Evidence below.

2.6.1 The Internet

The scope of this work does not allow for a full explanation of the Internet, yet a basic understanding is essential in order to grasp certain of the copyright and censorship problems which this relatively new phenomenon has given rise to and which have already been referred to above. Apart from the fact that copyright struggles to cope with the digital nature of intellectual property on the Internet, enforceability is also a major issue.

Basically the Internet is a worldwide network of computer users. Up to the present, it has mainly been used for research and the exchange of academic information. With the use of a more graphical interface, the 'World Wide Web' has now captured the world's imagination and more and more products and services are being offered, mostly in the form of programs, graphics[104] and data. At the moment of writing this, a furious debate is raging on the Internet copyright discussion group as to whether one makes a 'copy' when downloading a file[105] from the 'home page' of an Internet information provider, whether the latter is actually making the copy upon the 'request' by the visitor to the Web site,[106] and whether by making the file available on his or her 'home page', the user has actually put

---

103 ITEC Law Alert (McBride, Baker Coles) February 1998 at 5: 'With Digital Watermarks, Cracked Doesn't Mean Broken.'

104 The higher resolution of computer screens has caused an upsurge in 'on-line' pornography, which is virtually impossible to control at state level, since the pictures enter the country in an encrypted form via the telecommunications network.

105 Saving the file to one's own computer from the host computer.

106 Very often these processes are automated anyway.

it into the public domain. This issue was raised, but not resolved, at a recent conference in Geneva.[107] The matter goes even so far as to include replication (caching) on a different server in order to speed up transmission. In the case of *Religious Technology Ctr v Netcom On-Line Communications Servs, Inc,*[108] it was held that the use of Netcom's computers in this way was not direct infringement, but should be viewed as contributory infringement.

Whatever the outcome of this debate, it seems fairly clear that it will be very difficult to enforce copyright on the Internet without losing the free flow of information which has made it such a success in the first place. Traditional wisdom has been that the solution to making copyright pay would lie in encrypting the most valuable material and handing the encryption key to paid-up members. It would now begin to appear as if the solution might lie in advertising, which will allow free access to Web pages on which the sponsor's product is advertised.[109]

At a conference entitled 'Cyberlaw' held in Sandton on 21–2 October 1997 a paper by Mr Webster (of the firm of attorneys Spoor and Fisher) was read; it was entitled 'Guardianship of Third Party Rights on the Net'. Personally, I found most interesting that part of the paper dealing with the registration of Internet domain names. Mr Webster was of the opinion that this was analogous to trade mark protection but pointed out that there were also important differences:

> 'Trade marks may be registered in one or more of forty two classes, depending upon the goods or services for which protection is sought and it is not uncommon for the same mark to be used and registered by different parties for entirely different products or services. On the other hand only one domain name can be registered on an internet domain name space. Often more than one person will have a legitimate claim on the registration of a domain name but due to the technical requirement that each name must be unique, such registration will be dealt with on a "first come first served' basis. The timeous registration of a company name, trading style and important trade marks as domain names can therefore not be overstressed.'

For safety's sake, the firm of Spoor and Fisher registered all of the following as their domain names: 'spoor.co.za', 'fisher.co.za', 'spoorandfisher.co.za', 'sf.co.za'

107 Which is discussed in greater detail below in section 2.7.3 Intranational and Supranational developments. See also the discussion in sections 2.3.5 Use (transient reproduction) and 2.4 The Rapid Development of Technology above.

108 F Supp 1361 (ND Cal 1995).

109 In some of their latest manifestations these advertisements often resemble a rather large postage stamp, which revolves every few seconds, showing another sponsor's blurb on the flip side. So called 'banner-ads' are even more intrusive and increase download times considerably.

and 'sandf.co.za'! This matter receives further attention in the next chapter, dealing with trademarks.

Another interesting question is whether the use of a 'framed' link to another Web site constitutes copyright infringement. Some of the previous cases in which this question arose have been settled before final decision, such as the Scottish case of *Shetland Times, Ltd v Dr Jonathan Wills*, et al.[110] In the latest decision *Futuredontics, Inc v Anagramics, Inc*[111] the facts were as follows. Futuredontics had created a Web site to promote its dental referral business. Sometime after, Anagramics created its own site and included a hypertext link to the Futuredontics site. This procedure is quite normal and typical of the interrelations which enrich the Web; it is usually done by means of some highlighted text on the referencing page. In the present instance, however, Anagramics had used a portion of the Futuredontics site, 'framed' by a panel containing information about Anagramics. The judge denied Anagramics' motion to dismiss and this has given Futuredontics the chance to prove that Anagramics has created a derivative infringing work.

Before leaving the Internet and copyright it may be wise to memorize Lee & Davidson's[112] ten commandments in this regard:

'1. Copyright law *does* extend to the Internet—albeit tough questions regarding which country's copyright laws apply will arise;
2. Do not assume that any material posted is public domain, particularly since the 1989 amendment to the Copyright Act[113] makes clear that lack of a copyright notice does not affect whether copyright subsists in a work;
3. Fair use remains a consideration, but does not make any use permissible merely by virtue of posting material on the Net;
4. When a person forwards material to others, such conduct *may* be viewed as a distribution, reproduction, publication, public display, or performance, or even as an importation;
5. The transmission of audiofiles may involve the rights of both the author of the underlying musical work and the recording company (this latter twist is due to the Digital Performance Right in a Sound Recordings Act[114] of 1995);

110 1996 Sess Cas (Scot Outer House).

111 45 USPQ 2d 2005 (CD Cal 1998).

112 L C Lee & J S Davidson *Intellectual Property for the Internet* (Wiley Law Publications 1997) at 141.

113 Of the United States.

114 Of the United States.

6. Before simply accessing and reproducing data from a site, consider both any potential compilation copyright under US law, as well as the source of the data—current United Kingdom law provides for a database protection, and the European community (EC) Database Directive requires member states to implement national law by January 1, 1998 (even if a database is not protectable under United States law as an original expression under the *Feist* decision);
7. In addition to copyright, take note of any restrictions which may purport to limit use of material or data on a site. The significance of such restrictions should be read with an appreciation of the Seventh Circuit's decision in *ProCD*;
8. Even if you are merely an Internet access provider or online service provider acting solely as a retransmitter, take note that at least one court, albeit most likely in an aberrant decision, has held a BBS liable as a direct—as contrasted with indirect—infringer. At a minimum, consider adopting procedures for addressing scenarios where you are given notice of potentially infringing material. The current procedures of Netcom are an example, and they are a direct result of the suit by the Church of Scientology against Netcom relating to material transmitted by a Netcom subscriber, a former Scientologist, over the Netcom system;
9. Review carefully whether content suppliers have the necessary rights (either as owner or licensee) to permit you to post or transmit the content;
10. Do not assume that use for one purpose equates with use for any purpose. One use may be covered by a licence or be a permissible fair use, and another, seemingly similar, use may be infringement. Accordingly, each use should be analyzed in its context to determine if the use is lawful.'

Scary, isn't it! Particularly the fourth paragraph gives food for thought. Forwarding any material on the Internet (and *a fortiori* making it available for the first time, say as a service provider) *may* constitute one of the prohibited copyright actions. And then again, it may not. Even if it did, the problems of scale and jurisdiction might mean that this particular brand of copyright may not be enforced very well. One is again left with a feeling of something being stretched to the limits in order to accommodate something else that was never meant to be dealt with in this way.

None of the above paragraphs really cover the situation where the creator of a site inserts a hypertext link to another (possibly copyrighted) site. Hofman covers just this situation in his work *Cyberlaw*:[115]

'The problem is real but the legal solution is not obvious. In the few cases that have come before the courts, the courts have, probably wisely, avoided

115 Julian Hofman *Cyberlaw* (Ampersand Press 1999) at 92.

pronouncing on the main issue. It would certainly be possible to treat linking without permission as a breach of copyright or as a breach of the author's moral rights or as passing of. But to require permission for every link would be to deprive the Web of much of its flexibiity and potential for growth.'

Hofman then plumps for the opinion that 'the rights of the copyholder should give way to the general good', on other words that mere linking to other sites would not constitute an infringement of copyright.

In a recent case in the Netherlands, a court found exactly the opposite. In the case of *Scientology v Spaink/XS4all*[116] it was decided that creating hyperlinks to an infringing site would in itself constitute an infringement of copyright, whether it is done by creating a clickable link or by providing an address on one's own site. Interestingly enough, the service provider to the linker would not be held responsible since the reproductions made by his machines are dictated by technology.[117] The judge referred to the care which every participant owes to the rest of the community. One of the Dutch commentators comments in despair:

'Internet is teneinde. En snel toestemming vragen voor de links op je site.'[118]

He also makes the very relevant point that certain automated search engines create links on your site to what they have found automatically. Perhaps they can use the words of the court against itself—the search engine links might also be 'dictated by technology'! Still, this is a very worrying decision with huge implications for the Internet if the impact of the judgment spreads to other countries.

Finally, the Internet has also made a bit of a nonsense of the worldwide emphasis on standards. It has simply developed so quickly that the relatively slow-moving world of developing and accrediting standards has not been able to keep up. Lee & Davidson[119] point out that most of the Internet is run on *de facto* standards. However, they are impressed by the work of the IETF,[120] which they consider 'less formal, more responsive' than 'traditional organizations such as ISO'.[121]

---

116 Reported on the Internet at http://www.xs4all.nl/kspaink/cos/dag3eng.html.

117 This argument might also serve well for some other sticky situations in which service providers find themselves.

118 'Internet has come to an end. And get consent quickly for the links on your site.' (My translation.)

119 Op cit 163.

120 Acronym for Internet Engineering Task Force.

121 Acronym for International Standards Organization.

2.6.2 Databases

One of the points of criticism by Pistorius & Visser[122] of the 1992 amendments to the South African Copyright Act concerns the fact that it does not provide specific protection for databases. The original European Community Guidelines on copyright for computer programs, mentioned above, also failed to do so. It is a measure of the value of a database, notwithstanding that it might not represent a lot of originality, that an EEC 'common position' was adopted by the council on 24 July 1995, with a view to adopting a Directive of the European Parliament on the legal protection of databases and that the Directive itself was in fact adopted on 11 March 1996.[123] In its short lifespan, it has so far had an effect not only in the EU itself but even in the United States, as will be seen below when dealing with the latter country.

Given the fact that South Africa has often followed the lead of the United Kingdom in matters pertaining to copyright, it might perhaps be hoped that South Africa will now also properly provide for copyright in databases.[124] If the example of the EU is followed, it would also make for consistency with some of South Africa's most important trading partners. A philosophical problem does exist with regard to the requirement of originality or creative effort, when often a mere accumulation of data may have considerable commercial value. This is illustrated by the *Feist* decision in the United States,[125] which is dealt with below. For this reason too, the latest European Union directive (also dealt with below) had to go outside normal copyright to create a *sui generis* right with regard to the protection of databases. The initial EU common position was as follows:

> '1. Member States shall provide for a right for the maker of a database which shows that there has been qualitatively and/or quantitatively a substantial investment in either the obtaining, verification or presentation of the contents, to prevent acts of extraction and/or re-utilization of the whole of or a substantial part, evaluated qualitatively and/or quantitatively, of the contents of that database.'

A database was also defined quite adequately:

> '2. For purposes of this Directive, "database" shall mean a collection of works, data or other independent materials arranged in a systematic or

---

122 (1992) 4 *SA Mercantile Law Journal* at 346.

123 96/9/EC 'European Directive on the Legal Protection of Databases'.

124 A 1997 amendment has widened the definition of 'literary work' in section 1 of the Copyright Act, 98 of 1978, to encompass 'tables and compilations of data stored or embodied in a computer or a medium used in conjunction with a computer'.

125 111 S Ct 1282 11 L Ed 2d 358 (1991).

methodical way and capable of being individually accessed by electronic or other means.'

Both these statements were adopted without change in the Directive. The above definition now forms art 1(2) and the 'common position' constitutes a *sui generis* right under art 7(1). It would seem that the creation of a special right, additional to copyright, might be to overcome the strong emphasis placed on originality in the American case of *Feist Publications Inc v Rural Telephone Service Company Inc*,[126] with dealt specifically with databases. Before moving on to a closer look at that decision, one should perhaps pause to reflect again on the adequacy (or lack of it) of copyright law to provide the legal background for the growing commoditization of information referred to in the introduction above. Too many exceptions and *sui generis* inventions are often a sign that the limits of a present paradigm are being exceeded and that the whole field should perhaps be conceptually reconsidered.

The *Feist* decision turned on a list of the customers of a telephone company which was published as a directory. The company (plaintiff in the case) had listed the names of all telephone customers in alphabetical order, with their city of residence and telephone number. The defendant had prepared a competing nationwide directory, which included the plaintiff's customers and others. After the trial court and the federal court had found in favour of the plaintiff, the matter came before the Supreme Court, where these findings were reversed.

O'Connor J noted the tension between two fundamental premises of copyright.[127] On the one hand, facts are not subject to copyright; on the other hand, compilations of facts may be copyrighted. The learned judge resolved this by going back to the roots of copyright and the fact that copyright protection is limited to *original* works of authorship. This originality implies that the work must also possess a certain degree of creativity—facts are therefore not protectable because they are not created by the author. If compilations involve independent create effort they may however, qualify for copyright protection. O'Connor J rejected the alternative 'sweat of the brow' motivation which underpinned the lower court's acceptance of the plaintiff's claim. This theory rewards the compiler of data because of the significant time and effort which a compiler has to expend in accumulating data, no matter that little or no originality was involved. The defendant therefore triumphed because originality, not effort, was the true basis of copyright protection.

126 Supra.

127 According to *Harper & Row Publishers, Inc v National Enterprises* 471 US 539, 556 (1985) '[n]o author may [copyright] his ideas or the facts he narrates'.

According to Cross, an insightful commentator on the case,[128] this decision undercuts copyright protection for one of the three main types of computer databases. Cross distinguishes between:

- the 'free-format' type of database, where not much *a priori* ordering of data by the compiler is necessary since the computer does the searching;
- the 'hierarchical' type, where the compiler has to determine in advance exactly which categories he is going to use for classification;[129] and
- the 'field management' type, where any characteristic of a data object can start off a separate list containing other data objects with that same characteristic.

It is interesting that only the hierarchical type can be maintained without using a computer at all. It is also the type where it is easiest to find the required original creative effort needed to provide copyright protection. The field management model might also qualify, since the process of defining the field which contain relevant characteristics also requires the compiler to exercise some creativity and independent judgment. However, the free-format model, which is most useful in conjunction with a computer's considerable processing capabilities, does not require significant creativity from the human being operating it. As Cross puts it: 'This does not mean that compilers of free-format databases are somehow lazy. Instead, because of the inherent nature of the free-format database, arrangement serves no real purpose.'[130] Unfortunately this also means that this type of database will probably not qualify for copyright protection, since the compiler has not exhibited enough creativity or originality.

This is an upsetting development and may explain the development of a so-called *sui generis* right to prevent extraction from, and re-utilization of, databases by the legislature of the European Community.[131] It may also explain why the United States has embarked on its own database protection legislation and had refused to incorporate the database recommendations by the 1996 WIPO treaty.[132] A good example of a European country attempting to implement the EU Directive is the new Belgian draft law. This is discussed thoroughly in an article entitled 'Rechtsbescherming van databanken: het Belgisch wetsontwerp'.[133] The definition of 'database' is taken directly from the European directive—the countries are left with little choice in this regard. The concept changes domestic Belgian copyright

128 John T Cross in I Carr & K Williams (eds) *Computers and Law* (Intellect 1994) 113.

129 This reminds one of the older type of database program where one not only needed to define fields in advance, but also had to specify what the maximum of characters used by that field would be.

130 Op cit 123.

131 See section 2.7.3 below.

132 See the specific treatment of the United States in section 2.7.1 below.

133 By P Goethals & J Dumortier in (1998) 3 *Computerrecht* 127; freely translated as 'Legal protection of databases: The Belgian draft law'.

law to accommodate the EU copyright concepts, but enacts new legislation to provide for the *sui generis* right discussed above. Even a transient reproduction needs to be authorized by the copyright holder. An interesting development is a clause which authorizes the use of electronic databases in teaching and scientific research. The *sui generis* right applies only within the EU and lasts for 15 years from the completion of the database. The authors see many potential legal problems with regard to the future interpretations of this 'gloednieuwe' (brand-new) right.

2.6.3 Multimedia and video games

Although this is a 'buzzword' which helps to sell more expensive computers, it simply means using more than one medium. This usually boils down to fitting a computer with a CD-ROM drive, a sound card and speakers, and perhaps a video card. Equipped with this more attractive user interface, these machines are most often used for training or for entertainment, or for the new concept of 'edu-tainment'.

The central copyright problem seems to be the fact that it is so easy to incorporate digitized 'chunks' of other people's graphics, sound, animation and film into multimedia programs, even though it might be only one or two seconds' worth. Even apart from the problem of determining whether a 'substantial' portion has been taken, one may also encounter considerable problems of 'proof' to show that a specific snippet of 'multimedia' content was taken from a copyrighted work.

One of the solutions for creators of multimedia content is to buy disks filled with 'public domain' drawings, or video and sound clips, which are specially produced in order to provide for the growing demand for this type of multimedia content. Another solution is to 'roll your own' (a cigarette metaphor) by manufacturing your own multimedia content. For instance, a Unisa video production (to illustrate criminal procedure and evidence) was made in-house at the Unisa studios, with Unisa-drawn graphics and some 'public domain' music. It could, however, drive up the costs of a multimedia production considerably if one does not have in-house facilities. In such an eventuality it may be a better proposition to pay licensing fees and have Mickey Mouse, or some other copyrighted creature, to enliven your production legally.

Video games,[134] like databases, form an interesting integration of programming and data, but add a lot of digital literary work, digital artistic work, and digital musical work. This integration can obviously not be protected as a computer program alone, especially given the reasonably restrictive definition given to a

134 Although I shall be using this term for convenience, it is not very accurate. Most computer games make use of graphics, some of graphics and video, and only one or two of video alone. The last category is actually an example of the 'interactive video' genre, where the reactions of the users lead to different video clips, such as *Psychic Detective*, one of the rare examples of a video game in the narrower sense.

program in the South African Copyright Act.[135] Because of their considerable commercial importance, video games, in fact, constitute the acid test for copyright's ability to cope with digital multimedia.

Video games fall into the category of cheap, mass-marketed programs that even Breyer[136] concedes should receive copyright protection. Formerly they mostly appeared as ROM chip-operated 'arcade games', but now many games are available in loadable format[137] for private computers and are subject to extensive piracy. In an interview, the chairman of FAST, D Maclean, expressed the opinion that the very success of a company's software could spell its death, because its products are the favourite targets of home copiers and professional counterfeiters.

In an article based more on the older arcade games, G Dreisbach[138] points out that video games are protected as audio-visual works under the United States Copyright Act. The 'visual' part is important because the design of the screens on which the games are played often constitutes the greatest asset of the game. The idea behind a game cannot be protected, thus there are countless variations of the original 'Pac-man', a sphere with a gobbling mouth which spends its life in a maze, alternately eating or being eaten by ghosts. Dreisbach discusses a few cases which were brought to court as a result of variations on the basic idea, such as 'Mighty Mouth', 'Jawbreakers', 'K C Munchkin', and 'Packri Monster'. In all these cases the court had to struggle with the test for 'substantial similarity' (explained in a previous section) and the only conclusion which may safely be drawn is that the outcome of these cases is very uncertain!

An American case illustrating some of the practical problems is *Atari Games Corp v Nintendo of America Inc.*[139] In contrast to loadable games on a personal computer (PC), Atari and Nintendo manufacture so-called 'home video game systems' where the user buys a game cartridge which he or she inserts into a dedicated console from the same manufacturer. The console and the cartridge in fact contain programmed ROM chips which interact with one another. Atari had unsuccessfully tried to reverse engineer Nintendo's chips, paid licence fees and then fraudulently obtained the score code from the US copyright office. This enabled them to develop a similar program called 'The Rabbit'. They then had the gall to sue Nintendo for unfair competition, patent infringement, copyright infringement and trade-secret violations! The court used the *Nichols* abstractions

---

135 Act 98 of 1978, where s 1 defines a computer program as 'a set of instructions fixed or stored in any manner, and which, when used directly or indirectly in a computer, directs its operation to bring about a result'.

136 May/June 1985 *Computer Law and Practice* at 146.

137 Whether by CD-ROM or by a number of floppy disks.

138 (1984) 10 *Rutgers Computer and Technology Law Journal* at 127ff.

139 975 F 2d 832 (Fed Cir 1992).

test and the *Altai* filtration test[140] in order to find that Atari had engaged in unlawful copying. It is interesting to note, however, that this decision was based mainly on the illegal copying of the code at the Copyright Office. The court actually found that the reverse engineering fell under the fair use exception[141] and prevented Atari from using the copyright misuse defence[142] only because they had 'unclean hands' as a result of their attorney lying to the Copyright Office. In a case discussion,[143] Susan E Dallas points out that the court's dicta on reverse engineering actually narrowed copyright protection to such an extent that 'software developers will continue to attempt to protect their products with methods other than copyright'.[144] She also found a delightful quote from Goldberg & Bernstein: 'Old doctrines and principles are being stretched to unprecedented dimensions to accommodate developing software copyright issues.'[145] She suggests other possibilities such as 'patent, trade secret, misappropriation, and trademark law'.[146]

Coupled with this is the problem, mentioned above, that a video contains more protectable categories than that of a computer program alone. Visser & Pistorius[147] discuss this problem at the hand of some American and (unreported) South African cases. They find that computer-game displays are protected in the United Kingdom as 'cinematograph films' and in the United States as 'audiovisual displays'. By contrast the 1992 amendments to the South African Copyright Act[148] specifically exclude a computer program from the definition of cinematograph film. The authors therefore find the protection of video displays generated by computer programs 'obscure'. Even though these may be protected individually as static artistic or literary works, the authors are not very excited about this form of protection 'since the movements and mannerisms of some figure may be of the utmost importance, such as the 'gobbler effect' of 'Pac-man' or 'the effectiveness of the evasion manoeuvers of a defending aircraft'.[149] They suggest that trade-mark protection might be used if this is displayed on the screen.

And yet one wonders if the change in the definition of 'cinematograph films' and the expansion of the definition of 'author' to include 'a literary, dramatic, musical or artistic work or computer program which is computer-generated' does

---

140 Discussed more fully in section 2.7.1 below.

141 See section 2.6.5 dealing with fair use below.

142 See section 2.7.1. below.

143 (1994) 71 *Denver University Law Review* at 739ff.

144 Op cit at 755.

145 Op cit at 755.

146 Ibid.

147 (1992) 4 SA *Mercantile Law Journal*.

148 Act 98 of 1978 as amended by Act 125 of 1992.

149 Op cit at 356.

not mean that a new category of multimedia work, constituted by these types of work, is perhaps created. It would take a brave and technologically astute court to wring this interpretation out of s 1 of the present Act and it would probably be much better for the legislature to step in and protect multimedia works and video games properly and explicitly.

The initiative to do so has now perhaps been diminished by an influential Appellate Division case in South Africa in the shape of *Golden China TV Game Centre v Nintendo Co Ltd.*[150] Harms JA did an extensive technical analysis of a 'video game':

> 'A video game is, as its name implies, a game played on a video screen. An apparatus containing integrated circuits (usually two microchips) [is] connected to it. When the machine is in operation, a visual page appears on the screen. The display has the general appearance of an animated cartoon strip, save that the game player is able, up to a point, to control the game sequence with a control mechanism. In other words, the game sequence is not finitely fixed.'[151]

Harms JA then goes into the history of the copyright protection of cinematograph films in South Africa (since the appellants claimed that a video game did not constitute a film). Under the Patents, Designs, Trade Marks and Copyright Act[152] a 'cinematograph' was protected under the category of 'dramatic work'. Under the Copyright Act of 1965[153] (which was based on the United Kingdom. Copyright Act of 1956) films were protected in their own category. The latest Copyright Act[154] (which, according to Harms J broke to some extent with the United Kingdom tradition)[155] kept its own category, but in an 1992 amendment, specifically excluded computer programs from the definition of a film. This did not bother Harms JA as it did Coenraad Visser (see above), since '[i]t was common cause that the video games are not computer programs although computer programs were used during their creation and although they may have been fixated by way of such programs.'[156]

To the present writer, this seems to be somewhat of an over-simplification. Computer programs are necessary to access the game all the time and the game would be unplayable without the underlying computer programs. The value of

150 1997 (1) SA 405 (E).

151 Supra at 409DBE.

152 Act 9 of 1916.,

153 Act 63 of 1965.

154 Act 98 of 1978.

155 'This Act, influenced somewhat by the Continental approach to copyright, broke to some extent with the English legal tradition on copyright' (at 411).

156 At 415E.

a computer program to the playing of a video game[157] is more striking when one realizes that probably half of these games are actually played on a personal computer and not on the type of proprietary playstation based on ROM-chips described above. Of course, the program has to be modified to run on a proper computer, but this usually brings with it even better sound, graphics and even video. It is, in fact, a typical multimedia computer product such as we have been discussing in this paragraph.

It is also interesting to note some of the other findings made by Harms JA. He found that a reproduction, in the context of copyright, 'refers to the copying of the *work* (ie the cinamatograph film) in question and not to ephemeral versions, renditions or applications of a work'. He relied on the American case of *Midway Mfg Co vs Arctic International Inc*,[158] where it was pointed out that although the end user could change the order in which certain sequences of images were presented, the user could not change the images themselves. The video game therefore remained within the definition of a film. The appellants were therefore guilty of copying a film in contravention of the present Copyright Act, both before and after the 1992 amendments.

Although I would not want to quarrel with the final result in the present case, Justice Harms' definition of a reproduction would probably not hold good for items which are created digitally in the first place, such as a Web page on the Internet. If it did, the 'ephemeral' reproduction by someone downloading it onto another computer would then not be considered a 'reproduction in the context of copyright' and if this were the case, South African law has taken a different course to the EU, and probably to most of the rest of the world.

In a recent Belgian decision[159] it was found that MIDI-files[160] are subject to copyright, since they are in the same situation as computer programs.

2.6.4 Government information

In the South African Copyright Act,[161] s 5 provides that copyright subsists in a work which has been made by or under the direction of the state. The Government Printer has been designated[162] as the person in whom the govern-

157 In view of this misleading effect, perhaps these phenomena should rather have been called 'computer games'.

158 (1983) 704 F 2d 1009 at 1011B12; (1983) 218 USPQ 791 at 792–3.

159 'Arondissmentsrechtbank Utrecht' on 7 May 1997, reported in (1998) 6 *Computerrecht* at 261.

160 A music file in digital format, which makes it easily transportable over the Internet.

161 Act 98 of 1978.

162 By Proc R24 1979 in *GG* 6299 dated 9 February 1979.

ment's copyright vests for administrative purposes. On the other hand, s 12(8)*(a)* provides that

> 'No copyright shall subsist in official texts of legislative, administrative or legal nature, or in official translations of such texts, or in speeches of a political nature or in speeches delivered in the course of judicial proceedings, or in news of the day that are mere items of press information.'

Reading the two sections together, a reasonable conclusion would seem to be that, although the government does enjoy copyright in some of its own creations, this does not extend to the text of the statutes or even to the text of court judgments. This impression is strengthened by the fact that the interim Constitution of the Republic of South Africa[163] provided as follows (in s 32):

> 'Every person shall have the right of access to all information held by the state ... or another person ... in so far as such information is required for the exercise or protection of any of his or her rights.'

Section 32(2) also requires the government to pass legislation in this regard, and at the time of writing draft legislation for an 'Open Democracy Act' is circulating.

This is the 'freedom of information' clause, so-called since the same effect was achieved in the United States by a 'Freedom of Information Act'. At the moment another furious debate is raging on the international computer network 'the Internet', as to whether this freedom of access should not be extended to a positive duty of providing such legal information electronically or, at any rate, not granting private companies a monopoly in making available certain classes of government information. According to one of the participants, Ejan Maackay, of Montreal, Canada, the Netherlands does not believe in *Kroonauteursrecht*, which Canada, strangely enough, still does, in imitation of the UK. 'The latter has even strengthened that position by recent legislation.'

What it does seem clear is that certain countries, such as Canada and the United Kingdom are much more restrictive in trying to preserve copyright in government publications. It may well be asked if this does not impair the right to information of its citizens, and whether an attempt will not perhaps be made to challenge the government in the constitutional court. (South Africa would probably be classified as resorting under on the Canada/UK approach rather than under the position pertaining in the Netherlands.)

In the United Kingdom Her Majesty's Stationery Office (HMSO), the government's official publisher, was privatized on 1 October 1996. However, a small residuary body was left 'official', mainly to handle government copyright. Crown and parliamentary copyright is therefore now in the hands of the Copyright Unit

---

163 Act 200 of 1993.

of Her Majesty's Stationery Office, proving that some importance is still attached to government copyright.

2.6.5 Libraries and universities—the 'fair use' problem

Some progress has been made by the Universal Copyright Convention (UCC), where the role of libraries was emphasized in providing access to information. On the other hand, the possibility of rapid digital multiplication has filled publishers with dread and this has led to some strange resolutions being adopted. For instance, at the 25th Congress of the International Publishers Association[164] a resolution was passed 'which in effect stated that, because the analogue and digital environment works differently, all uses of copyright work which conflict with the normal exploitation of the work should be discarded'.

This would, in effect, mean that all 'fair dealing' or 'fair use' exceptions which have developed in favour of academic or library use will need to abrogated. There are fears among publishers that libraries will buy only one copy of a work, which could then be distributed electronically around the world, with the effect that sales of analogue books would cease and the paper publishing industry would collapse. In the view of Sandy Norman, this is a myth: on the contrary, and libraries and publishers need each other. Publishers also hope that since digital copying has the potential to be tracked (and therefore controlled), the exceptions allowed for photocopying in libraries would no longer have to apply. These were apparently only conceded to because there was no way to police their use. 'Although the battle had been lost with the photocopier, they were not prepared to lose the battle in the digital environment.'[165]

It is interesting to note that some special provision had been made for university research by the latest Belgian draft legislation (see section 2.6.2 dealing with databases above). By contrast, the right of private use and for research which exists in South African copyright law for literary works and which states as follows:

> '(1) Copyright shall not be infringed by any fair dealing with a literary or musical work—
>
> *(a)* for the purposes of research or private study by, or the personal or private use of, the person using the work;'

has specifically been removed by s 19A of the South African Copyright Act[166] with regard to computer programs.

---

164 Held in Barcelona on 26 April 1996.

165 From a speech by Sandy Norman in Johannesburg on 17 March 1997 entitled 'Copyright Removing the barriers?'

166 Act 98 of 1978.

2.7 THE SPECIFIC SITUATION WITH REGARD TO DIGITAL COPYRIGHT IN CERTAIN COUNTRIES

2.7.1 The United States

In this section we look at some United States-specific legislation as well as at a range of United States case law on the thorny expression/idea issue. The issue of the protection of databases, although addressed under the general part above, has also undergone some development in United States law and this it expanded on further below.

At the time of the previous edition and for a number of years thereafter, copyright in the United States was governed by the 1976 Copyright Act. After a report from CONTU,[167] President Carter signed into effect the Computer Software Amendment Act of 1980. This Act was followed by the 1984 Semiconductor Chip Protection Act. Like ordinary copyright in the United States,[168] it required registration. However, protection lasts for only ten years as opposed to the life plus 50 years for ordinary copyright.

The very latest legislative development in the United States has been the so-called 'Digital Millenium Copyright Act' (DCMA), which was signed into effect by President Clinton towards the end of 1998.[169] One of the reasons for the passing of the DCMA is to enable the United States to meet its obligations which it incurred from subscribing to the latest WIPO copyright treaty, signed on 20 December 1996 in Geneva.[170] The treaty itself is discussed in greater detail in section 2.7.3 below. The DCMA consists of five titles which deal with the following topics:

- I Implementing the WIPO treaty;
- II Establishing safe harbors [sic]for OSP's (Online Service Providers);
- III Permitting temporary copies of programs to be made during computer maintenance;
- IV Miscellaneous provisions, inter alia amendments which facilitate Internet broadcasting;
- V Creating unique provision for boat hull design.

It is interesting to note that a controversial clause, art 5 of the WIPO treaty, providing for the protection of databases, has not been implemented by the United States.

---

167 Acronym for Committee on New Technical Uses.

168 But unlike the position in the United Kingdom or South Africa.

169 As new Public Law 105–304.

170 The WIPO treaty on performances and phonographs was approved at the same time and place.

In a new s 1201 the DCMA pursues two lines of attack. In the first place, gaining unauthorized access to a work by circumventing a technological protection measure put in place by the copyright owner is prohibited.[171] So is manufacturing or distributing technologies, products and services, which may be used to defeat the technological protection mentioned in the previous sentence. Whereas the unauthorized access provision comes into force only two years from the publication of the Act,[172] the prohibition on making or making available overriding devices comes into effect with immediate effect.

Although the present writer had hoped at first that topic (III) above would solve the 'transient copy by using' problem, it transpires that this topic was left to be dealt with by an abortive art 7 of the WIPO treaty, which was not accepted by the Conference in Geneva leading up to the treaty.[173] One could perhaps argue that by limiting permitted use to maintenance periods, it excludes all other use, according to the principle of *inclusio unius est exclusio alterius*.[174] It is also interesting to note that s 1201*(f)* makes specific provision for reverse-engineering in order to ensure interoperability (a matter which has already been touched on above).

In the general section above, some time has been spent on the idea/expression test for copyright—the idea carries no protection, the expression is protected by copyright. The Geneva Conference mentioned above actually included an article on the 'Scope of Copyright Protection', which is not very helpful in providing a test:

> 'Copyright protection extends to expressions and not to ideas, procedures, methods of operation or mathematical concepts as such.'

One of the first cases of this nature in the United States was *Baker v Selden*.[175] Being decided in 1880, it obviously had nothing to do with computers, but it is important to the distinction between idea and expression. The United States Supreme Court held that when there is sufficient 'merger' between the idea and the expression of it, so that the expression cannot be protected without giving a monopoly in the idea itself, the expression is not copyrightable. Therefore the blank forms supplied to implement a new system of accounting are not copyrightable since they are 'neccessary incidents' to implementing the idea, they were part of the operation, and thus still formed part of the idea and not the expression. Reference has already been made in the general section to *Nichols v Universal Pictures Corporation*,[176] which turned on protecting the plot idea of the Jewish and Catholic

---

171 This is to give effect to art 11 of the December 1996 WIPO treaty.

172 In other words, towards the end of the year 2000.

173 For the full story see section 2.7.3 below.

174 'The inclusion of one is (or implies) the exclusion of others.'

175 101 US 99 (1880).

176 45 F 2d 119 (2nd Cir 1930).

families becoming romantically involved. This could be done by differentiating between increasing levels of generality and not protecting the most general levels, since these consisted of an unprotectable idea, and not protectable expression.

In *Synercom v University Computing*[177] the program concerned made use of a certain sequence of formats obtained from the plaintiff's material. The court held that this constituted 'ideas expressed' and not the 'expression of an idea' and therefore the program itself was not entitled to copyright protection. However, because the defendant's accompanying material contained too much material from the plaintiff's manual, the court was still able to protect the plaintiff.

The case of *SAS Institute v S & H Computer Systems*[178] illustrates that even though only 44 specific instances of copying could be proved (from a background of 186 000 lines of program code) this was not insubstantial and that the defendant's software was 'substantially similar' to that of the plaintiff (SAS Institute). It was therefore held to be a derivative work, infringing the plaintiff's copyright.

Since the advent of the computer, courts have started to develop an alternative to the 'expressed idea' test by moving onto the slippery slopes of the 'look and feel' test. In the case of *Whelan Associates v Jaslow Dental Laboratory*,[179] a programmer recoded a computer program so that it would run on another model. Although the actual coding differed completely, the organization and structure of the program remained (understandably) the same. After referring to the 'idea' of the programs (to provide a service for dental laboratories), the court applied the following test for distinguishing idea from expression: 'everything that is not necessary to that purpose and function would be part of the expression of the idea.'[180] Since the structure, sequence and organization of the programme belonged to the realm of expression, rather than to that of idea, the court held these aspects to be copyrightable and found that the second programme had infringed this copyright. The 'look and feel' of the program therefore had nothing to do with the actual screens produced by it, but everything with the structure of the written programme and the way in which it was organized, something which could only be 'looked at' and 'felt' by a fellow programmer.

Becker J was also quite critical of the decision in *Synercon*, above, where it was held that a certain sequence of formats was not protectable. From the general tenor of the Copyright Act of 1976 the learned judge deduced that sequencing and ordering were intended to be protectable and that computer programs should not be an exception to this rule.

---

177 462 F Supp 1003 (ND Tex 1978).

178 605 F Supp 816 (MD Tenn 1985).

179 797 F 2d 1222 (3rd Cir 1986).

180 Supra at 1236.

This decision has, in turn, been criticized, the most trenchant piece of criticism coming, in my opinion, from Nimmer, who finds a fatal flaw in Becker J's reasoning, in that 'it assumes that only one "idea", in copyright terms, underlies any copyright program, and that once a separable idea can be identified, everything else must be expression.' Nimmer would prefer the test to be whether 'the fundamental essence or structure of one work is duplicated in another'.[181]

The *Whelan* case was also criticized in *Computer Associates International, Inc v Altai*,[182] which found the former's proposed test (of separating the idea and leaving the rest subject to copyright), 'simplistic' 'inadequate' and 'inaccurate'. The court in *Altai* revived the old *Nichols* test of abstracting 'patterns of increasing generality' (see the general section at the beginning of this chapter), but perfected this into a so-called 'abstraction—filtration—comparison analysis'. This process is well described by Reed:[183]

> 'First, the courts should break down the allegedly infringed program into its constituent structural parts. Secondly, the court should examine each of these parts for such things as incorporated ideas, expression that is necessarily incidental to those ideas, and elements that are taken from the public domain, thus sifting out all non-protectable material. Thirdly, left with a kernel, or possibly kernels, of creative expression after following this process of elimination, the court's last step would be to compare this structure with the structure of an allegedly infringing program.'

This 'triple test' has become the major rival to the 'look and feel' test of Whelan, even in the United Kingdom, as we shall see below.

In an article entitled 'Copyright Infringement of Protected Computer Software: An Analytical Method to Determine Substantial Similarity'[184] Donald F McGahn II finds the abstractions test of *Nichols* to be eminently suited to the creation of a computer program, which is 'top-down':

> '[T]he genesis of a particular program is its intended purpose. A specific outline is then created, based upon the end user's particular needs. Data structures and algorithms are developed for this outline. The entire logic of the program is then flow-charted. This chart serves as a guide to develop sub-routines. Finally, the source code, incorporating all the prior parts, is encoded.'[185]

---

181 Melville B Nimmer & David Nimmer *Nimmer on Copyright* (Matthew Bender and Co 1994) 13-29 and 13-44.

182 982 F 2d 693 (2nd Cir 1992).

183 Op cit 137.

184 (1995) 21 *Rutgers Computer and Technology Law Journal* at 88ff.

185 Op cit 131.

Applying the abstractions test to this procedure, McGahn then argues that the 'initial general description is an unprotectable idea, while the final program is protectable expression'.[186]

Based on a distinction by Nimmer between 'comprehensive nonliteral similarity' and 'fragmented literal similarity', McGahn then continues to classify the different tests applied by United States courts to prove substantial similarity. The first is 'a similarity not just as to a particular line or paragraph or other minor segment, but [where] the fundamental essence or structure of one work is duplicated in another'. The second is 'sporadic "word-for-word" similarity'[187]

He then goes on to indicate that courts have used three tests to determine the first kind of (non-literal) similarity. The first is the 'ordinary observer' test, where 'an ordinary reasonable man' would find overall similarity between two works, despite 'minute differences between the two works'. This test was applied in *Atari Inc. v North American Philips Consumer Electronics Corp*,[188] where the court compared the plaintiff's 'Pac-man' with the defendant's 'KC Munchkin' and found 'that an ordinary observer could conclude only that North American copied plaintiff's Pac-man'.[189]

The second similarity test is the so-called 'extrinsic—intrinsic' test. This is a two-pronged test where the extrinsic (second) prong depends on 'specific criteria which can be listed and analyzed' and where expert testimony is allowed. Once the first test has determined sufficient similarity between the *ideas* behind the programs, the second prong determines whether substantial similarity between the *expressions* exist, and here the 'ordinary reasonable man' test (as described in the previous paragraph) may also be used. The second stage has to be carried out without any expert testimony. This test was applied by the court in *Broderbund Software, Inc v Unison World Inc*,[190] where defendant's 'Printmaster' incorporated the interface and parts of the screen display of the plaintiff's 'Print Shop'. In the chapter on copyright in *Computer Law*,[191] Christopher Millard finds the citation of *Whelan's* case (in support) by the judges surprising:

> 'The last part of this statement is rather surprising, given that the *Whelan* case was about infringement of copyright in program code (ie, a literary work), not infringement of copyright in screen displays (ie audiovisual works). Moreover, in place of the structural analysis conducted by the *Whelan* court, the *Broderbund* court was more concerned with whether "the

186 Ibid.

187 Op cit 113.

188 672 F 2d 607 (7th Cir 1982).

189 Op cit 114.

190 648 F Supp 1127 (ND Cal 1986).

191 Chris Reed (ed) *Computer Law* (Blackstone Press 1996) 134ff.

> infringing work captures them 'total concept and feel' of the protected work". Noting "the eerie resemblance between the screens of the two protected programs", the court found that infringement had indeed occurred.'[192]

It is interesting to note that the screens resulting from the operation of the program have to protected under a different heading from the program itself, namely 'audio-visual works'. That is why screens themselves can never give the look and feel of a copyrighted program, one has to look at the structure of the coding itself.

The third similarity test amounts to the 'total concept and feel', which has already been mentioned in the previous paragraph. Another case which made use of it was *Digital Communications Assocs, Inc v Softklone Distrib. Corp*,[193] where screens were literally placed side by side to prove their substantial similarity. McGahn comments that this test may be useful with computer screens, but not with comparing a program's structure, sequence and organization, where there are no aesthetic aspects to compare and where 'a computer program could be copied from another program, while looking nothing like the original to the untrained eye'.[194]

He also gives an example of the 'fragmented literal similarity' test mentioned above. This is the so-called 'iterative approach', where the program is not borrowed as a whole but certain portions are copied exactly. Besides the *SAS Institute* case mentioned above, this test was also applied in *Williams Electronics, Inc v Artic International, Inc.*[195] The court was able to find direct copying in the fact that certain errors had been copied, as had certain 'high scores' achieved by previous (Williams) players, as had a 'buried' copyright notice, which was printed out from an Artic memory device by Williams' employees.

The wheel turned a full historical circle when a series of decisions involving the menu structure of the famous spreadsheet programme (Lotus 1.2.3.) was finally resolved on appeal with reference to one of the earliest cases on the scope of copyright, *Baker v Selden* (discussed above). This happened in the case of *Lotus Development Corporation v Borland International Inc*,[196] which was reported on in *Computer Law and Security Report*.[197] After Lotus had triumphed in two prior decisions on the same point by courts *a quo*,[198] the appeal court finally held that the Lotus menu hierarchy, or tree structure, was not copyrightable, since it was

192 Op cit 97.

193 659 F Supp 449 (ND Cal 1986).

194 Op cit 118.

195 685 F 2d 870 (3d Cir 1982).

196 49 F 3d 807, 34 USPQ 2d 1014.

197 [1995] 11 *CLSR* 224ff, entitled 'Lotus Menu Commands Uncopyrightable'.

198 *Lotus Development Corporation v Paperback Software International* 740 F Supp 37 (Mass 1990).

a 'method of operation', excluded from protection by a piece of American legislation.[199] Counsel for Borland relied on the *Baker v Selden* decision and argued that '[T]he only difference is that the "user interface" of Selden's system was implemented by pen and paper rather than by computer'. Although the *Lotus* court did not want to go that far, it did hold that the menu structure was as uncopyrightable as the buttons on a Video Cassette Recorder (VCR) in that:

> 'If the users wish to copy material, for example, they use the "copy" command. If users wish to print material, they use "print" command.'[200]

The court also rejected the three-part test of 'non-literal' copying laid down in the *Altai* case, above, probably because the present case was one where literal copying was in issue, the main issue being whether the copied expression fell within one of the categories excluded from copyright protection by s 102*(b)*.

According to Reed,[201] the most recent trend in the United States Courts seem to be towards following the three-part *Altai* test. He cites cases such as *Gates Rubber Co v Bando Chemical Industries Ltd*,[202] *Kepner-Tregoe v Leadership Software Inc*,[203] and *Engineering Dynamics Inc v Structural Software Inc*[204] to bolster his argument that *Altai's* abstraction—filtration—comparison test has 'tended to be applied more or less as a matter of course to determine the scope of copyright protection in cases involving non-literal copying'.[205]

In conclusion, the present writer hopes that the careful distinctions drawn by McGahn above will be kept in mind by courts treading this intellectual minefield. At the very least, courts should only quote in support those cases which really support their conclusion and not vaguely classify cases into a borderless 'look and feel' category, which the original *Whelan* decision never had in mind.

Another interesting development in American copyright law has been the so-called 'copyright misuse' doctrine originating from the case of *Lasercomb America, Inc v Reynolds*.[206] Here the court ruled that a software manufacturer could not enforce its copyright in CAD/CAM[207] software against an infringer because its standard licence agreement barred licencees from creating their own CAD/CAM products. It was viewed as an attempt by Lasercom 'to use its copyright to control competition in an area outside the copyright' and therefore

---

199 17 USC s 102*(b)*.
200 Supra at 815.
201 Op cit 137–9.
202 (1993) 4 CCH Computer Cases at 46, 971.
203 (1994) 4 CCH Computer Cases at 65,812.
204 (1994) 4 CCH Computer Cases at 47,095.
205 Supra at 139.
206 911 F 2d 970 (4th Cir 1990).
207 Acronyms for Computer Aided Drawing/Computer Aided Manufacturing.

a 'misuse of copyright'. This case had been followed in *DS Comms Corp v DGI Technologies Inc*.[208]

A significant new development has been the adoption of the copyright misuse doctrine by a court of the 'influential Ninth Circuit, the largest of the 12 US Courts of Appeal'.[209] In *Practice Management Information Corp v American Medical Association*[210] the prestigious AMA was barred from enforcing its copyrighted system of codes that identify over 6 000 medical procedures against PMI. The court held that the 'AMA misused its copyright by licensing the CPT[211] to HCFA[212] in exchange for HCFA's agreement not to use a competing coding system'. As a result, the AMA could not enforce its 'tainted' copyright and PMI was able to use the CPT without paying any licence fees to the AMA.

The ITEC *Law Alert* mentions that this case serves as a warning to software companies 'whose licence agreements may contain the seeds of their own copyright's destruction'.[213] This matter will be raised again in the chapter on contracts below.

Mention has already been made above[214] of the *Feist* decision with regard to the protection of databases. In this case O'Connor J laid down a requirement of creativity or originality in compiling the database. The mere 'sweat of the brow' in accumulating a great amount of data was held to be not sufficient to obtain copyright protection for a database of this nature. This has shed fresh light on some earlier decisions with regard to the compilation of legal information. For instance, in *West Publishing v Mead Data Central*[215] the court held that the copyright in the compilation of West reporters extended also to the page numbers used in the series of law reports. According to the court, the page numbers reflected the 'arrangement' selected by West in its compilation of the database. This decision was followed in *Oasis Publishing Co v West Publishing* Co.[216]

Apparently the tide has now turned. In the case of *Matthew Bender & Co v West Publishing Co*[217] the court held that West has no copyright either in its page numbers or in the changes which it makes in case opinions before publishing them in its law reports:

---

208 81 F 3d 597 (5th Cir 1996).

209 According to April 1998 ITEC Law Alert (April 1998) at 2.

210 121 F 3d 516 (9th Cir), cert denied, 118 SCt 339 (1997).

211 Acronym for Current Procedural Terminology—the copyrighted system of codes.

212 Acronym for Health Care Financing Administration—a third party precipitating the dispute between the AMA and PMI.

213 Op cit at 2.

214 Section 2.6.2 above, dealing with specific problems arising from the use of databases.

215 799 F 2d 1219 (8th Cir 1986).

216 924 F Supp 918 (DMinn 1996).

217 1997 US Dist Lexis 6915, 42 USPQ 2d 1930 (SDNY 1997)

> 'On November 22, 1996 the court first ruled that page breaks resulting in the page numbers used by West were an accident of production, not an act of authorship. In its second decision, issued May 19, 1997, the court found that the changes made by West to opinions it received from courts did not represent sufficient creative effort to warrant copyright protection. The changes included the addition of parallel citations, alterations of case captions to conform to West's established format, information concerning the attorneys representing the parties, and occasional corrections to text.'[218]

According to a later edition of the same source[219] the House of Representatives recently passed the 'Collections of Information Antipiracy Act'.[220] This Bill,

> 'which is of keen interest to the publishing and information industries, would create a broad regime of protection for databases, both electronic and printed, and would largely nullify existing copyright law prohibiting the protection of information appearing in a database.'

An accompanying House Report claims that the present Bill would avoid constitutional problems associated with an earlier Bill on the same subject, by modelling protection on unfair competition or misappropriation law rather than on copyright law.[221] The Report also states that the Bill 'would restore a modified form of the "sweat of the brow" protection' (an obvious reference to the *Feist* decision mentioned above, and discussed previously under the database section).[222] The Bill provides a 15-year term of protection to 'information that has been collected and has been organized for the purpose of bringing discrete items of information together in one place or through one source so that users may access them'. 'Information' includes 'facts, data, works of authorship, or any other intangible material' but expressly excludes computer programs.

According to the latest information to hand at the time of writing, (the end of December 1998), the Bill has been passed by the House and has been received and read twice in Senate, before being passed to the Committee on Judiciary.

2.7.2 The United Kingdom

Here the influence of the European Union has made itself felt during the years intervening since the previous issue of this work (1986). This is manifested especially in legislation.

---

218 August 1997 *ITEC Law Alert* at 4.

219 August 1998 *ITEC Law Alert* at 4.

220 HR 2652.

221 Here I have to repeat my earlier misgivings that the 'commodification of information' mentioned in chapter 1 would exceed the parameters of existing intellectual property law—the reference to 'misappropriation law' sounds much like the law of things, or even criminal law.

222 See section 2.6.2 above.

At the time of writing the previous edition of this work, the old Copyright Act of 1956 still held sway. Amendments had addressed some of the more pressing computer problems. The government had appeared reluctant to find room on the parliamentary timetable for software copyright legislation. The pressure group FAST (Federation Against Software Theft) persuaded the Tory MP William Powell to introduce a private member's Bill to amend the Copyright Act on this subject. The Act then came into operation on 16 September 1985, as the Copyright (Computer Software) Amendment Act of 1985.

A major new step has been the enactment of the Copyright, Designs and Patents Act (CDPA) in 1988. Most provisions have come into force on the first of August 1989. It has been described by Reed as 'an attempt to start again with a clean slate' and 'a far more coherent, comprehensive and accessible statement of the law than the statutes which it replaced'.[223] According to Reed it is not clear to what extent case law based on the old Act would still be relevant, since the provisions of s 172 of the new Act are ambiguous in this regard.

In the previous edition of this work the author referred to the first criminal conviction for software piracy in the United Kingdom.[224] The proprietor of a computer software hire business using pirated software was convicted under the Trades Description Act and the Copyright Act, and also of forgery. Tuckett found the penalty disappointing, though—a fine of £40 with £50 costs. In terms of the 1956 Copyright Act, the unauthorized importation or manufacture of a copy of a program might have have resulted in a maximum fine of £2 000 on summary conviction or an unlimited fine (or two years' imprisonment) on indictment. A year later, editorial comment in the September/October 1985 issue of *Computer Law* ran as follows:

> 'In a jurisdiction which not so long ago, hanged a man for stealing a sheep and sent his cousin to the penal colonies for picking a pocket, the felonious infringer will scarcely be quaking in his boots at the worst that the judiciary can throw at him, but it is clear that, unless there are extenuating circumstances, he will be meted out a severer punishment than the man who parks on yellow lines or avoids his bus fare. Owners of software which is pirated at the rate of millions of pounds a year will doubtless draw a great comfort from this.'[225]

As far as the statutory confirmation that software is a 'literary work' was concerned, that simply brought England to the same level of development which South Africa had already reached, thanks to the decision of *Northern Office Micro Computers v*

223 Reed op cit 106.

224 Based on a note by R Tuckett in September/October 1984 *Computer Law and Practice* at 9.

225 September/October 1985 *Computer Law and Practice* at 1.

Rosenstein.[226] Otherwise, the decision apparently confirmed that the storage of a work in a computer amounts to copying that work (a point left open in the *Rosenstein* case) and that the conversion of a program into or out of a computer language is an 'adaptation', which is also something which had to be permitted by the copyright owner.

All these points have been cleared up by the 1988 Act. Section 3(1)*(b)* of the CPDA explicitly includes a computer program in the definition of a 'literary work'. (It is interesting to note that this was the position in South Africa after the *Rosenstein* decision, but before the 1992 amendments to our Copyright Act.) The work has to be recorded 'regardless of the method by which or medium in or on which it is recorded', according to the definition of 'writing' given in s 3(2) of the CDPA. Another interesting definition is that of 'copying', which includes storing the work in any medium by any electronic means, and includes thereby the making of copies which are transient or incidental to some other use of the work.[227]

In 1992 the United Kingdom incorporated the 1991 European Software Directive into its local law.[228] Although British implementation has not altered the general principles of their own copyright law, some commentators have been sceptical about the result:

> 'The excruciating gestation[229] of the Directive left it with some strange marks, and its subsequent conversion into United Kingdom law has added others.'[230]

The United Kingdom has had some interesting cases on the old idea/expression test. Reference has already been made to the *Elanco v Mandops*[231] decision in the general section above. Here the plaintiff was protected because of the skill and judgment which he had exercised in assembling the data for a database.

In the case of *John Richardson Computers v Flanders*,[232] the defendant had rewritten a competitive computer program in a different language.[233] Ferris J then attempted to undertake the triple 'abstraction, filtration and analysis' laid down in the United States' *Altai* case. In the end he found that although there were seventeen apparently similar elements, only three of them were actually infringing on the plaintiff's copyright.

---

226 1981 (4) SA 123(C);

227 CDPA (1988) s 17(1), (2), (3).

228 Through Copyright (Computer Programs) Regulation 1992, SI 1992 No 3233.

229 The consultations had started in December 1988 but finally bore fruit only in May 1991!

230 Cornish *Intellectual Property* 443.

231 28 1980 RPC 213.

232 [1993] FSR 497.

233 One must assume that this was at least one step removed from a simple 'translation', which is clearly prohibited.

According to s 3(1) of the CPDA, copyright can subsist in a table or compilation (subsumed under the category of a literary work) even though the matters compiled may bear copyright on their own. In *Ibcos Computers Ltd v Barclays Mercantile Highland Finance*[234] Jacob J stated that '[t]here is no reason why a compilation of computer programs should not itself acquire a separate copyright'. With what Cornish calls a 'Whelanesque flourish',[235] he also rejected the American development of a 'merger' of expression into idea. Cornish proceeds to comment further on the differences between American and British law in this manner:

> 'The *Ibcos* judgment is right to point out some essential differences between British and American copyright doctrine. The former, applying its strictly limited requirement of "originality", has not hesitated to protect compilations of information against copying, even where there is little real scope for alternative expression. Likewise it has not feared to trespass on the territory of the "functional". Nonetheless the caution exhibited in Computer Associates (Altai) is not without its resonances for the assessment of substantial taking under British law.'[236]

In the end the problems with regard to United Kingdom databases will have to be resolved by means of the solution put forward by the European Union. A 'Directive on the legal protection of Databases' was issued on 11 March 1996 with an implementation date of 1 January 1998. One of the greatest problems is a lack of sufficient originality and, according to Cornish,[237] the Directive makes use of 'a highly elaborate strategy' to get around this:

> 'It allows copyright in a database (as distinct from its contents), but only on the basis of authorship involving personal intellectual creativity (a new limitation, so far as common law countries are concerned, and one which must presage a raising of the standard of originality throughout British copyright law). Intellectual judgment which is in some sense the author's own must go either into choosing contents or into the method of arrangement (the selective dictionary will doubtless be a clearer case than the classificatory telephone directory, but each may have some hope; the merely comprehensive will be precluded—that is the silliness of the whole construct).'[238]

The European Union Directive is addressed again under the next heading—International and supranational groupings.

234 [1994] FSR 275.

235 Op cit 449.

236 Ibid.

237 Op cit 458.

238 Ibid.

2.7.3 International and supranational groupings (eg the European Union)

One of the other changes that has occurred since the previous edition of this work is the 'internationalization' of copyright. It no longer serves much purpose to deal with the different European countries one by one, since they almost all have to conform to European Union directives at some stage. This type of development is now taking place internationally, either in other supranational groupings or by way of international treaties sponsored by the United Nations or other international organizations. In these days of the Internet and instantaneous worldwide communications such developments are more necessary than ever.

The first of such treaties dealing specifically with copyright was the Berne Convention of 1886.[239] At present 121 states are party to it. What complicates matters is the fact that there have been many revisions of this convention and that not every signatory has accepted and acceded to every revision. This means that different countries have different Berne 'regimes'. The last of such revisions took place in Paris in 1971.

Because the Berne Convention is complex and demands a big commitment from governments, many countries have not signed it. A notable absentee had been the United States, until a few years ago. To try to be more inclusive, a Universal Copyright Convention was agreed on at a UNESCO[240] Conference in Geneva. It is less extreme than Berne but recognizes the need for developing countries to gain access to information. In case of conflict, Berne will be the overriding treaty.

The major copyright conventions are administered by a United Nations body called WIPO, except for the Universal Copyright Convention, which is administered jointly by WIPO and UNESCO. One of the main purposes of WIPO is to encourage all countries to accede to the latest revisions of the international copyright treaties. Another important international development is TRIPS. After the realization that the protection of intellectual property was a vital component in International Trade, TRIPS adopted the obligations of Berne and added even more protection. TRIPS is managed by the recently formed WTO,[241] which is seen by some as a rival to WIPO.

After a long period of consultation, preceding conferences and other international gatherings, a diplomatic conference was organized in Geneva in December 1996. It led to a new Copyright Treaty which took into account the

239 For some of the following overview use was made of a speech by Sandy Norman 'Copyright: Removing the Barriers?' given in Johannesburg on 17th March 1997.

240 Acronym for United Nations Educational, Scientific and Cultural Organisation.

241 World Trade Organization.

dissemination and use of copyrighted materials on the Internet. In the Preamble the treaty referred inter alia to new technological developments and 'the profound impact of the development and convergence of information and communication technologies on the creation and use of literary and artistic works'. Article 2 finally laid down the internationally acceptable position with regard to the scope of copyright protection:

> 'Copyright protection extends to expressions and not to ideas, procedures, methods of operation or mathematical concepts as such;'.

As we have seen above, however, this might be begging the question: distinguishing between idea and expression is not that easy!

Article 4 makes specific provision for the protection of computer programs:

> 'Computer programs are protected as literary works within the meaning of Article 2 of the Berne Convention. Such protection applies to computer programs, whatever may be the mode or form of their expression.'

In terms of this clause South Africa has perhaps painted itself into a corner by creating a separate category for computer programs and removing them from the category of literary works, as will now be the international norm (see below).

Article 5 deals with the protection available to databases:

> 'Compilations of data or other material, in any form, which by reason of the selection or arrangement of their contents constitute intellectual creations, are protected as such. This protection does not extend to the data or the material itself and is without prejudice to any copyright subsisting in the data or material contained in the compilation.'

Article 11 specifically targets devices designed to override technical protection:

> 'Contracting Parties shall provide adequate legal protection and effective legal remedies against the circumvention of effective technological measures that are used by authors in connection with the exercise of their rights under this Treaty or the Berne Convention and that restrict acts, in respect of their works, which are not authorized by the authors concerned or permitted by law.'

(This would include devices to override the dongles and other copyright locking devices which we have discussed under the heading 'technical protection' above.)

Article 12 puts an obligation on the contracting countries to provide 'adequate and effective legal remedies' against persons removing or altering 'any electronic rights management information' without authority, or distributing, broadcasting or communicating to the public such 'denuded' works. 'Rights management information' is defined as:

> '[I]nformation which identifies the work, the author of the work, the owner of any right in the work, or information about the terms and conditions of use of the work, and any numbers or codes that represent such information, when any of these items of information is attached to a copy of a work or appears in connection with the communication of a work to the public.'

Although the present art 7 deals with 'Rights of Rental', an abortive article which was to have dealt with a 'Right of Reproduction' was withdrawn after strong reservations were expressed by inter alia the delegates representing librarians. The article would have reserved rights to the copyright owner which included the right to authorize 'direct and indirect reproduction ... whether permanent of temporary, in any matter or form'. This clause would have reserved the right to the copyright holder to authorize even the temporary reproductions which are required to store a work in a digital form in an electronic medium. If every such transient reproduction had to be authorized, it 'would have slowed down the traffic on the Information Superhighway considerably'.[242] It was left out of the final treaty in spite of a proposed limitation:

> 'In cases where a temporary reproduction has the sole purpose of making the work perceptible or where the reproduction is of a transient or incidental nature, provided that such a reproduction takes place in the course of the work that is authorized by the author or permitted by law.'

The exception to art 7 was felt to be too narrow and likely to be open to differing interpretations internationally.

Mention has already been made in this chapter[243] of Coenraad Visser's view that persons permitting their copyrighted works onto the Internet are tacitly agreeing to the transient copy necessary for viewing, but not for saving to disk or for making printouts. This is roughly equivalent in effect to the aborted art 7 described above, but is in conflict with one of Lee & Davidson's 'laws of copyright on the Internet':[244]

> 'Do not assume that any material posted is public domain, particularly since the 1989 amendment to the Copyright Act[245] makes clear that that lack of a copyright notice does not affect whether copyright subsists in a work;'

The rest of the treaty contains much more of interest and should be studied by itself, since it has in the meantime led to legislative efforts on the part of the United States and the United Kingdom (to name but two) in order to bring domestic legislation into line with the treaty provisions.

---

242 From the speech by Sandy Norman.

243 See the text accompanying note 86 above.

244 See the text accompanying note 113 above.

245 Of the United States.

Probably the most active of subgroupings of blocs of countries trying to harmonize their intellectual property regime, has been the European Union. On 14 May 1991 the Council of the European Communities issued a Directive on the Legal Protection of Computer Programs.[246] After 29 'Whereases' (in typical bureaucratic fashion!), the Directive was adopted. Some of these illustrate the typical problems which we in Africa also face, and have perhaps not been tackling systematically enough:

> 'Whereas computer programs are at present not clearly protected in all Member States by existing legislation and such protection, where it exists, has different attributes;
>
> Whereas the development of computer programs requires the investment of considerable human, technical and financial resources while computer programs can be copied at a fraction of the cost needed to develop them independently;
>
> Whereas computer programs are playing an increasingly important role in a broad range of industries and computer program technology can accordingly be considered as being of fundamental importance for the Community's industrial development, etc.'

The rest of the directive determines inter alia that computer programs be protected as literary works (again South Africa is out of line with its *sui generis*[247] protection), that only the expression (not the idea behind it) is protected, and that the program has to be original. Other articles deal with authorship and the beneficiaries of protection and define the exclusive rights of the copyright holder. The latter shall include the right to do or to authorize:

> '*(a)* the permanent or temporary reproduction of a computer program by any means and in any form, in part or in whole. Insofar as loading, displaying, running, transmission or storage of the computer program necessitate such reproduction, such acts shall be subject to the authorisation by the rightholder.
>
> *(b)* the translation, adaptation, arrangement and any other alteration of a computer program and the reproduction of the results thereof, without prejudice to the rights of the person who alters the program;
>
> *(c)* any form of distribution to the public, including the rental of the original computer program or of copies thereof. The first sale in the Community of a copy of a program by the rightholder or with his consent shall exhaust the distribution right within the Community of that copy, with the exception of the right to control further rental of the program or a copy thereof.'[248]

---

246 91/250/EEC.

247 'Of its own (unique) kind.'

248 Article 4 of the Directive, dealing with 'Restricted Acts'.

(This clears up and standardizes many of the procedures with regard to computer programs which have hitherto been causing uncertainty in European countries, including the United Kingdom.)

Article 5 of the Directive excerpts certain activities from the need of authorization in terms of the aforegoing, namely if the restricted acts are 'necessary for the use of the computer program by the lawful aquirer in accordance with its intended purpose, including error correction', for the purpose of making back-up copies (this may not be excluded by contract) and to study the functioning of the program in order to determine the underlying ideas and principles. Article 6 deals with decompilation and art 7 forces member states to provide appropriate remedies against persons committing the following acts:

'*(a)* any act of putting into circulation a copy of a computer program knowing, or having reason to believe, that it is an infringing copy;

(b) the possession, for commercial purposes, of a copy of a computer program knowing, or having reason to believe, that it is an infringing copy;

(c) any act of putting into circulation, or the possession for commercial purposes of, any means the sole purpose of which is to facilitate the unauthorized removal or circumvention of any technical device which may have been applied to protect a computer program.'

Article 8 fixes the term of protection for the life of the author (or last surviving author, if there were co-authors) plus 50 years. If the program is created by a legal person, it shall be 50 years from the time the program was first made available to the public. Member states were forced to comply by 1 January 1993.

In similar fashion, the European Parliament and the Council of the European Union issued a European Directive on the legal protection of databases. After 60 (!) 'Whereases', the Directive was adopted. The most interesting one reads as follows:

'Whereas the increasing use of digital recording technology exposes the database maker to the risk that the contents of his database may be copied and rearranged electronically, without his authorization, to produce a database of identical content which, however, does not infringe any copyright in the arrangement of his database.'

The Directive itself defined 'database' as 'a collection of independent works, data, or other materials arranged in a systematic or methodical way and individually accessible by electronic or other means'.[249]

Article 2 makes it clear that the protection does not extend to the computer programs used in making the databases accessible, while Article 4 indicates that the

249 Article 1.

protection does not extend to the individual content of the databases. Article 5 has the normal restricted acts, such as temporary or permanent reproduction, in whole or in part; the translation, adaptation, arrangement or any other alteration of the database, any form of distribution or copies of it and any form of communication to the public of the database itself or the result of any the above activities.

Article 7 is very interesting in that it creates a '*sui generis* right' with regard to 'extraction' or 're-utilization' of the whole or a subtantial part 'evaluated qualitatively and/or quantitatively'. The forbidden activities are defined as follows:

> ' "extraction" shall mean the permanent or temporary transfer of all or a substantial part of the contents of a database to another medium by any means or in any form.'

and

> ' "re-utilization" shall mean any form of making available to the public all or a substantial part of the contents of a database by the distribution of copies, by renting, by on-line or other forms of distribution.'

Reassuring to librarians should be the fact that 'public lending' is not seen as a form of either of these acts.

These prohibitions shall not affect the rights and obligations of lawful users and there are further exceptions to the *sui generis* rights, amongst others, 'the case of extraction for private purposes of the contents of a non-electronic database' and 'the case of extraction for the purposes of illustration for teaching or scientific research, as long as the source is indicated and to the extent justified by the non-commercial purpose to be achieved'.[250] Member states were given until 1 January 1998 to give effect to these provisions in their domestic legislation.

2.7.4 South Africa

Because the old version of the South African Copyright Act[251] did not expressly make provision for the protection of computer programs, it was left to the courts to make provision for this need. This they did excellently in the classic decision of *Northern Office Micro Computers (Pty) Ltd & others v Rosenstein*.[252] This case has been quoted in many overseas journals, usually with a plea for a similar development in the country concerned.

The facts were that a programmer, the respondent in this case, finished an uncompleted suite of programs for the applicant. The programs consisted of an accounting and administrative system for doctors and dentists and had a fair commercial value. After this the respondent resigned from the services of the

250 Article 9.

251 Act 98 of 1978.

252 1981 (4) SA 123 (C).

applicant and claimed that copyright in the suite of programs vested in himself and that the applicant should pay him royalties for each program sold.

Marais AJ held a program for computers to be eligible for copyright protection as a 'literary work' as defined in s 1 of the Act. Section 2(2) further required that the work be original and that 'the work has been written down, recorded or otherwise reduced to material form'. Marais J took the view that sufficient effort and skill had been expended by the respondent to comply with the originality requirement. (This requirement has since been dropped anyway, by a 1980 amendment of the South African Copyright Act). In the light of overseas developments, it is interesting to note that the original (pre-1980) version of s 2 read as follows:

> '(2) A literary, musical or artistic work shall not be eligible for copyright unless—
>
> *(a)* sufficient effort or skill has been expended on making the work to give it a new and original character; and
>
> *(b)* the work has been written down, recorded or otherwise reduced to material form.'

(This reminds one of the 'sweat of the brow' test which has been yielding ground steadily to the 'originality and creative effort' test in the United States, especially after the *Feist* decision. Once again, South Africa seems to have been ahead of overseas developments in that the 1980 amendment[253] basically required only that the work be original and reduced to some kind of material form.)

The judge in *Rosenstein* also held that the second requirement had been complied with, since some of the formulae and supporting documentation had been reduced to writing and a listing of the program had been printed out by the computer. He left open the possibility that the recording of the program on the floppy disk itself could be seen as a 'recording' in terms of s 2. However, notwithstanding the fact that the respondent had copyright in the suite of programs, he restrained the respondent from copying and distributing the program in terms of trade-secret law. (This aspect is covered in the following chapter.)

Comment on the case has generally been favourable[254] and probably lessened the pressure for legislative reform. Nevertheless such reform has come in the shape of amendments to the South African copyright system[255] specifically to accommodate computers. It has introduced a new category of work, namely 'a computer program'. It has defined this concept[256] and specifically excluded it from the

253 By Act 56 of 1980.

254 See locally, Horwitz (1983) 100 *SALJ* 301, Visser in 1984 *CILSA* 32 and Price in *Computerweek* 23 January 1984; and overseas, Tapper op cit at 34 and 62.

255 By Act 125 of 1992.

256 It means 'a set of instructions fixed or stored in any manner and which, when used directly or indirectly in a computer, directs its operation to bring about a result;'.

definition of 'literary work' (thus negating the effect of the *Rosenstein* decision and flying in the face of the latest European Union and international copyright directives and legislation).

The concept of archival copies has been borrowed from the 1984 Australian amendment and has been formulated as follows:[257]

> '(2) The copyright in a computer program shall not be infringed by a person who is in lawful possession of that computer program, or an authorized copy thereof, if—
>
> *(a)* he makes copies thereof to the extent reasonably necessary for back-up purposes;
>
> *(b)* a copy so made is intended exclusively for personal or private purposes; and
>
> *(c)* such copy is destroyed when the possession of the computer program in question, or authorized copy thereof, ceases to be lawful.'

(I have always wondered how many computer users follow these instructions carefully. Software grows old terribly quickly and is probably thrown away or languishes forgotten in some cupboard. Is the possession still lawful if one has already forgotten about the original, which has been returned to one's employer, where it is languishing in an even bigger forgotten cupboard?)

Other controversial questions are also dealt with, for instance adaptation and translation of programs. 'Adaptation' (which needs to be authorized) with regard to computer programs now includes—

> '(i) a version of the program in a programming language, code or notation different from that of the program; or
>
> (ii) a fixation of the program in or on a medium different from the medium of fixation of the program;'.[258]

As may be seen, translation is now specifically incorporated into the concept of adaptation.

The term 'protection' is defined in s 3 as follows with regard to:

> 'cinematograph films, photographs and computer programs, fifty years from the end of the year in which the work—
>
> (i) is made available to the public with the consent of the owner of the copyright; or
>
> (ii) is first published,

257 By s 19B of Act 98 of 1978.

258 Section 1 of Act 98 of 1978.

> whichever term is the longer, or failing such an event within fifty years of the making of the work, fifty years from the end of the year in which the work is made;'.

The definition of 'author' of a program has now also changed. When programs were still protected as 'literary works' in South Africa, the author was simply the person who first made or created the work. Now the author is the 'person who exercised control over the making of the program'.[259] According to s 21 of the Act, the author of the program will in most cases also be the first owner of the program, except where the program is made in the course of his employment, or made under the direction or control of the state.

As far as infringment of copyright is concerned, the courts have held that taking even a small piece of the work may be 'substantial'.[260] South Africa does not have the extended 'fair use' doctrine, which permits the United States judges to insert some 'equity' into proceedings. In fact, our own exemptions seem to be even skimpier than those of the United Kingdom, upon which they appear to be modelled.

The South African provisions relate mostly to reviewing, demonstrating or taking quotations or exerpts from programs. Using a programme for teaching is allowed, however, provided it is in accordance with 'fair practice' and proper acknowledgement is given.[261] This hardly seems to make up for the loss of 'research, private study, personal and private use' however, which are from now on reserved for literary works alone.

It is also permitted to make back-up copies of programs 'to an extent reasonably necessary' and provided they are made 'exclusively for personal and private purposes' and destroyed when the licensed use terminates.[262]

Commentary on the Act has been mixed. In an article entitled 'Protection of Computer Programs by Copyright in South Africa'[263] O H Dean is of the opinion

> 'that computer programs, having been fitted out in tailor-made clothing under the Copyright Act, are now adequately protected by South African law and that the basis has been laid for this form of intellectual product to develop and thrive in South Africa.'

Reflecting another shade of opinion, T Pistorius & C Visser have written an article entitled 'The Copyright Amendment Act 125 of 1992 and Computer Programs:

---

259 Section 1*(f)* of the Act.

260 As was decided in the (South African) cases of *Galago Pulishers (Pty) Ltd & another v Erasmus* 1989 (1) SA 276 (A) and *Fax Directories (Pty) Ltd v SA Fax Listings CC* 1990 (2) SA 164 (D).

261 Section 19B of the Copyright Act, read with s 12(4) *mutatis mutandis.*

262 Section 19B of the Act, read with various subsecs of s 12.

263 (1995) 1 *Stellenbosch Law Review* at 87ff.

A Preliminary Overview'.[264] They point out that the South African approach of leaving the well-known waters of protecting computer programs as a 'literary work' and protecting it as a separate category of work is 'clearly a minority one'. The authors are also alive to the fact that only the final form of a program will be protected as such, and that preliminary stages of a program, such as specification sheets and flow charts (which are much more relevant in terms of development costs) will still have to be protected as 'literary works'. They also point out that protecting the 'literal elements' of a computer program alone is not very effective if the 'non-literal elements' (all those elements other than the bare source code and object code itself) still have to be protected as 'literary works. It is probable that other non-literal elements of the program—for instance, products of the program, such as screen displays—may also not be protected in the same form as the program itself.

The latter problem (copyright protection of computer screens) came to a head in South Africa in the decision of *Pastel Software v Pink Software (Pty) Ltd*.[265] The matter turned on the program 'TurboCASH', which was being marketed by 'Pink Software' and which 'Pastel Software' claimed copyright. The latter firm also had contractual claims and, in the third place, claimed that the former company was competing with it unfairly.

Eloff J dealt with the copyright issues as if the program was a 'literary work'.[266] 'Pink' had argued in the first place that it had reproduced only screen images which are ephemeral and cannot found a copyright claim. The court decided that the original creation had been recorded as manuals 'and that those were converted in the form of screens and printouts' and that even the screens formed part of the program and 'may not be imitated'.

Apart from showing a lack of understanding of the series of processes which underlie the creation of a computer program, this finding flies in the face of the American experience, where the screens are protected as 'audiovisual works'. It also goes against the trend embodied in the latest South African Copyright Act, where neither the preliminary flowcharts and notes nor the final product of the program itself, such as screens, are protected as part of the program.

In the second place, Pink argued that there was nothing wrong with looking at Pastel's screens and then writing a different program to generate a similar end-product. This seems to be a reference to American cases, like those of *Altai* above, where the screen represents the unprotectable idea, or goal, and the program itself represents the protectable expression, as a specific and unique means to attain

264 (1992) 4 *SA Mercantile Law Journal* 346ff.

265 M Stranex (ed) *Judgments on Copyright* (The Law Publisher 1993) 399 (T).

266 The latest amendments had not yet come into operation at the time of the trial.

the general goal. The court confessed quite candidly: 'I am not sure that I understand the point.'

By focusing on the manuals, instead of on the program (which seems to have been the basis of Pink's argument), Eloff J disposed of the matter quite handily:

> 'If Pastel in law acquired copyright in Katz's manuals, it in law enjoyed the sole right of making reproductions and of resisting efforts to make imitations of its reproductions. There is everything wrong in someone examining the reproductions and imitating them. An imitation is a copy of a reproduction of the screenimage in regard to which Pastel enjoys copyright.'[267]

Rather disconcertingly, the court further justifies its finding of illegal copying by personally comparing screens from the two different programs. Although this is an example of the American 'total concept and feel' approach, as embodied in the *Softklone* decision above, it will not work in cases where the structure and sequence of the 'hidden' program itself are in issue (as it probably was in the present case). It will also no longer work in terms of the latest South African Copyright Act, where 'computer program' is restrictively defined as

> 'a set of instructions fixed or stored in any manner and which when used directly or indirectly in a computer, directs its operations to bring about a result.'

It seems obvious to state that 'screens' can never be squeezed into the above definition. In that sense, at least, the new Act should have brought greater clarity by specifically addressing this question. This point is made by Pistorius & Visser, who also criticize the Act for not dealing with copyright in databases and for declaring that copyright is indirectly infringed by acquiring an infringing copy of a computer program with the knowledge that it is an infringing copy.[268]

At a conference on Cyberlaw[269] Mr Michau of Spoor and Fisher was asked about the specific protection of databases by the present Copyright Act. While conceding that a database would not be protected in the category of 'computer program', given the narrow definition of the latter, he was of the opinion that it might be protected as a 'compilation', in the category 'literary work'.

The matter has probably been settled by a 1997 amendment which has widened the definition of 'literary work' in s 1 of the Copyright Act, 98 of 1978, to now also encompass 'tables and compilations of data stored or embodied in a computer or a medium used in conjunction with a computer'.

The point has been made above that technical protection might be a realistic means of protecting the commercial interest of the persons providing the creative

267 Op cit 86n264.

268 Section 23(2)*(d)* of the Act.

269 'Cyberlaw-Beyond 2000' held at Midrand from 31 March to 1 April 1998.

input, not only with computer programs, but with any product which is to be used or stored digitally. One form of 'technical protection' is to make popular programs, such as games software, available on CD-ROM. Certain parts of the program may be copied to one's hard disk to speed up use of the system, but usually the entire system cannot be copied.[270] It is also much more stable and reliable than when stored on the magnetic medium of floppy or 'stiffy' disks. Pistorius & Visser make the point that the South African Copyright Act's permission to make back-up copies probably does not apply in the case of CD-ROM disck, since this should not be necessary for legitimate use.[271]

2.8 Conclusion

Copyright has always been international and is being governed more and more by international agreement. It would therefore seem the ideal vehicle to protect one of the most valuable rights in the 21st century, namely commoditized information. Nevertheless, some doubt still remains as to whether it has not bitten off more than can it chew with digital copyright. In most countries its protection shows its roots as being grounded in creative, artistic work. Having to protect computer programs and products, which smack more of machinery and technical things, seems like a bridge too far. Its requirement of creativity makes impossible the protections of compilations, such as databases, leading to the development of a *sui generis* right which has to exist alongside ordinary copyright. It has great difficulty in coping with the Internet, which requires millions of transient copies to be made in milliseconds, simply in order to operate. By focusing on the procedure of copying, instead of on the rights which are supposed to be protected, copyright has almost made itself unenforcable.

On the other hand, it is almost all that we have. The degree of international consensus (and thereby jurisdiction) would be difficult to achieve with any other field of law. If applied by its adherents in a restrained way, it could become a facilitator of instead of a roadblock to Internet traffic. Matters such as the scope and subsistence of digital copyright as well as the march of modern technology have created much food for thought in this field of copyright.

---

270 This does not address the situation where the installation software is simply placed on a CD-ROM disk instead of on floppies, but applies when the CD-ROM itself has to be used in the operation of the program.

271 Op cit 358.

CHAPTER THREE

TRADE SECRETS AND UNFAIR COMPETITION

The interrelation between trade-secret law, competition law and information as a legal object is fascinating and is proving to be a melting pot in the law's efforts to deal adequately with information.

III TRADE SECRETS AND UNFAIR COMPETITION*

The title of this chapter has been changed from its equivalent in the previous edition of this work, where it was simply called Trade Secrets. It is interesting that Tapper[1] has also amended the title of the corresponding chapter in his latest edition. In prior editions it used to be Trade Secrets and Confidentiality, but this has been changed to Trade Secrets and Unfair Competition in the latest edition. This foresight is to his credit, since English law in general is still using a scatter gun approach in trying to systematize the law of trade secrets in the United Kingdom. Tapper uses the following citation to illustrate this:

> 'A cursory study of the cases, where the plaintiff's confidence has been breached, reveals great conceptual confusion. Property, contract, bailment, trust, fiduciary relationship, good faith, unjust enrichment have all been claimed, at one time or another as the basis of judicial intervention. Indeed some judges have indiscriminately intermingled all these concepts. The result is that the answer in [sic] many fundamental questions remains speculative.'[2]

Nevertheless, Tapper's title is still amazingly accurate as far as South Africa is concerned. Not happy with the more casuistic English approach, our courts have analysed this phenomenon from the perspective of the Roman-Dutch common law (the field of trade secrets being one part of intellectual property law which has not yet been legislated). As we shall see, the *actio legis Aquiliae,* based on unfair competition, is the action which underlies the uncodified part of the South African law of intellectual property. This makes the concept more flexible than legislation, since it can be developed and fine-tuned by our courts.

The present chapter also acts as a hold-all for those statutory parts of the law of intellectual property which have not yet been dealt with in the chapters on patent and copyright, such as the law of trade marks and designs. Under trademark law the typical Internet problem of registration of domain names is also dealt with, whereas design is relevant to the protection of semi-conductor chips and chip mask designs.

The interrelation between trade-secret law, competition law and information as a legal object is fascinating and is proving to be a melting pot in the law's efforts to deal adequately with information.

* *Including trade marks and designs.*

1 Colin Tapper *Computer Law* 4 ed (Longman 1989) 76.

2 Gareth Jones, as quoted by Tapper op cit 76–7.

3.1 TRADE SECRETS

3.1.1 Introduction

The law of trade secrets forms a distinct part of intellectual property law and in practice plays a more important role in the field of computer law than either patent or copyright. The CONTU[3] report referred to in the previous chapter contains a chart comparing the relative merits of these three fields, specifically with regard to the protection of computer software. From the chart it is apparent that protection by trade secret is usually dependent on entrance into a contractual relationship,[4] as against copyright, which flows automatically from the act of creation. The former is still better than the lengthy application procedure for patents, however.

In the work *The Legal Protection of Computer Software* it is acknowledged that trade secrets must be the most commonly adopted means of protecting computer software, although the contributors are also not blind to the problems attendant on this form of protection. Nevertheless, with regard to the United States at least, the authors are of the opinion that 'in general trade secret law provides better protection than patents for computer software'.[5]

On the other hand, the CONTU report finds trade secrets more expensive to maintain and to enforce against violators than the other two options. In the event of successful litigation, statutory damages and attorneys' fees are not available from infringers. Finally, trade-secret protection is not at all suitable for software which will be subject to mass distribution.

Other problems with trade-secret protection are enumerated by Michael C Gemignani.[6] He mentions that the law on this point is not uniform throughout the United States, that it has never fully addressed the novel problems created by computer technology, that failure to protect the confidentiality of a program is fatal in a suit for damages and that once secrecy has been lost, one is not even left with the limited protection of copyright. Furthermore, the great mobility of programmers on the labour market makes protection by means of secrecy difficult and raises problems of competition law. Finally, a developer encounters problems in determining whether his or her program has been misappropriated and then of proving this in court, because none of the normal copyright or patent presumptions applies.

---

3 Acronym for Committee on New Technical Uses.

4 Even though secrecy is sometimes treated as an implied term of the contract, or as a duty of confidentiality resting on the recipient (the United Kingdom equity action), it is risky not to provide for it explicitly in the contract.

5 H Brett & L Perry (eds) *The Legal Protection of Computer Software* (ESC Publishers 1981) viii.

6 (1980) 7 *Rutgers Computers and Technology Law Journal* 269 at 306.

To the above, one might add the fact that litigating just once will reveal the secret anyway! It is significant to note the mention of competition law in the above paragraph in the same context as trade secrets.

Linda N Flewellen[7] points out another problem with trade secrets. Because of the secrecy necessary to prevent the misappropriation of programs, much time is invested in 're-inventing the wheel', or in writing software which has already been developed by someone else, although it is being kept secret. This has a detrimental effect on the industry because of the duplication of effort.

In a paper delivered at a conference on *Computer Technology and the Law*,[8] E Price mentioned certain requirements set by South African courts in this regard such as secrecy, novelty, the conferring of an advantage and 'a use in business'. He also mentioned such disadvantages as the need for continual vigilance and the inappropriateness of this type of protection to mass-marketed products. He did explain, however, why trade-secret protection remains so popular in spite of the many disadvantages. According to Price, this is one of the few fields which really protect ideas. Furthermore, there are no technical requirements (for instance, copyright's demand that there should have been an initial reduction to material form or that an actual copying be proved).[9]

Of these advantages, the present writer consider the first to be the most important. It has already been shown that neither the law of copyright nor that of patent really protects ideas. I find support from the views of Joseph E Root[10] in this regard:

> 'Trade secrecy certainly will not wither away in the near future. Its primary strength, the ability to protect the algorithm of a program, makes it highly attractive.'

Besides the practical problems with trade secrets, this field also presents lawyers with theoretical conundrums, the biggest one being the choice of a legal pigeonhole in which to file the law of trade secrets. In other words, what is the legal basis for holding a person liable for disclosure and, depending on this answer, what should he be held liable for?

The situation is complicated by the fact that the relatively international homogeneity of copyright does not apply to the field of trade secrets. In England, therefore, a special tort has been developed in the field of equity, based upon

---

7 (1981) 8 *Rutgers Computer and Technology Law Journal* 273 at 279.

8 Organized by the associations ALASA and LES in Johannesburg on 11 and 12 September 1985.

9 E Price 'Computer Software: Protection in SA Law by way of Copyright and Trade Secrets'. Paper presented at the *Computer Technology and the Law* Conference, 1985.

10 (1981) 8 *Rutgers Journal of Computers, Technology and the Law* 215 at 226.

considerations of good faith in relationships between parties.[11] In South Africa, with its emphasis on the more general actions of the Roman-Dutch law, the *actio legis Aquiliae* has been considered apposite where such lack of good faith has led to the unlawful interference with trade or business. In other words, delictual liability flows from the common law of competition, since the divulgement of entrusted or discovered confidences interferes with free competition.[12] In the United States and on the European continent the law of trade secrets has also been linked to the right to free and fair competition. This basis also consists in England, together with alternative grounds such as the right of property in the information itself and the field of contract.

Christopher J Millard makes the same point when he states:

> 'Yet the uncertain conceptual basis of such rights has significant implications for the breadth of protection which can be secured and for the types of remedies that are available. Secrecy rights have variously been attributed to equity, contract, tort and property.[13]'

He discusses each of these briefly and makes the point that the last category could also give rise to criminal sanctions for the 'theft' of trade secrets: ' ... yet it is precisely the availability of enforcement 'teeth' which makes the proprietary model attractive to software developers.'[14] Millard mentions that English courts seem to prefer the equitable basis whereas there is more support for the property basis in the United States and Canada. Although all these may have a role to play, he feels that a 'general taxonomy' is crucial. He suggests that trade secrets as a form of intellectual property be distinguished from the duties of confidentiality based on equitable tort principles and that the law of contract could then come into play to modify both types of protection.

Guy Vandenberghe[15] states that on the Continent there is not one single form of trade-secret protection but a fan ('waaier') of such protection:

> 'Aldus kan contractueel een geheimhoudingsverplichting worden opgelegd, of deze kan van rechtswege op basis van het sociaal recht rusten op de werknemer; ook kan er strafrechtelijke aansprakelijkheid gelden, of er kan opgetreden worden wegens oneerlijke concurrentie, onrechtmatige daad, of zelfs vermogensverschuiving zonder rechtsgrond.'[16]

---

11 See, for instance, *Seager v Copydex* [1967] 2 All ER 415 at 417.

12 See, for instance, *Dun and Bradstreet (Pte) Ltd v SA Merchants Combined Credit Bureau (Cape) (Pty) Ltd* 1968 (1) SA 209 (C).

13 Christopher J Millard *Legal Protection of Computer Programs and Data* (Sweet and Maxwell 1985) 25.

14 Op cit at 131.

15 Guy Van den berghe *Becherming van Computer Software* (Kluwer 1984) 154.

16 'Therefore an obligation of secrecy may be imposed contractually or it may rest on an employee by law on the basis of social law; criminal liability may also arise, or

The last ground raises the fascinating possibility of utilising enrichment as a possible ground of protection for computer software. This has also been mooted in an article by Rudolf Callmann entitled 'He who reaps where he has not sown: unjust enrichment in the law of unfair competition'.[17] Although space and time and my lack of knowledge of the law of enrichment do not permit me to pursue this aspect here, the subject may well be worthy of further investigation.

In the next rubric this topic is considered country by country, in the same sequence followed in the preceding chapter. In the following sections the topics of trade marks and design will be dealt with. Finally, an overview and conclusion is attempted with regard to IPR[18] in general (the entire first part of this book), with an assessment of the role it can play to protect computer hardware and software, both mainframe and micro.

3.1.2 The United States

(1) Trade secrets

The Americans have specifically dealt with trade secrets in their First Restatement of Torts of 1939. Section 757 determines that:

> 'One who discloses or uses another's trade secret, without a privilege to do so, is liable to the other if:
>
> (a) he discovered the secret by improper means, or
>
> (b) his disclosure or use constitutes a breach of confidence reposed in him by the other in disclosing the secret to him, or
>
> *(c)* he learned the secret from a third person with notice of the facts that it was a trade secret and that the third person discovered it by improper means or that the third person's disclosure of it was otherwise a breach of his duty to the other, or
>
> *(d)* he learned the secret with notice of the facts that it was a secret and that its disclosure was made to him by mistake.'

The 'breach of confidence' and 'breach of duty' are typically the phrases used in the Anglo-American torts for infringement of trade secrets. In discussing the basis of liability for disclosure, the Restatement seems to reject property and unfair competition:

> 'Analogy is sometimes found in the law of "literary property", copyright, patents, trade marks and unfair competition. The suggestion that one has

action may be taken on the grounds of unfair competition delict or even transfer of assets without legal ground' (latter probably refers to unjust enrichment).

17 (1942) 55 *Harvard Law Review* 595.

18 Acronym for 'intellectual property rights'.

> the right to exclude others from the use of his trade secret because he has a right of property in the idea has been frequently advanced and rejected. The theory that has prevailed is that the protection is afforded only by a general duty of good faith and that the liability rests on this duty; that is breach of contract, abuse of confidence or impropriety in the method of ascertaining the secret. Apart from breach of contract, abuse of confidence or impropriety in the means of procurement, trade secrets may be copied as freely as devices or processes which are not secret.'

From the Second Restatement of Torts, a bird's-eye view of litigation related to s 757 may be obtained. In *United States v International Business Machines Corp*[19] it was decided that s 757 would be the standard in determining whether the information in question rises to the level of a trade secret. In quite a few of the other decisions, in many of which computers were involved, the claims were carefully couched to allege the misappropriation of trade secrets *and* unfair competition.[20] Even if conceptually confusing, practically the matter is quite simple. The infringers of trade secrets are usually ex-employees of the plaintiff, whereas the unfair competitors are their new employers!

Richard H Baker[21] suggests the following question to help determine whether information in possession of the ex-employee has risen to the status of a trade secret: could the employee have learned this anywhere else? If so, the information was probably general knowledge and no protection would follow. Another rule of thumb is that the higher up in the echelons of the company the ex-employee had been, the more likely he is to have been privy to trade secrets. This could help to explain the action instituted by Apple Computers against its own co-founder, Steven Jobs, when he left with some key personnel to set up the NEXT company. As some readers may know, Steve is now back with Apple again and setting sales records with the new i-Mac machine!

Even though the Second Restatement contained a record of litigation in terms of the First Restatement, it did not take over its substantive provisions with regard to trade secrets because of doubt whether that was their proper place. This led to the National Conference of Commissioners on Uniform State Laws adopting a Uniform Trade Secrets Act (UTSA) in 1979, based largely on the provisions in the First Restatement.[22]

---

19 67 FRD 40 at 46.

20 Amongst others *Telex Corp v IBM Corp* 46 L Ed 2nd 244 (1975) and *Sperry Rand Corp v Pentronix* Inc 311 F Supp 910 at 913 (my emphasis in the main text).

21 Richard H Baker *Scuttle the Computer Pirates* (Tab Books 1984) 40.

22 This has been adopted in the states of Arkansas, Kansas, Louisiana, Minnesota, North Carolina, Utah and Washington.

An effort to consolidate differing state approaches has been made by UTSA, which defines a trade secret as follows:

> '"Trade Secret" means information, including a formula, pattern, compilation, program, device, method, technique or process, that:
>
> (i) derives independent economic value, actual or potential, from not being generally known to, and not being readily ascertainable by proper means by other persons who can obtain economic value from its disclosures or use; and
>
> (ii) is subject of efforts that are reasonable under the circumstances to maintain its secrecy.'[23]

It has also been informally defined as 'confidential information that is valuable to a company by providing an advantage in the marketplace over those who do not know the secret'.[24] It should be borne in mind that there is no federal application of UTSA: it acts as a guide to state legislatures who do not have to adopt it, or who have adopted it but with changes to its content. 'Thus, each state has slightly different trade secret laws.'[25]

The above definitions are interesting when compared to the definition of information settled upon in the first chapter of the present work. 'Information' means '(desired) items of knowledge' and 'knowledge' in turn means 'a person's range of information'. This means that information is something which a person would like to bring within his range of personal knowledge. This is borne out by the fact that trade secrets (which usually consists just of information) have an economic value as long as they stay desired. Once they become common knowledge they are still useful but no longer have economic value for their original 'owner'. This diminution in value to the owner has led to the phrase 'theft of information'.

A problem unique to the United States, with its powerful Constitution, was whether or not the *federal* patent and copyright law pre-empted the application of the *state-based* trade-secrecy laws. Even though this question was answered negatively in *Kewanee Oil Co v Bicron Cotp*,[26] at least with regard to patent, the enactment of new copyright legislation, which abolished the old common-law copyright, cast new doubt on the matter. This was apparently resolved, however, by the decision in *M Bryce and Associates, Inc v Gladstone*,[27] where the Court of Appeals held that federal copyright law does not pre-empt state trade-secrecy laws.

---

23 Section 1.

24 L C Lee & J S Davidson *Intellectual Property for the Internet* (Wiley Law Publications 1997) 14.

25 Op cit at 15.

26 416 US 470 (1954).

27 319 NW 2d 907.

A leading United States case on unfair competition is also relevant to trade secrets because it involved the 'theft' of news[28] by one news agency from another, apparently by bribery of the victim's officials. In *International News Service v Associated Press*[29] the court commented as follows:

> 'In doing this defendant, by its very act, admits that it is taking material that has been acquired by complainant as a result of organisation and the expenditure of labor, skill and money, and which is saleable by complainant for money, and that defendant in appropriating it and selling it as its own is endeavouring to reap where it has not sown, and by disposing of it to newspapers that are competitors of complainant's members is appropriating to itself the harvest of those who have sown.'

For the way in which Continental courts, such as the French, for instance, deal with the misappropriation of news, see section 3.1.4 below.

(2) Competition law

Because unfair competition seemingly bears a close relationship to trade secrets, it may be wise also to take a brief look at United States competition law. There it is termed 'antitrust law' and the matter was first addressed by the Sherman Act of 1890. The name and impulse for legislation came from so-called 'trusts' which were dominating the American business scene towards the end of the 19th century.[30] Amazingly, the Act is still in force, although expanded upon.

Section 1 states that:

> 'Every contract, combination in the form of trust or otherwise, or conspiracy, in restraint of trade or commerce among the several States, or with a foreign nation, is declared to be illegal.'

Section 2 forbids monopolies, or attempts or conspiracies thereto, with regard to 'any part of the trade or commerce among the several States, or with foreign nations'.

In 1914, Congress passed the Clayton Act, which contained some clauses specifically clarifying the Sherman Act. In 1950 the Clayton Act was amended to prohibit mergers or acquisitions where 'the effect of such acquisition may be substantially to lessen competition or to tend to create a monopoly' in commerce, anywhere in the country.

Merdes et al [31] take up the interesting argument as to whether there is tension between patent, which bestows a (limited) monopoly, and antitrust law, which is strongly anti-monopolistic. In the end the authors resolve the problem by

28 Note that 'news'is part of the definition of 'information' dealt with above.

29 248 US 215 (1915).

30 R P Merdes, P S Menell, M A Lemley & T M Jorde *Intellectual Property in the New Technological Age* (Aspen Law and Business Publications 1997).

31 See note 28 above.

pointing out that a patent usually only covers one product, whereas that product is only a small part of the entire product market (which is protected by antitrust law). Yet, they warn that where innovation has created an entirely new market, patent is likely to confer an economic monopoly entirely. One is here reminded of Bill Gates, who is more of a marketer than an innovator, but is at present fighting antitrust proceedings because of the pervasiveness of his Windows operating system.[32] His company has already been involved in the prior case of *United States v Microsoft, Inc.*[33] Here the facts were that Microsoft required computer manufacturers to pay royalties on each machine they shipped, whether or not the Microsoft operating system software had been installed on it. The manufacturers then installed the operating system as a matter of course, since they had already paid for it on behalf of the client. The US Antitrust Division utilized s 3 of the Clayton Act which prohibits 'exclusive dealing'. The Microsoft position roughly boils down to the following threat: 'If you want *some* of my products, you buy *everything* from me!' Microsoft settled the case and agreed to stop claiming universal royalties.

3.1.3 The United Kingdom (trade secrets and competition)

As has been pointed out in the general section, some conceptual confusion exists as to the true basis of the protection of this field:[34]

> 'Property, contract, bailment, trust, fiduciary relationship, good faith, unjust enrichment, have all been claimed, at one time or another, as the basis of judicial intervention.'[35]

Tapper also feels that the basic tension is between a proprietary and a personal approach, but that 'there is much less coherence than in the purely statutory domains of intellectual property'.[36] He mentions that this field could go further than patent or copyright by protecting an idea before it has been hard-wired into a program, or a list of customers committed to memory but not yet written down. This is borne out by Niblett,[37] who states that the equitable jurisdiction of the action for breach of confidence is wider than copyright,[38] because it protects ideas and concepts.

32 Actually the charges are more specifically that he tried to leverage his near monopoly in operation systems (Windows) to force clients to buy his Internet browser (Explorer) rather than the competing product (Communicator) from his rival (Netscape).

33 159 FRD 318 (DDC) and 56 F 3d 1448 (DC Cir 1995).

34 Since Tapper calls it 'Trade secrets and unfair competition', it may be misleading to refer to either of the two in isolation. The term 'this field' will therefore be used.

35 Tapper *Computer Law* 76.

36 Op cit 77.

37 Brett & Perry *The Legal Protection of Computer Programs* 61.

38 And wider than patent too?

In the case of *Fraser v Evans*[39] Lord Denning stated that a cause of action for breach of trade secret was founded 'not so much on property or a contract, but rather on the duty to act in good faith'. According to Gutterman & Anderson,[40] however, courts at present tend to treat claims of breach of trade secrets by taking into account whether a contractual relationship existed.

Tapper[41] describes the full spectrum of trade-secret protection, from a personal proprietary basis ('owning' the information) through a gradual shift in emphasis towards the behaviour of 'a defendant who may have competed unfairly' (by stealing staff from a competitor). In the latter case there is 'little trace of the proprietary element'. The only common element between the two ends of the spectrum, according to Tapper, is 'an element of unfairness'. This unfairness has led to stress being placed on the equitable character of some of the remedies that are provided and has led to an equitable action for breach of confidence, which may be distinguished from trade-secret protection by the stress which it places on the relationship between the parties. Tapper concedes that it may sometimes be difficult to distinguish between a secret (protected by trade-secret law), a confidence (protected by breach of confidence) or a situation where neither obtains. This is to be expected, however, in the light of the 'protean nature of information, as opposed to physical objects' and the lack of statutory guidance which makes for a field which 'defies simple conceptual characterization':

> 'It cannot be explained or understood solely in terms of contract, property or confidence, but all have their part to play in the inter-relation of liabilities and remedies. It can indeed be argued that it is this diversity which particularly fits this area for a flexible and innovative role in dealing with a new technology which cannot easily be pigeon-holed into an established area of intellectual property, or characterized by a historic theory of liability.'[42]

The 'confidence' in the above quotation refers to the action for breach of confidence, an equitable action typical of English law. This equitable protection of trade secrets has been developed in a series of judicial decisions, the most important being *Saltman Engineering v Campbell Engineering*[43] and *Seager v Copydex*.[44] In the *Saltman* case Lord Greene demarcated 'confidential information' as something which is not public property or public knowledge. From this Reed[45] deduces that absolute secrecy is not required—'[r]elative secrecy may suffice'. This puts the law

39 [1969] All ER 8 at 11.

40 Alain S Gutterman & Bentley J Anderson *Intellectual Property in Global Markets* (Kluwer 1997) 214.

41 Op cit 77.

42 Op cit 78.

43 [1963] 3 All ER 413; [1948] 65 RPC 203.

44 [1967] 2 All ER 415; [1967] RPC 349.

45 Chris Reed (ed) *Computer Law* (Blackstone Press 1996) 212.

onto a slippery slope in trying to determine how far disclosure may go while retaining enough 'secrecy' to qualify for trade secret protection. In the so-called '*Spycatcher*' case,[46] reported as *Attorney-General v Guardian Newspapers Ltd (No 2)*[47] it was decided that once information is in the public domain it can no longer be protected by confidentiality law at all.

Reed further distinguishes between three categories of confidential information, namely personal information (which involves privacy issues), government information (which involves security issues) and trade secrets (which involves commercial issues). The thrust of the present book is towards the last-mentioned since that has to do with the 'commodification of information' discussed in the first chapter. Nevertheless it is useful to keep this triple distinction in mind in order to avoid conceptual confusion. The right to information which the South African Constitution[48] bestows deals with government information and so will the Freedom of Information Act once it becomes law in South Africa.

Reed has the following to say on trade secrets:

> 'Trade secrets are valuable commercial assets and to a large extent they are protected for the same reasons as other intangible commercial assets such as patents and copyrights. These include rewarding innovation and effort, allowing recoupment of expenditure and development and curtailing unfair competition by limiting the opportunities for piracy. In the context of computing, trade secrets may include software or hardware specifications as well as more standard business information such as pricing policies, lists of customers and suppliers, the company's payroll, quotation and investments, any or all which may be kept on an in-house computer or may be held on behalf of a client on the computer of a specialist bureau.'[49]

Interesting in the above is the mention of unfair competition and the distinction between computer-related specifications of commercial value and ordinary business data. Reed also quotes a Canadian[50] definition of trade secret:

'... trade secret means information that

(i) is, or may be, used in a trade or business,

(ii) is, not generally known in that trade or business;

(iii) has economic value from not being generally known, and

(iv) is the subject of efforts that are reasonable under the circumstances to prevent it from being generally known;

---

46 This was the title of a work which the Thatcher Government in the United Kingdom tried to suppress on the grounds that it divulged state secrets.

47 [1990] 1 AC 109.

48 Act 108 of 1996, s 32.

49 Op cit 214.

50 From a draft statute adopted by the Canadian Uniform Law Conference in 1988.

(2) For the purposes of the definition, trade secret "information" includes information set out, contained, or embodied in, but not limited to, a formula, pattern, plan, compilation, computer program, method, technique, process, product, device or mechanism.'

The latter section indicates again what an amorphous concept 'information' really is. As with the United States section, the reader is again referred to the definition of 'information' in chapter 1 as '(desired) items of knowledge, news', which illustrates the 'economic value' mentioned in the Canadian definition.

England has never had the problems of overlapping and pre-emption between copyright and confidentiality that the United States has; in fact, the United Kingdom Copyright Act specifically states that 'nothing in this Act shall affect the operation of any rule of equity relating to breaches of trust or confidence'.[51] This selfsame section has been borrowed by the South African legislature, even though this country does not really have the equitable jurisdiction which has underpinned the English section!

3.1.4 Other countries and supranational groupings (trade secrets and competition)

In countries such as Germany and the Netherlands trade-secret protection seems to be linked to unlawful competition and in Germany the statute law specifically prohibits such practices as false advertising, bribery, disparaging a competitor or his goods, imitating, defamation, disclosure of trade secrets, etc.

Vandenberghe[52] cites a French and a Dutch decision to illustrate the use of the criminal law in protecting trade secrets. In the first case the accused copied programs of his former employer on to his own disks and was convicted of theft, even though nothing had been physically removed. In the second, an Arnhem decision, an employee who had copied 'gegevens',[53] which included programs, was convicted of 'verduistering' (theft by conversion). Vandenberghe realizes that this implies that software is capable of bearing personal real rights of ownership which he sees as going too far: 'Bescherming die de softwarebeschermingsbehoeften ruimschoots overstijgt.'[54]

Japan has been involved with trade secrets in a negative way in that the Japanese manufacturer of mainframe computers, Hitachi, has been charged with and convicted of stealing design secrets from IBM. Nevertheless, the Japanese Ministry of Technological Affairs (MITI), seems to have more faith in trade secrets

---

51 Copyright, Designs and Patents Act (1928) (UK) s 171(1)*(e)*.

52 Op cit 157.

53 See the Geldenhuys definition of 'gegevens' in the introductory part of this book as facts which have come to the notice of somebody.

54 'Protection which totally exceeds the need of protecting software'.

and licensing the use of these, than in copyright protection: in 1990 Japan amended its Unfair Competition Prevention Act (Law No 14) to protect trade secrets, and recognized a cause of action for unfair competition when there is an unauthorized use or disclosure of a lawfully acquired trade secret.[55]

As has been seen with the United States above, the protection of fresh news is a major problem. A further complication arises with the latest media of news distribution, such as the Internet, for instance. In an article entitled 'News on the Internet: Legal Implications of *Union Syndicale des Journalistes Français CFDT v Sté Plurimédia*',[56] a trade union for journalists sought the equivalent of an interdict against an Internet service provider in order to compel her to remove certain articles from the Internet. The facts were that certain journalists had signed agreements with a daily French regional newspaper (called 'DNA' for short)[57] which gave the paper the right to publish these articles in its pages. When the same articles were now made available on the Internet, the journalists claimed that this was another medium, not covered by the contract. It was pointed out that a new means of communication is employed, that the clientele catered for was different on the Internet[58] and that the on-line manipulations gave the newspaper a different character.

In the end the 'TGI'[59] decided in favour of the journalists.[60] What was perhaps harsh on the part of the court was to find against Plurimédia, even though they had signed contracts with DNA by which they were assured that DNA had full copyright for the Internet transmission of the relevant material. Lindner puts it as follows:

> 'Indeed, the court's perception, if confirmed by higher courts, would have the effect that contractual assurances regarding the ownership of intellectual property would not be enough; the addressee of a contractual assurance would have to verify its factual and legal correctness, which could ultimately result in an obligation to seek complex legal advice. If this case law was upheld, would it not mean that in future contractual guarantees regarding the ownership of rights are worthless?'[61]

The decision would seem to indicate that even the law of contract is not really the final answer when dealing with news, the latter constituting an excellent

55 Gutterman & Anderson op cit.

56 By Brigitte Lindner in 1998 *European Intellectual Property Review* (*EIPR*) 410ff.

57 Standing for *Dernières Nouvelles d'Alsace* (*Daily News from Alsace*).

58 Much larger and more international!

59 *Tribunal de Grande Instance* at Strasbourg, reported in (1998) 176 *RIDA* 466ff.

60 Also on a related claim which had to do with making the visual material from a television broadcast available on the Internet.

61 Op cit 413.

example of a (very short-lived) trade secret.[62] Millard's opinion (discussed in the general part of this chapter) that contract will have the final say in this field is perhaps over-optimistic.[63] In my opinion, competition law may have a better chance of finding an optimal solution because it is embedded in the general principle underlying the protection of trade secrets, namely unfairness.

3.1.5 South Africa (trade secrets and a lot of competition)

Even though computers have not often formed part of the subject-matter, there has been a fair amount of litigation on trade secrets in South Africa. As mentioned above, s 41(3) of the South African Copyright Act has directly taken over the corresponding British section dealing with a 'rule of equity relating to breaches of trust or confidence', even though this action is foreign to the Roman-Dutch common law. Copeling discusses this action, albeit critically, using such words as 'inadequate' and 'obsolete'.[64] The authorities cited in his footnotes seem to be mostly British.

In *Coolair Ventilator Co (SA) Ltd v Liebenberg & another*,[65] reference was made to the fact that the Romans employed mostly slaves and pieceworkers, but no wage-earners. For this reason, the development of the concept of good faith in an employee's dealings with his employer took place only in English (and later American) law. Although reference was made to unfair competition, an implied term of contract seems to have been the basis of the liability for the disclosure of a trade secret in that particular case.

Another South African case in which trade secrets came under close scrutiny was *Dun and Bradstreet (Pte) Ltd v SA Merchants Combined Credit Bureau Cape (Pty) Ltd*.[66] Corbett J referred to the legislative borrowing of the South African legislature from the British, but continued:

> 'It seems obvious that these savings clauses in our legislation cannot be construed as introducing the English equitable remedy for breach of trust or confidence or as creating such a remedy where previously none existed in our law.'[67]

The judge recognized that part of the problem was that English courts were still struggling to assign this action to a 'particular juristic niche':

> 'Apart from emphasising that it does not depend upon breach of contract, express or implied, the English courts have generally refrained from assigning the action to any particular juristic niche. Although, in the

62 Compare again our own definition of 'information', which includes 'news'.

63 See also the statement by Lord Denning in *Fraser v Evans* (supra).

64 (1965) 28 *THRHR* 12.

65 1967 (1) SA 686 (C).

66 1968 (1) SA 209 (C).

67 Op cit 215A.

> circumstances, tort seems to be the most appropriate niche, neither the Courts not [sic] the leading text-book writers in England appear to have classified the action in this way.'[68]

Corbett J[69] did mention, however, that the United States seems to regard the action as a tort remedy. Turning to the law of competition, the judge referred to several decisions as well as to the works of overseas and local academics, the latter being 'Grondslae van die Mededingingsreg',[70] the doctoral thesis of H J O van Heerden. This basis was found to be the true one for the protection of trade secrets in South Africa and to be in accordance with trends of legal development elsewhere. The claim is Aquilian in character and the causation of damage by the unlawful competition is therefore an essential ingredient to the claimant's cause of action. The present writer agrees that this is the true philosophical basis for the protection of trade secrets, even if not necessarily for personal and public secrets.[71] On the other hand, as Esmé du Plessis points out,[72] not all factual situations can be relayed to a right to goodwill being injured unfairly (thus leading to unfair competition), because the right may be injured by someone who is not a business competitor of the person affected. She prefers a wider remedy based on a right to incorporeal property in the form of confidential information, which, if 'misappropriated', could lead to delictual remedies, including an interdict.[73] As was shown in the treatment of trade secrets in the United States and the United Kingdom, there is a strong proprietary argument to be made out with regard to the true legal status of information. In the previous edition of this book the present writer also argued strongly for this basis to the treatment of information and trade secrets. (This matter is fully dealt with in the next chapter, which tries to draw a conclusion with regard to immaterial 'property' as a whole, in the context of private law.)

In *Oude Meester Group v Stellenbosch Wine Trust*[74] Diemont J confirmed the Aquilian aspects of this action and stressed the criteria of fairness and honesty in competition. This was particularly apposite in the present case, where the one wine company had apparently obtained the label as well as the launch information of the new wine of its competitor from the latter's printing firm!

---

68 Ibid.

69 As he then was; he became Chief Justice of South Africa later.

70 'Fundamentals of Competition Law' (my translation) (unpublished doctoral thesis, University of the Orange Free State 1958).

71 See the three kinds of information distinguished by Reed in the United Kingdom section above.

72 (1985) *MB* vol 7 61 at 69.

73 She does concede that her views are in conflict with the *Dun and Bradstreet* decision (supra), though.

74 1972 (3) SA 152 (C).

Unfortunately, the court cast back to the British equity basis in the South African decision of *Harvey Tiling Co v Rodomac.*[75] Although it referred obliquely to competition, and to the *Oude Meester* decision (supra), it ignored the strong Aquilian base for the action laid down in the *Dun and Bradstreet* decision (supra), looking rather to British and Australian decisions, including the decision in *Saltman Engineering* (supra; being the British *locus classicus* on the equity action, as was indicated above).

The well-known case of *Northern Office Micro Computers (Pty) Ltd v Rosenstein,*[76] discussed above for its impact on copyright, was actually decided substantially on the law of trade secrets. Although it was found that the respondent had copyright in the suite of programs he had written, the applicants based their claim mostly on the right of an employer to require an ex-employee to respect and maintain the employer's trade secrets.

Unfortunately Marais AJ was vague in establishing the precise legal basis for this action. He refers to the *Harvey Tiling* case (supra) (which rests on a rather shaky basis, as indicated), the *Coolair* decision (which was decided on a basis of contract), and to s 41(3) of the South African Copyright Act[77] (which has been copied directly from its British equivalent). He does feel uneasy about the warning in the *Dun and Bradstreet* decision (supra), namely that this provision cannot introduce into South African law principles of the English common law which do not exist here, but feels that some effect has to be given to the section. It is indeed a great pity that he did not follow the firm Aquilian base in competition, laid down by Corbett J in the same *Dun and Bradstreet* decision, to explain the protection of trade secrets in Roman-Dutch law.[78]

With respect, Marais AJ did much better on the related questions of what exactly amounted to a trade secret and in how far the possessor of knowledge could be restrained from using it without being unreasonable. The judge has no doubt that computer programs qualify for the protection which the law accords to confidential matter and trade secrets, provided that the program is not commonplace. The bare concept of a suite of programs to assist the day-to-day running of a medical or dental practice is not novel enough to be protected as a trade secret, but:

> 'It is common cause that much work, skill or time is needed to produce a suite of programs of this kind. If respondent were permitted simply to copy it, he would be unfairly nullifying the advantage of the "long start"

75 1977 (1) SA 316 (T).

76 1981 (4) SA 123 (C).

77 Act 98 of 1978.

78 He does at least refer to 'common-law rights'.

> over anyone else to which applicants are entitled. To that limited extent, the suite of programs is, in my opinion, a trade secret.'[79]

What is interesting in the above decision is that the judge here refers to a form of 'sweat of the brow' justification, which could take the place of originality, as has been argued with regard to databases in the United States, at least up to the *Feist*[80] decision. Even though the respondent was prohibited from copying the programs, the court refused to restrain him in the form prayed for by applicant:

> '[F]rom communicating all computer language instructions relating exclusively to the accounting and administrative requirements of doctors and dentists, whether in writing or otherwise, embodied in the suite of programs designed by respondent for the purposes of producing an accounting system for doctors and dentists irrespective of the nature or type of computer in conjunction with which such instructions may be used.'[81]

The judge felt that the respondent could not be expected to clear his memory because this would halter the respondent's use of his own training, skill and experience to an unacceptable degree, even if he were restrained only for a limited period.

In *Prok Africa & another v NTH & others*[82] Goldstone J quoted a paragraph from the *Oude Meester* decision (supra), in which Diemont J described the English equity action with reference to *Seager v Copydex* (supra), before he (Diemont) accepted that the 'equivalent remedy' for Roman-Dutch law was based on 'unlawful interference with trade or business', in other words, competition law. Goldstone J perceived that 'our law does not recognise any such "broad principle of equity" and the equivalent remedy is Aquilian'.

Unfortunately Mullins J, in the decision of *Butt v Schulz & another*,[83] quoted the same paragraph from the *Oude Meester* case (supra)—without, however, adding that the English equity action does not exist in our law. At any rate, he decided the matter by making use of the law of unfair competition. It is therefore submitted that this decision is not out of line with a clear South African trend to found liability for the disclosure of trade secrets on an Aquilian action, based on unlawful interference with trade or business.

---

79 137D.

80 *Feist Publications Inc v Rural Telephone Service Company* 111 S Ct 1282 L Ed 2d 358 (1991).

81 137B–D.

82 1980 (3) SA 687 (W).

83 1984 (3) SA 568 (C).

3.2 TRADE MARKS AND DESIGNS

Although similar sounding and also part of IPR,[84] trade marks differ appreciably from trade secrets. They probably have more in common with patent—being statutory and giving the holder worldwide legal protection against any other claimant, in return for registering[85] with a central authority. The same could be said about the protection of designs; in fact, they probably have even more in common with patent, as well as often overlapping substantially with copyright protection. Nevertheless, judged on the deeper philosophical ground of promoting fair competition in trade, the law of trade marks and the law of designs carry out exactly the same function as the law of trade secrets.

Although this topic is covered more thoroughly in section 3.2.2 below[86] one should bear in mind that the original treaty dealing with international patent also made provision for the protection of trade marks.[87] It is important to understand also that there has been a groundswell movement towards treating Intellectual Property Rights (IPR) as a trade-related issue and thus moving it into the world of GATT[88] and TRIPS.[89] This has led to a corresponding lessening of importance of the traditional standard-setting bodies such as WIPO[90] and the older IPR treaties—primarily the Berne Convention and the Universal Copyright Convention for copyright and the Paris Convention for patents and trademarks. As a result of (mainly United States) pressure, a WTO[91] has come into being and by becoming a member a country also has to assume certain responsibilities, through TRIPS, with regard to IPR, including trademark and design rights.

The world of the Internet has led to renewed interest in trade marks because of the practice of registering so-called 'domain names' for Web addresses. Certain 'cybersquatters' have adopted the practice of registering as domain names the brand names of internationally known products and then demanding payment from the company for selling them 'back' the domain name. A normal World Wide Web[92] address on the Internet usually resembles something like this: 'http://www.unisa.ac.za'. The *first* part represents 'hypertext transfer protocol' and is usually 'understood' (that is, not even mentioned when the address is given to

---

84 Acronym for Intellectual property rights.

85 Although in many jurisdictions a trademark may be also be obtained by mere use.

86 'Other countries and international groupings'.

87 The Paris Convention on Industrial Property of 1883. A number of successive 'Paris' conventions have been held since, in various other cities.

88 Acronym for General Agreement on Tariffs and Trade.

89 Acronym for 'trade-related aspects of intellectual property rights'.

90 Acronyms for World Intellectual Property Organization and Intellectual Property Rights.

91 Acronym for World Trade Organization.

92 See the section on the Internet under Copyright above.

interested parties). The *second* part represents 'World Wide Web' (and is sometimes deliberately not used as part of the address). The *third* part is the 'brand name', which is usually in dispute, in this case representing the University of South Africa. If a firm, say the 'United Service Agency', is carrying on a business, it will probably register 'http://www.unisa.co.za'. The *fourth* field thus distinguishes the field of endeavour of the preceding name: 'ac' represents 'academic' and 'co' represents 'commercial'. The *fifth* field simply distinguishes the country in which one is based, namely 'za' for 'South Africa'. With a certain amount of high-handedness Americans do not feel the need to use 'us' as part of an address—if the fifth field is lacking one therefore usually assumes that it comes from the United States, subject to the following remark. The use of 'com' in the fourth field also indicates 'commercial', but it is not followed by any country qualifier, thus signifying something like 'We are the best in the world, we are truly international, we are unique!' Thus a dispute between the American computer manufacturer and the English record company concerning the address 'www.apple.com'[93] is quite likely!

Trade marks have existed for about 4 000 years and have traditionally served the following functions:

> 'First, they served as a form of advertising, allowing makers to get their name in front of potential customers. Second, they may have been used to prove that the goods were sold by a particular merchant, thus helping to resolve ownership disputes. Third, the marks served as a guarantee of quality, since a merchant who identifies herself with her goods puts her reputation on the line.'[94]

These functions and objectives remain valid at the end of the twentieth century, when we are entering upon a brave new world of commerce.[95]

The origin of design registration has been described by Cornish[96] as follows:

> 'The origins of design registration stretch back to the earliest period of industrialisation in some parts of the textile industry. The real impetus towards the modern system came in the 1830s. The poor quality of British industrial design, particularly when compared with the achievements of the French, incited middle-class radicals to press for a system of training designers and manufacturers to demand a more substantial legal monopoly.'

This led to a Copyright of Designs Act in 1842, but even though the name might indicate that this was merely another category of copyright, 'the need actually to prove that an alleged infringement was copied' was gradually done away with.

93 The American computer company and the English record company respectively.

94 Merdes et al op cit.

95 See the introductory part of chapter 1 above and chapter 7 Mercantile Law.

96 W R Cornish *Intellectual Property* (Sweet & Maxwell 1996) 486.

According to Cornish[97] the protection of designs acquired characteristics of a patent system and in 1875 the Patent Office took over the registration and administration of designs. The uneasy co-existence of copyright and a design right will be explored in the section on the United Kingdom below. Suffice it to say that these problems emigrated to South Africa and here have assumed a life of their own.

A final word on design. Even though the United States has adopted a specific Act towards protecting semi-conductor chip design, most other countries try to protect this as part of their general design protection (which has remained rather underdeveloped in the United States.)

3.2.1 The United States

(1) Trade mark

Trade-mark law was a late developer in the United States, perhaps because of the relatively low volume of trade in finished goods in the earlier part of the Union's existence.[98] The first federal trade-mark statute (1870) was struck down by Congress because it was thought that the statute would conflict with the fields of patent and copyright (the motivation had been grounded upon the copyright clause in the American Constitution). A second attempt in 1881, this time grounded in the commerce clause, had greater success. Today trademark protection is based on the Lanham Act,[99] enacted in 1946. Prior to the 1988 amendments of the Lanham Act, a requirement was that the party actually had to use the mark which he or she had registered, or lose it.[100] An applicant now only has to state a bona fide intention to use the mark, in commerce or in connection with products identified in the application. It should also be borne in mind that in the United States a distinction is drawn between a 'service mark', which identifies *service* only, and a 'trade mark', which identifies *goods*, but is often used as a generic term to cover both.

The 1988 amendments were brought about by the Trademark Law Reform Act of 1988 and one of the motives behind it had been to clear up the whole Web address/domain name mess explained in the general section above:

> '[I]t is my hope that this anti-dilution[101] statute can help stem the use of deceptive Internet addresses taken by those who are choosing marks that are associated with the products and reputations of others.'[102]

97 Op cit 487.

98 Merdes et al 524.

99 15 USC (art 1051ff).

100 'Use it or lose it'!

101 This term is explained two paragraphs below.

102 Senator Leahy as cited in Lee & Davidson *Intellectual Property for the Internet* 145.

In the United States domain name registration has been carried out by a non-governmental[103] organization called 'Network Solutions Inc' (NSI), which has also issued rules governing the registration of domain names. These provide inter alia that a registered trade mark will override a similar domain name reserved for an outside entity:

> '... that a United States or foreign trade mark registrant can contact NSI to seek cancellation of a domain with a name identical to a previously issued United States or foreign trademark registration. NSI will then contact the domain name reservant, and if the reservant does not present evidence of a prior United States or foreign trademark registration, NSI will give the reservant notice that the domain will be withdrawn. If a dispute arises between the trademark registrant and the domain reservant, NSI will "freeze" the domain until it receives a court ruling resolving the dispute.'[104]

Along with ordinary trademark infringement, certain state laws and a Federal statute (the Trademark Dilution Act of 1995) protect against the dilution of a trade mark. An example would be to call a poorly performing sportsman or woman 'the Rolls-Royce of all failures'. It comes down to using a famous mark in a way which might be seen as disparaging. According to the 1988 amendments to the Lanham Act, an action will lie against the use of a domain name incorporating a famous trade mark if it can be shown that this inclusion will dilute the trade mark.

This has been borne out by the decisions of *Hasbro v Internet Entertainment Group Ltd,*[105] where a preliminary injunction was given against the use of 'candyland.com' on a sexually *risqué* Web site, and the case of *Intermatic Inc v Toeppen,*[106] where summary judgment was given to the plaintiff (who was the trade mark registrant of the 'famous mark Intermatic') against the lesser-known registrant of the domain name 'intermatic.com'.[107]

The protection of domain names entered a new phase on 1 July 1997, when President Clinton instructed the Secretary of Commerce to transform the domain name system in a way that would increase competition and facilitate international participation in its management.[108] The Department of Commerce (DOC) issued a request for comments and on 30 January 1998, on the basis of comments received, the National Telecommunications and Information Administration

---

103 Although sponsored by the National Science Foundation (NSF).

104 Lee & Davidson op cit 145.

105 1996 WL 84853 (WD Wash 1996).

106 40 USPQ 2d 1412 (ND Ill 1996).

107 Lee & Davidson loc cit.

108 Most of the remarks in the following section are based on a paper entitled 'Developments with regard to the protection of domain names' delivered by Coenraad Visser on 8 April 1999 at the Seventh Annual Conference on International Intellectual Property Law and Policy, Fordham University School of Law, New York.

(NTIA), an agency of the DOC, published a Green Paper entitled 'A proposal to Improve Technical Management of Internet Names and Addresses'.[109] The NTIA followed this up by a White Paper entitled 'Management of Internet Names and Addresses'[110] and finally by the formation of the Internet Corporation for Assigned Names and Numbers (ICANN), a California non-profit public benefit organization. According to ICANN's Articles of Incorporation and Bylaws, the stated business purpose of ICANN is to:

(a) coordinate the assignment of Internet technical parameters as needed to maintain universal connectivity on the Internet;

(b) to perform and oversee functions related to the coordination of the Internet Protocol;

(c) to perform and oversee functions related to the coordination of the domain name system (DNS), including the development of policies for determining the circumstances under which the new top-level domains are added to the DNS root system;

(d) to oversee the operation of the authoritative Internet DNS root server system; and

(e) to engage in any other related legal activity in furtherance of items *(a)* to *(d)*.

In the meanwhile, the World Intellectual Property Organisation (WIPO) has also published an interim report on the topic of domain names, which will be discussed in greater detail below. In the present writer's opinion, this is a necessary counterweight to the United States' powerful administrative position with regard to all things Internet. Coenraad Visser believes the evolution of the international legal framework with regard to domain names described above will have a more important impact than national case-law.

By 9 September 1998, the DOC took over the NSF's co-operative responsibilities towards NSI, in connection with, inter alia, registration of domain names in the top level domains (TLD) of .com, .net and .org. As has been described above, the fourth field in a web address explains the field of endeavour and this is known as the TLD. Even though the fifth field specifies the country concerned, for instance 'org.za', firms prefer just having the fourth field registered as a suffix to their company names, since this enables and implies international recognition.

(2) Design law

Other than in the United Kingdom, where design law started off under the aegis of copyright and gradually moved closer to patent, although retaining its distinct

109 63 Fed Reg 8825 (1998).

110 63 Fed Reg 31741 (1998). Both papers are available at http://www.ntia.doc.gov.

character, design has always been seen as a form of patent in the United States. It seems to be limited to 'aesthetic' designs, since 'functional' designs would probably be indistinguishable from patent: 'Design patent law overlaps both copyright law and trademark and unfair competition law in its coverage of the nonfunctional features of useful objects.'[111] The original design patent law was passed in 1842 'to fill a gap that then existed between copyright protection for authors and patent protection for inventors in the mechanical arts.'[112]

Currently the Design Patent Act[113] covers 'any new, original and ornamental design for an article of manufacture' and makes most provisions covering patents for inventions also applicable to design patents. According to Merges et al[114] interest seems to be renewing in this form of IPR.

3.2.2 The United Kingdom

(1) Trade-marks and passing off.

Here the common-law action for 'passing off'[115] was shored up by the Trade Marks Registration Act of 1875. The defects of the common law were that it was often difficult or cumbersome to have to prove the required goodwill and that there was no way of knowing which names had been 'taken', thus risking the infringement of another's rights. A system of registration only came into being with a series of further statutes, culminating in the Trade Marks Act of 1938. At first registration was limited to marks for goods, but this was extended to service marks by the Trade Marks (Amendment) Act 1984.[116] The most recent legislation on this point in the United Kingdom is the Trade Marks Act of 1994, which came into effect on 31 October 1994. This Act brings the United Kingdom in line with the European Directive on Trade Marks (see below).

Under prior trade-mark law the applicant had to satisfy certain statutory requirements for registration. Under the 1994 Act the default position is that a trade mark will be registered unless one or more grounds for refusal are applicable.

Mention has been made above of the common-law action of passing off. This action exists (independently of the statutory action in terms of the Trade Marks Act) against anyone who 'represents his goods as the goods of somebody else', as had already been stated in the 19th century in the case of *Reddaway (Frank & Co Ltd) v George Banham & Co Ltd*[117] In the case of *Erven Warnink BV v J Townend*

---

111 Merdes et al 308.

112 Ibid.

113 35 USC art 171 (1988).

114 Op cit 309.

115 This term is explained two paragraphs below.

116 Tapper *Computer Law* 114.

117 (1896) 13 RPC 218.

and Sons (Hull) Ltd[118] the requirements for an action for passing of were set out as follows:

> '(1) a representation, (2) made by a trader in the course of trade, (3) to prospective customers of his or ultimate consumers of goods or services supplied by him, (4) which is calculated to injure the business or goodwill of another trader (in the sense that this is a reasonably foreseeable consequence) and (5) which causes actual damage to a business or goodwill to the trader by whom the action is brought.'

The legal interests to be protected against passing off, namely 'goodwill', seem to be pretty close to the legal interests protected by competition law, namely 'werfkrag'. (See the section on competition law at the end of this chapter.)

A recent Appellate Division case has confirmed that the registration of third parties' trademarks as well-known names as domain names amounted to passing off.[119]

(2) Design-rights

As has been mentioned in the general part above, the special design right has led an uneasy co-existence with the protection of design by copyright. The Copyright Act of 1911 introduced a concept of infringement of an artistic work by 'reproduction in a material form' but at the same time excluded copyright in registered designs which were to be used as models or patterns to be multiplied by any industrial process. According to Cornish,[120] '[t]his had the effect of keeping copyright out of most industrial territory', thus establishing a truce between copyright and design.

The 1956 Copyright Act laid down that copyright existed on all designs, but s 10 of that Act determined that the copyright would not be enforceable if a registration of the design had been applied for, or if the copyright owner had used the design on industrially produced articles. However, in the case of *Darling v Honnor Marine*[121] the court made a rather forced division between designs capable of registration in terms of the Registered Designs Act (1946), which were then subject to s 10 and the bar on copyright, and designs which were not so registrable.[122] The latter carried the extensive term of copyright protection, even where they had been used in industrial applications. A 1968 amendment gave

118 [1980] RPC 31.

119 The group of 'one in a Million Ltd'—cases reported at [1999] FSR 1 (CA).

120 Op cit 484.

121 [1965] Ch 1; [1964] 1 All ER 241; [1964] 2 WLR 195.

122 The court was perhaps over-fastidious in finding reasons why the assembly parts and the profile of a new type of yacht could not be registered.

the registrable designs 15 years of copyright while the non-registrable designs continued to enjoy their extensive period of copyright protection.[123]

According to Cornish[124] this over-generous treatment of the copyright holders led to a 'merry litigious bonanza', although reined in slightly by the House of Lords in *British Leyland v Armstrong*,[125] which in turn came to the right decision for the wrong reasons.

A major consolidating and innovative Act (the 1988 CDPA[126]) again separated the two fields and precluded artistic copyright from the design field, introduced an unregistered design right of limited duration to fill the gap and provided for 'the continuance of registered design partly in the territories of copyright and unregistered design, but partly in its own exclusive field'.[127]

3.2.3 Other countries and international groupings

The first important international treaty concerning the protection of industrial property was the Paris Convention on the Protection of Industrial Property of 1883, which has had many sittings in different cities since to debate amendments, for instance Stockholm in 1967. With regard to trademark procedure there has been the Madrid Agreement concerning the International Registration of Marks (1891) and the Protocol relating to the Madrid Agreement (1989).

As has been mentioned above, there has been a shift towards protection under the trade umbrella with a corresponding growth in the importance of organizations such as the WTO and its related TRIPS, with which WTO members all have to comply. The need for change has been expressed as follows:

> 'The existing international intellectual property regimes—primarily the Berne Convention and the Universal Copyright Convention for copyright and the Paris Convention for patents and trademarks—have helped to build an international framework for intellectual property protection. While some of the international intellectual property conventions have required adherents to provide high standards for foreign rights holders, others have not. Signatories to these conventions have merely been bound to provide national treatment. Furthermore, the conventions were never intended to be used as enforcement mechanisms for intellectual property rights. While they have ostensibly required governments to implement their provisions,

123 The designer's life and 50 years thereafter!

124 Op cit 485.

125 [1986] RPC 279.

126 Acronym for Copyright Design and Patents Act.

127 Cornish op cit 486.

> they have not provided either bilateral or multilateral dispute settlement provisions to ensure compliance.'[128]

In this respect TRIPS has been a major advance. Despite its strengths, WIPO simply lacked enforcement mechanisms. Unfortunately, developing countries (such as almost all African states) have looked with suspicion at TRIPS, believing that increased intellectual property protection would simply aggravate the 'information gap' between the First and the Third World. Nevertheless, these countries have come to recognize that the benefits in other areas such as agriculture and textiles would make the 'package deal' to their benefit.

As has been noted with most of the other branches of IPR above, the European Union has taken steps to harmonize the differing regimes of trade-mark law amongst the countries under its jurisdiction. Thus, on 21 December 1988 the European Council adopted a Directive[129] designed to harmonize trade-mark legislation in the member states. This directive does not apply to trade marks obtained by mere use, but only to those which have been registered in the name of the proprietors.

On 15 March 1994 Regulation 40/94 took effect[130] and provided for a so-called 'Community trade mark' which would have effect among the European Union member states alone. The community trade mark does not replace the system of national (or international) registration systems and trade mark proprietors retain the option to retain their trademark in existing fashion. Of course, this sets the scene for some horrific conflicts between, Community and other trade marks, especially since 'there is no requirement that the body with responsibility for examining applications for a Community trade mark conduct a search of national registers for any possible prior rights".[131]

Complicating matters even further is the fact that smaller supranational groupings have also made provision for special registration of trade marks, for instance the Uniform Benelux Trade Mark Act. This governs registration in Belgium, the Netherlands and Luxembourg. Registration may be made through a national office or through the central Benelux Trade Mark Office. Disputes will be resolved by the Benelux Court of Justice.

The question of domain names will probably be dealt with in terms of recent World Intellectual Propert Organization (WIPO) deliberations in this regard. In December 1998, WIPO published its interim report entitled 'The Management

128 G Gardine *Intellectual Property & International Trade—A guide to the Uruguay Round TRIPS Agreement* (International Chamber of Commerce 1996) 13.

129 89/104/EEC.

130 In terms of art 7 of Council Directive 89/104.

131 Gutterman & Anderson op cit 208.

of Internet Names and Addresses: Intellectual Property Issues.'[132] At time of publication of the present work, the final report will probably have been transmitted to ICANN[133] and to the member states of WIPO.

The report states that one should try and avoid having two autonomous systems living in isolation from another, the Domain Name System (DNS) in 'cyberspace' and the 'ordinary' intellectual property system of identifiers as developed before the coming of cyberspace (here, one probably thinks of the present registry system for trade marks.) It also remarks upon the fact that factors such as low entry barriers in the DNS system has made registration fast and easy and that this has encouraged the rapid growth of the Internet.

The recommendations of the interim report focused on the following areas:

(a) best practices for registration authorities;

(b) the availability of information relating to contact details;

(c) dealing with false or inadequate information; and

(d) the problem of uniqueness—technical measures.

Besides these, the report focuses on uniform dispute resolution procedures (a procedure which should be much more suitable than conventional litigation for disposing of disputes in this area) and on the problem of notoriety: famous and well-known trade marks. In the latter regard the report noted that this kind of trade mark has often been the target of 'a variety of predatory and parasitical practices on the Internet, such as cybersquatting and warehousing'.[134] This problem would be addressed by

(a) a mechanism for obtaining and enforcing an exclusion of the use of a famous or well-known mark in open TLD's;

(b) an evidentiary device for ensuring that the protection afforded by an exclusion can be extended to confusingly similar, as well as the same, domain name registrations; and

(c) the recognition of the abusive registration of a domain name as a ground for cancelling or transferring such a registration.

It is to be hoped that the WIPO recommendations will take care of the domain name problems that has attended the Internet boom over the last few years. In

---

132 Again, much of what follows comes from a paper entitled 'Developments with regard to the protection of domain names' delivered by Coenraad Visser on 8 April 1999 at the Seventh Annual Conference on International Intellectual Property Law and Policy, Fordham University School of Law, New York.

133 An acronym for 'Internet Committee for Assigned Names or Numbers'. See the United States section above.

134 According to Visser, 'warehousing' takes place when 'a person registers many famous and well-known trademarks as domain names, and so hoards a digital collection of marks that can be offered for sale.'

the opinion of the present writer, one of the future problems might be to facilitate co-operation between the United States ICANN-system described above and the more international WIPO system.

At the time of writing the European Union had imminent plans to establish and administer a system of Community-registered designs with a corresponding harmonization of the national design law of the constituent countries. According to Cornish,[135] it would follow broadly the new Community deal for trade marks.

3.2.4 South Africa

(1) Trade marks

According to B R Rutherford[136] the 1963 Trade Marks Act had been badly in need of reform, having been in force for nearly 30 years. He also stresses the need to conform with international developments, particularly the European Directive on Trade Marks and the TRIPS requirements of the Uruguay Round of the GATT negotiations (both discussed in the previous section). The United Kingdom enacted a new Trade Mark Act in 1994 to bring that country in line with the European Directive. As the United Kingdom is one of South Africa's major trading partners, it was important for South Africa also to get into line. The TRIPS agreement is also South Africa's passport to international trade and many of the TRIPS requirements in fact overlap with those of the European Directive.

The new Act[137] is then described by Rutherford as 'South Africa's attempt to modernize its trade- mark system and to keep abreast of the international developments mentioned above'. With this statement he encompasses the European Directive, the 1994 United Kingdom Act as well as the TRIPS requirements.

The term 'trade mark' is defined as:

> 'A mark used or proposed to be used by a person in relation to goods or services for the purpose of distinguishing the goods or services in relation to which the mark is used or proposed to be used from the same kind of goods or services connected in the course of trade with any other person.'[138]

By focusing on the distinguishing function instead of the original origin function, the definition is more in line with the international requirements as set out above.

The term 'mark' has been defined as:

> 'any sign capable of being represented graphically, including a device, name, signature, word, letter, numeral, shape, configuration, pattern, ornamen-

135 Op cit 307.

136 In Coenraad Visser (ed) *The New Law of Trade Marks and Designs* (Juta 1995) 1.

137 Act 194 of 1993, in operation since 1 May 1995.

138 Section 1.

tation, colour or container for goods or any combination of the aforementioned.'

Rutherford is of the opinion that the above definition is not exhaustive but creates the potential for the registration of sounds,[139] and even smells, as trade marks. If it is this wide, a domain name under the Internet could perhaps also be included (see the discussion below).

A brief look at the rest of the Act shows that by restricting infringement rights to goods or services in respect of which the trademark is actually used, the Act has made 'defensive' registrations impossible. Anti-dilution provisions have also been brought in, prohibiting the use of another mark which would be likely to take unfair advantage of, or be detrimental to, the distinctive character or repute of the registered mark.[140] By protecting 'well-known foreign trade marks' South Africa now also complies with its obligations in terms of the Paris Convention. According to Rutherford, this is a 'fundamental departure from the current legal position'. (On a practical note, he has mentioned to the present writer that the registration procedure is so far in arrears that there have not been enough new registrations yet to provide any decided cases on the new provisions.)

The purpose of the present work, however, is not to give an extensive analysis of the new Act, but to decide whether this relatively recent (1993) statute also addresses computer problems adequately—particularly the question of Web domain names.[141] In this respect *The South African Business Guide to Internet Law*[142] is more than useful. According to this work:

> 'A domain name is an important corporate identifier. Beyond being the name under which you send and receive e-mail, like any other trade mark or trade name it can be a symbol of your goodwill and recognition in the marketplace. Importantly, when attempting to locate an entity on the Internet, the domain name is often the first component of any search. It is accordingly of vital importance that your domain name reflects your full corporate and/or some or all of your product names, or at least a recognizable part thereof.'[143]

As has been explained in the previous section, the registered owner of a trade mark will usually be able to force the registrant of a similar domain name to give

---

139 The exhaust note of a Harley Davidson motorcycle is very distinctive and has not yet been equalled by Japanese clones. Perhaps trade-mark protection or patent has had something to do with this!

140 Section 34(1)*(c)*.

141 For a fuller discussion of domain names, see the general part at the beginning of this section.

142 *The South African Business Guide to Internet Law* (Werksmans 1997).

143 Op cit 8.

up the latter if there is a likelihood of confusion. The Werksmans guide points out that, whereas in the past it was possible for three companies, United Airlines, United Bank and United Van Lines, to co-exist in the trade-mark world,[144] only one www.united.com is available.

> 'The result is that, with names over which more than one trade mark owner has rights, those trade mark owners may find that they cannot prevent others from using their trade marks as domain names.'[145]

According to Hofman[146] cyberpiracy and cybersquatting with regard to domain names seem to be 'abuses of the DNS', althugh (the participants might see it to be 'valid commercial speculation'. If businesses have not yet registered their appropriate domain names, this might be seen by courts as negligence.[147]

Werksmans also describes exactly how one should go about registering a domain name, starting off with one's local ISP.[148]

(2) Design law

With regard to design, South Africa has received a new Designs Act[149] in tandem with the Trade Marks Act just discussed. According to M le Roux in *The New Law of Trade Marks and Designs*,[150] this Act is unique in the world by clearly distinguishing between aesthetic and functional design. 'Aesthetic design' is defined as:

> 'any design applied to any article, whether for the pattern or the shape or the configuration or the ornamentation thereof, or for any two or more of these purposes, and by whatever means it is applied, having the features which appeal to and are judged solely by the eye, irrespective of the aesthetic quality thereof.'[151]

On the other hand, the term 'functional design' is defined as:

> 'any design applied to any article, whether for the pattern of the shape or the configuration thereof, or for any two or more of these purposes, and by whatever means it is applied, having features which are necessitated by the function which the article to which the design is applied is to perform, and includes an integrated circuit topography, a mask work and a series of mask works.'

---

144 Because there was little likelihood of confusion, given the different areas in which they trade.

145 Op cit 9.

146 Julian Hofman *Cyberlaw* (Ampersand Press 1999) at 99.

147 Op cit 100.

148 Acronym for Internet service provider—M-Web, Yebonet, Internet Africa, the Internet Solution, etc.

149 Act 195 of 1993, in force since 1 May 1995.

150 Visser *The New Law of Trade Marks and Designs* 73.

151 Section 1(1)(i).

Whereas the prior Act[152] had required for a functional design features 'dictated solely by the function', the new Act requires features 'necessitated by the function which the article to which the design is applied is to perform.'[153] Whether this is such a major change is debatable.[154]

In the same work, O H Dean gives the sorry history of the 'interplay' (some would say, confusion) between copyright and design protection.[155] This follows the unhappy history in the United Kingdom to a great extent (South Africa usually taking its lead from the United Kingdom in the field of IPR), except for an interesting amendment in 1988. The full history is succinctly set out by Dean (also in *The New Law of Trade Marks and Designs*) and the following is a brief synopsis and attempt to link it with developments in the United Kingdom.

Besides the protection enjoyed in terms of the Designs Act, designs are also protected by s 1(1) of the Copyright Act[156] under the category of 'artistic work' which is defined[157] as meaning:

> 'irrespective of the artistic quality thereof—
>
> *(a)* paintings, sculptures, drawings, engravings and photographs;
>
> *(b)* works of architecture being either buildings or models of buildings;
>
> *(c)* works of craftsmanship not falling within either para *(a)* or *(b)*.'

Things are not what they may seem on the surface, however. 'Drawings' are further defined as including 'any drawing of a technical nature or any diagram, map chart or plan'. According to Dean, 'artistic work' includes visual representations of ideas or the results of intellectual effort in a material form. The 'drawings' and 'works of craftsmanship' categories would include design drawings of articles of manufacture or industrial products, and prototypes of such goods. 'Reproduction'with regard to an 'artistic work' (which is the category containing all these concepts) is defined to include making a three-dimensional from a two-dimensional version and vice versa. Making a reproduction of something which is already a manufactured reproduction of the original design or prototype (say an exhaust system for a motor car) would constitute an indirect reproduction of the original copyrighted design or prototype.

The draftsmen of the 1916 Patents, Designs, Trade Marks and Copyrights Act[158] appreciated that a design might enjoy double protection and therefore

152 Act 57 of 1967.

153 Section 1(1)(xi).

154 Op cit at 76–7.

155 Visser op cit 80ff.

156 Act 98 of 1978.

157 In s1(1) of the Act.

158 Act 9 of 1916.

provided that only if a design was not capable of registration as such would it enjoy copyright protection. The question as to which designs were capable of registration or not was discussed in the case of *Klep Valves (Pty) Ltd v Saunders Valve Co Ltd*[159] By the time the 1965 Copyright Act rolled around the idea was still to avoid double protection, but it was now done procedurally rather than substantially. Dean explains this as follows:

> 'The 1965 Act did not provide that no copyright subsisted in artistic works that were capable of registration as designs. Rather, it limited the right of the owner of the copyright in a relevant artistic work to sue for infringement of copyright in certain circumstances. The copyright continued to exist but became partly unenforceable. Section 11 provided that such part of the copyright as would have fallen within the scope of a corresponding registered design became unenforceable and was in fact 'forfeited'. Case law established that the forfeiture of the enforceability of the copyright in an artistic work occurred only where the design of the article depicted in the work was capable of registration as a design; where the design of the article was dictated solely by the function which the article had to perform and so could not be registered as a design, the forfeiture did not take place.'[160]

In other words, if the design was registrable in terms of the present Designs Act,[161] that part of copyright protection which was now no longer necessary (because of the design-right protection) became unenforceable. The last all-new Copyright Act[162] did not initially carry over the unenforceability provisions of its predecessor, but was amended in 1983 to again make copyright enforceable in certain circumstances. These were the following:

> 'when authorized three-dimensional reproductions of an artistic work had been made available to the public, inside or outside South Africa, and someone without the consent of the copyright owner made three-dimensional reproductions or adaptations of that artistic work by copying the authorized three-dimensional reproductions or adaptations of that work, provided that the authorized reproductions which serve as the basis for the copying primarily have a utilitarian purpose and are made by an industrial process.'[163]

This meant that a design could be reverse engineered from the finished product (say a motor car's exhaust system) without the holder of the copyright in the design being able to enforce his rights. Initially this block on enforcement came into effect

159 1985 (1) SA 646 (T).

160 Op cit 80.

161 Act 57 of 1967.

162 Act 98 of 1978.

163 Section 15(3A) of the Act.

only within ten years of the passing of the Act (1993) or ten years after the finished product had been placed on the market anywhere in the world, whichever date was the later. Indirectly, therefore, an overlap between the Copyright and Design Acts was avoided, although the Design Act was never mentioned by name. The ten-year delay for the block on enforcement was removed by a 1988 amendment of the Copyright Act[164] and the latter would come into effect immediately after the finished product has been placed on the market anywhere in the world.[165]

The requirement of 'making by an industrial process' is fortunate because so many computer graphics and animations (and even full-length animated features and computer games) are rendered in a three dimensional, yet virtual and pictorial, format these days. It was probably not the intention to treat these in the same fashion as manufactured articles by the common use of the word 'three-dimensional'. The latter term has now been overtaken by progress and should not be used in future legislation.

In summing up, Dean feels that copyright and design protection no longer complement each other and that each 'by itself leaves considerable scope for abuse of the manufacturer's position by competitors'. He feels that we should have followed the British and the European Directive's lead in this regard.

In closing, a few words should be said about the protection of Integrated Circuits (ICs). Since this falls in the category of a 'functional design', the new Designs Act should protect these circuits adequately, even though the Americans felt that they had to promulgate a specific Act in this regard.[166] C K Job, in the same work by Coenraad Visser cited above,[167] explains that even though the possibility existed of a *sui generis* right to protect ICs, or amendment of the Copyright Act in this regard, it was decided that the new Design Act would be the best vehicle in this regard:

> 'After all, despite being somewhat specialized, complex and minute, integrated circuits and their topographies are merely designs having pattern, shape and configuration, and their features are necessitated by the functions which the integrated are to perform.'

Therefore ICs and their corollaries—'mask works'—are now protected in South Africa, thus complying with our TRIPS obligations in this regard. In fact, we seem to have overshot, since TRIPS determines that a person will act lawfully if he or she did not know, or did not have reasonable ground to know, that the article

164 Act 13 of 1988.

165 Perhaps a throw-back to the South African sanctions era, when because of the international boycott, many things had to be locally produced?

166 In the previous edition of this work I made specific mention of the American Act as 'the latest thing'.

167 Op cit 90.

concerned incorporated unlawfully produced layout designs. The South African liability is strict, in other words, not dependent on 'guilty knowledge'.

3.3 THE LAW OF UNFAIR COMPETITION

3.3.1 Introduction

Competition law has been mentioned in the preceding section. It has specifically played a role in some trade-secret cases, where one firm has obtained information concerning, or from, a competitor. This information has then given the first firm an unfair advantage. It has also been shown above that with regard to trade secrets, South African courts have wavered between the Roman-Dutch Aquilian action and an English-derived equitable action based on breach of trust. For purposes of the present work, which is neither a specialized work on trade secrets nor one on competition law, it is assumed that the Aquilian action will form the basis of both of these in future and that the tort-based actions from England had been a temporary aberration.

3.3.2 The basis and scope of competition law

The theory of subjective rights has been explained above and it has been mentioned that this philosophy governs most Afrikaans-speaking law faculties. One theory that has been put forward is that a firm has a subjective right in 'werfkrag' (goodwill) which may not be infringed upon by a competitor.

This is the view held by H J O van Heerden & J Neethling, the authors of the leading work on competition law in South Africa:[168]

> 'It suffices to point out here that wrongfulness in the competitive sphere lies in the infringement of a competitor's right to the goodwill ('werfkrag'') of his business, and that the limits of this right are ascertained, first with reference to the competition principle, and secondly, as supplementary criterion with reference to reasonableness or *boni mores* criterion.'

Cases such as *Matthews v Young*[169] and *Geary and Son (Pty) Ltd v Gove*[170] paved the way for the statement by Van Dijkhorst J in *Organic Fertilizers (Pty) Ltd v Pikkewyn Ghwano (Pty) Ltd*[171] that:

> '[T]he law of South African recognizes and grants a general action against unlawful competition based on the principles of the *lex Aquilia*.'

168 H J O van Heerden & J Neethling *Unlawful Competition* (Butterworths 1995) 68.

169 1922 AD 492.

170 1964 (1) SA 434 (A).

171 1981 (2) SA 173 (T) at 186.

Even though authors such as Esmé du Plessis[172] agree that the matter turns on the infringement of a subjective right in goodwill, she extends the argument to other classes of subjective rights, since she does not believe that a *numerus clausus* of such rights exists. She foresees that statutorily the legislature might provide for subjective rights in new objects, such as computer programs.[173] She also expects the common law perhaps to expand and protect trade secrets as an independent subjective right. This would then protect trade secrets even in situations where the infringer was not a competitor who could be brought to court in terms of competition law, as described in the previous paragraphs.

A distinction may be made between (negative) private-law principles of discouraging unlawful competition and (positive) public-law rules in which the state tries actively to encourage lawful competition. An example of the latter would be the Maintenance and Promotion of Competition Act.[174]

Another statutory basis for the regulation of competition in South Africa is the new Competition Act.[175] The Act was assented to in November 1998 and is due to come into operation soon after the time of writing (early 1999). Its goals are set out in s 2:

- to promote economic efficiency, adaptability and the development of the economy;
- to provide consumers with competitive prices and product choices;
- to promote international competitiveness, and
- to ensure market access for small and medium-sized enterprises.

It is also clear that the overriding objective is not the integration of economic systems, as with the European Union, but to promote the diversification of ownership for the upliftment of historically disadvantaged communities and to create new employment opportunities.

The Act leaves the common-law system and the criterion for competition intact, and kicks in only once those minimum criteria have been met.

3.3.3 The criterion for unlawful competition

According to Van Heerden & Neethling[176] the real competition principle can be defined as follows:

---

172 Van Heerden & Neethling *Unlawful Competition* at 89ff.

173 As they did by amending the Copyright Act, 78 of 1988, by Amendment Act 125 of 1992, which made specific provision for computer programs. See chapter 2 Copyright above.

174 Act 96 of 1979.

175 Act 89 of 1998.

176 Op cit 130.

> 'The real competition principle is ... that the competitor who delivers the best or fastest (most reasonable) performance, must achieve victory, while the one rendering the weakest (worst) performance, must suffer defeat.'

This principle has been accepted by courts, although 'fairness and reasonableness' nd the *boni mores*[177] have to be reconciled with it. This was done rather well in the case of *Van der Westhuizen v Scholtz*[178] where some pharmacists (the respondents) had advertised 25% discounts on prescription medicines to the public. The applicant (who was also a pharmacist, but not part of the deal) tried to obtain an interdict to stop the advertising on the grounds that it transgressed the Advertising Code of the Pharmacy Board and therefore constituted unlawful competition. Hattingh J found that the Advertising Code was not only in conflict with the *boni mores* by preventing the public from being informed,[179] but was also against the competition principle since it prevented the competitor (the advertiser) who was competing fairly, from emerging victorious out of the 'competitive struggle'. The respondents were therefore competing fairly by advertising and the interdict was refused.

3.3.4 Competition and the Constitution.

Even though the interim South African Constitution[180] left open the matter whether it was to be applied 'horizontally' (in private-law relationships) in addition to its true métier of 'vertical' application (in public-law relationships), indications are that the final Constitution[181] will be more amenable to horizontal application. This is the opinion of Dawid van Wyk in an article entitled ' 'n Paar Opmerkings en Vrae oor die Nuwe Grondwet'.[182]

This should be good news to Van Heerden & Neethling,[183] who argue that if the Constitution also operates horizontally, the fundamental rights are applicable to the public law of the maintenance and promotion of competition as well as to the private law of unlawful competition. These latter rights would include:

> 'the right to equality, the right to dignity, the right to privacy, the right to freedom of expression, the right to association, the right to property, and most importantly, the right to free economic activity.'[184]

177 Literally, 'the good morals'.

178 1992 (4) SA 866 (O).

179 Here information raises its unruly head yet again!

180 Act 200 of 1993.

181 Act 108 of 1996.

182 'A Few Remarks and Questions Concerning the New Constitution' (1997) 60 *THRHR* 377 at 386n28.

183 Op cit 13 and 14.

184 Op cit 14–15.

Annexure: IIIa General Conclusion with regard to IPR and Computers

Working through the different divisions of IPR, one is struck by the almost random way in which it has come into existence. Without the invention of the printing press, it is doubtful whether we would have had copyright. Without the Industrial Revolution, with its sparking of a slew of new technological ideas, it is doubtful whether we would have had a law of patent. The law of trade marks and the law of designs were likewise reactions to factual historical situations. Only the law of trade secret, which has not yet been codified, seems to have a kind of general and long-lasting formative principle behind it. One wonders whether we would not have been better off had a development corresponding to IPR taken place in private law itself with regard to the dematerialization of assets.

This question is particularly relevant in South Africa, where the local legal system has always prided itself on developing in line with principle and not casuistically. This is in line with systems on the continent of Europe, whence our Roman-Dutch common law has come, but without the impediment of a totally codified system. South African private law and criminal law are almost entirely based on a further development of Roman-Dutch principles. Significantly, the South African law of immaterial property has, up to the last Copyright Act,[185] been based almost exclusively on the more casuistic British law as a result of regular adoption (with modification) of the then current British copyright statute.

As far as computers and law are concerned, it is only in the area of trade secrets where South African law has had the chance to develop by means of principle. After the *Dun and Bradstreet* decision it is clear that our law of trade secrets is based on the delictual action that goes by the name of the *actio legis Aquiliae*, theoretically grounded in the law of unfair competition. On the other hand, our law of patents, copyright, trade marks and design are all based on more or less successful copies of corresponding UK legislation. This is not necessarily negative, since it has brought a degree of internationalization which is very important in the transborder world of the Internet and other computer networks.[186] It is also obvious that the world has decided that IPR, in one form or the other, will have to be the solution to the commodification of information. Which it probably will be, although it will not be an elegant solution, with many strained analogies and quite a few *sui generis* exceptions. Nevertheless, if South Africa wants to participate in global commerce, it will have to see that its legal infrastructure is put in place and that it does not look too different from that of other countries.

---

185 Act 98 of 1978.

186 That is why South Africa, in striking out alone with its latest amendments to the Copyright Act as far as computers are concerned, may be painting itself into a corner.

Many of the initial computer-related problems, such as the incidence and scope of copyright in computer programs, have gradually been solved—some by perspicacious judges and others by enlightened legislatures. Long may this process continue.

CHAPTER FOUR

PRIVATE LAW

The present journey through the the world of private law leaves one with the sense of a legal system which has not quite kept pace.

IV PRIVATE LAW

This chapter attempts to clarify the interface between computers and the field of private law. The latter is a complex, multi-faceted area of law and we shall therefore concentrate on the following areas:

In the law of things, the question of real rights in immaterial goods and the commodification of information are explored.

In the law of contract the question of electronic offer and acceptance as well as special problem areas such as EDI,[1] the year 2000 (Y2K) phenomenon[2] and e-commerce are dealt with.

Under the law of delict (tort) we explore the borders between contractual and delictual liability by means of practical examples such as the Year 2000 (Y2K) problem.

Privacy is also dealt with — an important factor as far as the Internet is concerned, especially when considering e-commerce on this medium.

Another personality right which is threatened by the Internet is defamation and some attention is devoted to this topic.

Finally the importance of international private law is explored as a possible means to solving the major jurisdictional problems which may arise from a medium as international as the Worldwide web.

Because Roman-Dutch law is alive and well in South Africa as far as private law is concerned, the latter is very much a home-grown affair. This means, first, that comparative law is not that useful in order to solve typical South African problems. Historical research is often more rewarding in South African private law, but in the area of computer law would still have limited value. In the second place, most of South African private law is formed by the courts interpreting the Roman-Dutch law and this field is not as regulated by statute as many others. This gives the system an enviable flexibility and ability to adopt change. Whether it is able to cope with computers still remains to be seen. Throughout one should also bear in mind that South Africa now is a *Rechtsstaat* (a country governed by law as the ultimate authority) and that we have a Constitution[3] (with teeth) to protect the human rights of the individual. Particularly where technology threatens a personal right, such as privacy, for instance, the Constitution may well be called upon to play a role.

1 Acronym for 'electronic data interchange'.
2 Popularly expressed as 'the Y2K problem'.
3 Act 108 of 1996.

4.1 PRIVATE LAW — COMPUTERS AND THE LAW OF THINGS

In the introduction to this work, mention was made of the discomfort experienced by the law of things in dealing with incorporeal matter such as electricity, information and even money in its modern sense. The present writer first explored these matters in an article which initially was supposed to deal with the theft of information from a criminal law perspective, but then found that the trail led to private law and to the doctrine of subjective rights, imported from Continental Europe.

The doctrine of subjective rights and their accompanying competencies was first popularized in South Africa by W A Joubert.[4] This long-held foundation of all legal debate from the Afrikaans universities has been overtaken by recent events, specifically because of its insistence that the law of things ('sakereg') confine its attentions to material, movable things thus leaving all immaterial things, from electricity to information, to be handled by the law of immaterial property. The first such challenge came form the present writer in an article entitled 'Diefstal van Onliggaamlike Sake met Spesifieke Verwysing na Rekenaars'.[5] Here he argued that the problem of 'theft of information' was not really a problem of criminal law, but that had originated from the failure of private law, notably the law of things, adequately to deal with immaterial things. This was followed by Duard Kleyn's contribution to the 1992 edition of *Silberberg and Schoeman's The Law of Property*[6] as well as L C Coetzee's 'Die Rol van die Onstoflike Saak in die Sakereg'[7] and, finally, another article from Kleyn entitled 'Dogmatiese probleme rakende die rol van onstoflike sake in die sakereg'.[8] Kleyn argues that the concept of a 'thing' should be extended to 'anything whether corporeal or incorporeal that is of use and or value to man and which is regarded as *in commercio*'.

In the first article the present writer quoted an article[9] by Eksteen J, who (already in 1984) foresaw the problems to which the interfacing between computers and law was likely to lead:

---

4 See his articles in (1958) 21 *THRHR* at 12ff. It is worth noting that Joubert does not like the expression 'intellectual *property*' because this would seem to imply real rights.

5 Translated as 'Theft of Immaterial Goods with Specific Reference to Computers' in 1985 *SACC* 129.

6 Chapter 2.

7 Translated as 'The Role of the Immaterial Thing in the Law of Things' (unpublished LLB thesis University of Pretoria 1992).

8 Translated as 'Dogmatical Problems with regard to the Role of Immaterial Things in the Law of Things' in 1993 *De Jure* 1ff.

9 1985 *Obiter* 1 (law journal of the University of Port Elizabeth).

'The computer is such a novel concept in itself and one so far removed from the contemplation of the founders of our legal system, that the application of the principles framed by them often presents considerable difficulty when seeking to apply them to the behaviour of people using computers.'[10]

In pursuing the question whether information may be stolen I was led to attempt answering the question whether information (or other immaterial goods) could be made subject to real rights such as ownership and possession in terms of the law of things. The answer seemed to be that only corporeal objects could be subject to these rights, although a few anomalies gradually became apparent. Thus in C G van der Merwe's work *Sakereg*[11] the author admits that Roman law did distinguish between *res corporales* and *res incorporales*[12] but that he still prefers to confine the law of things to corporeal matters, for two reasons. The first is that this facilitates the categorization of the different kinds of subjective rights into four categories, namely real rights, personal rights, personality rights and immaterial property rights. The second is that a real right should imply direct physical control over the object to which it applies. (To this one might reply that any systematization should be reviewed in the light of new developments which do not fit neatly into existing paradigms ('back to the drawing board'). Later on, Van der Merwe has to admit that in certain 'exceptional cases' immaterial goods may form the object of a real right[13]; at another juncture he describes similar cases as 'anomalies',[14] and thirdly[15] he admits that certain incorporeal things may form the object of theft and the legal rules which are 'analogous' to those applicable to corporeal matters should be applied. Finally,[16] he tries to explain that one may obtain only *quasi*-possession and *quasi*-ownership with regard to these incorporeals.

As I have remarked above with regard to the *sui generis* right having to be developed with regard to the protection of databases — if too many examples of special cases or exceptions start occurring, it may be time to go back to the drawing board and revamp the entire system. Unfortunately, the first stop-gap solution to the problem of immaterial goods, namely the law of intellectual property, has become so ingrained into the very warp and woof of international and national law, that such a total rethink seems unlikely. More likely is a recurrence of 'special cases', *sui generis*-protection and *quasi*-rights. The full implication

10 Op cit 3.

11 C G van der Merwe *Sakereg* 2 ed (Butterworths 1989) 20.

12 'Immaterial things' as opposed to the previous 'material things'.

13 Op cit 5n14, where he mentions usufruct and using personal rights as surety.

14 Op cit 22.

15 Op cit 25.

16 Op cit 37.

of this may be a gradual lessening of the importance of the law of things, with its material objects, in favour of an increasing emphasis on the law of intellectual property. The latter can at least claim the capacity to protect immaterial objects, including the most valuable asset of the late 20th century and beyond, namely information. Criminal law is likely to find application as isolated islands grafted onto intellectual property statutes to give them 'teeth', as is already the case in South Africa (with the exception of the law of trade secrets).

To return to the article on the theft of information: the writer then tried to show that money has practically ceased to exist in corporeal form but that this 'incorporeal' could still be stolen under our present criminal law. A 'quick and dirty' solution to this would be for the criminal law to go its own way and simply define 'property' also to include intangibles, but this could lead to a dichotomy between criminal law and private law which may prove fatal to any coherent legal system. This matter is more fully discussed in chapter 5 Criminal Law below.

Fortunately this problem has attracted the attention of private-law academic Duard Kleyn, the present Dean of the Faculty of Law at the University of Pretoria. In his article entitled 'Dogmatiese probleme rakende die rol van onstoflike sake in die sakereg',[17] Kleyn also recommends that the concept of a thing ('saak') be extended to include incorporeals. He attributes the present clinging to the outdated concept of corporeal things to judicial conservatism and traditionalism even though in practice examples occur of real rights in incorporeal things. He does not want to go so far as to give the right holder to a patent the title of 'owner', however, and suggests that hear she be seen as the holder of a limited real right. After exploring the traditional features of a thing, such as controllability, separateness, etc, he recommends the following new definition of a thing:

> 'Anything whether corporeal or incorporeal that is of use of value to man and which is regarded *in commercio*.'[18]

Interestingly enough, this definition is so wide that it would quite probably include information too, with interesting implications for the law of intellectual property. If one could really buy and sell copyrighted computer programs, for instance, the whole licensing of use and (theoretical) return or destruction of floppy disks would probably come to an end.

The question of the ownership of information has also exercised the mind of a South African specialist in the field of the law of intellectual property. In an article which has already been cited,[19] Esmè Du Plessis argues that the right to information is actually an immaterial property right which has developed next to other similar rights, such as patent and copyright. This is, however, in conflict with the

17 (1993) Vol 1 *De Jure* 1ff (legal journal of the University of Pretoria).

18 Op cit 13.

19 1985 *MB* 61 at 69.

case of *Dun and Bradstreet v SA Merchants Combined Credit Bureau (Cape) (Pty) Ltd*,[20] where the basis of the action for trade secret was held to lie in competition law. Ms Du Plessis' viewpoint appears to be rooted in the subjective rights school of legal theory, since she specifically mentions that confidential information has an independent existence from its bearer and that it has inherent economic value. In an article entitled 'Vruggebruik ten aansien van Ontginningsregte',[21] P J Badenhorst distinguishes between this 'subjective rights approach' and the 'traditional' approach[22] as far as the law of things is concerned, with regard to the proper classification of a usufruct in respect of mineral rights. He does not feel that it is necessary to widen the traditional definition of a thing to include incorporeal matter (as Kleyn did), since his own particular problem with a usufruct on a mineral right may also be solved by means of the subjective rights theory. In fact, he feels that the Kleyn definition may be so wide as to run the risk of vagueness. Nevertheless, Badenhorst's own approach simply puts forward a possible solution for rights on other rights and he does not venture a solution for rights in information.

This has been attempted by Tertius Geldenhuys, also building upon the foundation of subjective rights. In his doctoral thesis, entitled 'Die Regsbeskerming van Inligting'[23] he explores the question whether information can ever be the subject of rights. By applying the subjective rights test for a legal object, he finds that certain categories of information, such as trade secrets, do comply. The test is that the object

'(1) has to be of value to some or other legal subject and fulfil a need of that subject;

(2) has to be 'toedeelbaar' (apportionable) to a legal subject to the exclusion of other legal subjects — which means that something which is freely available such as air (and information in general) would not qualify;[24]

(3) if the apportionment serves a 'gemeenskapsordenende funksie' (orders society).'[25]

---

20 1968 (1) SA 209 (C).

21 Translated as 'Usufruct in respect of Mineral Rights' 1993 *Stellenbosch LR* 394ff.

22 Of which Kleyn is considered to be an exponent.

23 Unpublished LLD thesis, Unisa 1993.

24 This theory does not adequately reflect the commodity-like nature of information, which may be of value to a society. Cf the so-called 'information gap' which an entire continent such as Africa could be suffering from.

25 In a quaint remark, which dates the subjective rights theory badly, Geldenhuys cites the subjective rights argument that possession of pornography can never be true law, since it does not 'order society'. This would mean that one could with impunity remove merchandise from a Hustler shop since it does not enjoy legal protection. These items might be morally repugnant, but that does not mean that one can arbitrarily deprive them of their undoubted economic value.

The further development of the subjective rights approach also to encompass information[26] seems conceptually more promising than developing a number of *quasi-* and *sui generis*-rights in the law of things, but the question remains whether this solution would be acceptable internationally. In Germany an argument has been made out for a right to '*Daten*', which is described as '*informationellen Rechtsgutes*'[27] and which has developed as a result of new information techniques. In her work entitled *Der Strafrechtliche Schutz der Computerdaten gegen die Angriffsformen der Spionage, Sabotage und des Zeitdiebstahls*,[28] Ingeborg Schulze-Heiming argues that, whereas the first Industrial Revolution replaced human muscle power by machines, the second Industrial Revolution[29] is replacing human '*Geisteskraft*'[30] with machines. As a result of the corresponding increase in the value of '*Computerdaten*', possession of this has become a new right which is analogous to the older real rights. On the other hand, society needs a free flow of information and the author thus categorizes general information as '*ein freies (öffentliches) Gut ein Allgemeingut und wird nur ausnahmeweis in Form des Immaterialgüterschutzrechts individualrechtlich zugeordnet*'.[31] In dealing with the legal position of '*Daten*', the law will have to make use of the law of things, intellectual property rights as well as the '*Geheimnissphäre*'[32] which every individual (and legal person?) possess. (The author's argument seems to boil down to the fact that the fields of private law and intellectual property law (including trade secrets) will have to co-operate creatively in order to deal with information.)

To sum up, the whole legal foundation for protecting information still seems to be built on concrete which has not set yet, and this will probably not change until we have more clarity on the precise nature of information. Certain representatives from the traditional approach as well as the subjective approach to the law of things seem willing to extend their definition of thing to also include incorporeals, but there is still some resistance to this from equally respected experts in the field. Authors such as Geldenhuys and Tony Twine have wildly disparate ideas of concepts such as 'data', 'knowledge' and 'information'. For what it is worth, the present writer will reiterate his own[33] definition of information in the first

---

26 Or, at least, some kinds of information.

27 '(An) informational legal thing.'

28 Ingeborg Schulze-Heiming *Der Strafrechtliche Schutz der Computerdaten gegen die Angriffsformen der Spionage, Sabotage und des Zeitdiebstahls* translated as 'the ciminal law protection of computer data against the forms of attack of espionage, sabotage and the theft of time' (Waxmann 1995) 1.

29 Which I would prefer calling the Third Wave or 'the Information Revolution'.

30 Roughly translatable as 'mental power'.

31 Op cit 4 and freely translatable as: 'A free (public) good, a common good which only in exceptional cases is reducible to individual disposition by means of intellectual property law.'

32 Literally 'sphere of secrecy'.

33 On loan from the *Concise Oxford Dictionary*.

chapter: "Information' is defined as 'knowledge', (desired) items of knowledge, news;' Read with the definition of 'knowledge', it would again seem to be centered around a specific person's spectrum of knowledge (range of information), but to go further than that by including desired items of knowledge. Information therefore implies a potential marketability, which will be reverted to below when the so-called 'commodification of information' is dealt with.' Marrying this to Schulze-Heiming's views above, it seems that information should be a free-flowing commodity to which everyone should have a right (*'Gemeingut'*). When this has been transmuted into a private individual's range of knowledge, however, that knowledge deserves protection since it is a marketable good.

Unless the law of things starts dealing satisfactorily with the marketability side of incorporeals, and specifically with information as a commodity, it runs the risk of being overtaken by events.

4.2 PRIVATE LAW — COMPUTERS AND THE LAW OF CONTRACT

4.2.1 Introduction

In the previous edition of *Computers and the Law*[34] contracts were dealt with by means of a checklist, which was more useful with the then current system of contracting for bespoke, turnkey,[35] mainframe computer systems. These systems were made up of huge mainframe computers which had to be installed permanently in a specially prepared location and had to be serviced exclusively by the original provider. Security was easy because of physical access control (which is much easier than controlling electronic access) and the fact that the computer was connected only to in-house dumb terminals.[36] This means that much of what was written in the previous edition is now of little value. One set of rules still hold good, however: it is likely that both hardware and software will be sold by means of standard form contracts and the skeleton of this contract could form a good basis for negotiation. According to the previous edition of this work, the characteristics of standard form contracts were as follows:

Ideally, all such contracts should have an introduction, setting out the purpose of the contract and identifying the principal parties to it. The purpose should indicate the type of legal relationship that is being created, for instance, whether a lease of licence is intended, but should also describe the subject-matter accurately and completely. In the case of many computers the only solution to the latter problem is to append a complete technical specification as a schedule to the contract.

---

34 Dana van der Merwe *Computers & the Law* 1 ed (Juta 1986).

35 Like a car, a complete self-contained system is delivered — it is ready to start at the turn of a key (turnkey).

36 A dumb terminal means that it has no procession power in itself but has to receive it from the network. The so-called 'network' computer is simply a modern reincarnation of it.

In the second place, the contract should set out the buyer's obligations, which usually consist of paying the contract price (possibly staggered), also according to an appended schedule. The buyer may also be obligated to co-operate with the vendor on topics such as site-preparation, testing etc.

The third category consists of two series of obligations by the vendor, one being to meet the contractual deadline for delivery, installation, testing, etc, and the other being to give the required technical support in the form of training, maintenance, updating of software, etc. It is quite important to marry any deadlines to easily determinable dates, for instance, a given period following an 'effective date' which is set by signing of the contract.

Fourthly, an unrelated number of topics is usually included, often dealing with matters such as ownership, the passing of risk, insurance and confidentiality.

The present writer also suggested making use of a checklist to ensure that everything has been taken care of. The above considerations still hold good when buying a mainframe computer which will be permanently installed in a given location, operated by means of proprietary dedicated software written by a group of dedicated programmers. However, the world has changed a lot in 12 years. Nowadays even the most powerful servers are movable machines which are also usable as personal computers, except that they spend most (or all) of their 'lives' hooked up to the umbilical cord of a network. Even though Intranet[37] also existed in mainframe days, these were linked to dumb terminals (see above) which had no independent processing power. Nowadays personal computers serve as the terminals and these are quite capable of working independently from the network, provided the proper software is installed.[38] Software is mostly sold over the counter as commercial packages and no longer has to be painstakingly programmed in-house. We are facing threats, technical and legal, from problems such as Y2K which were unthought of, way back in 1986. All this necessitates a fresh look at the question of computer contracts.

4.2.2 Hardware contracts

Computers may be sold, leased or rented. A maintenance contract would probably be part of the main contract but separate arrangements are often made. According to Karin Alheit, in her doctoral thesis 'Issues of Liability arising from the Use of Expert Systems',[39] contractual terms may be express[40] or implied. She described implied terms as follows:

---

37 A local area network within a particular organization.

38 Ignoring for argument's sake the possibility of the so-called 'network computer' which will almost be a reversion to the old 'dumb terminal'.

39 Unpublished doctoral thesis, Unisa 1997 at 93ff.

40 Express terms may come about expressly by words or tacitly by conduct.

> 'Implied terms describe the unexpressed provisions of a contract which are imported by law (*ex lege*) without regard to the intention of the parties, or they may consist of terms implied by the facts or circumstances of the case (*ex consensu*). The *ex lege* implied terms of a contract differ according to the form of contract entered into. Such terms are in fact one of the *naturalia* of the contract which apply automatically if they are not excluded.'

Some doubt with regard to terminology still remains, however. In a new work, *South Africa & The Millennium Time Bomb*,[41] Lance Michalson distinguishes between a 'tacit term' in contract, which corresponds with Alheit's *ex consensu* terms, and 'implied terms', which corresponds with her *ex lege* terms. In order to avoid confusion, I shall stick to the good Latin and use the expression *ex consensu* instead of 'tacit' and also use 'implied terms' in Alheit's wider sense as incorporating both *ex lege* and *ex consensu* terms.

Alheit also distinguishes between *essentialia* (prescribed terms of law that have to form part of a contract to give it a specific character), *naturalia* (the default terms unless excluded by the parties) and *incidentalia* (matters which the parties have freely negotiated amongst themselves without being prescribed to by law.[42])

With a contract of sale some of the *naturalia* are the obligation of the seller to deliver the goods, to prevent the buyer from being evicted from his or her title to the goods and to accept responsibility for latent defects in the goods. The last gives rise to the so-called Aedilitian[43] actions. These actions permit the buyer of a product with latent defects to cancel the contract and ask for his or her money back (with the *actio redhibitoria*) or at least claim a reduction in the selling price (with the *actio quanti minoris*.) They will apply only where the seller publicly claims to possess certain skills and/or expertise with relation to the product and the buyer therefore relied upon these in entering into transaction. Almost any computer dealer will fall within this category.

Something as technologically complex as a computer might easily show defects in use which were not apparent beforehand and therefore sellers of computer hardware are keen to exclude this kind of liability by means of exemption clauses (typical *incidentalia*) and, in exchange, to provide a maintenance clause. According to Alheit, these exemption clauses 'are used to empower contractants in a strong bargaining position to exploit c-contractants in a weaker position'.[44] South Africa also does not have legislative protection against unconscionable contract terms

---

41 Lance Michalson *South Africa and the Millenium Time Bomb: a Guide to the Legal Issues* (Francolin 1998) 32.

42 Op cit 94.

43 Named after the *Aediles Curules*, magistrates in Roman times who had to keep a watchful eye over commercial activities.

44 Op cit 94.

although the South African Law Commission has researched this topic[45] and has also produced draft legislation in this regard in the shape of the Bill on the Control of Contract Terms (1991). Michalson speculates on the question whether these kinds of exemption would be applicable in the case of Y2K problems and cites some chilling examples.[46] He mentions the (hopefully hypothetical) instance where a hospital had bought a dialysis machine which malfunctions because the supplier had not checked whether an embedded computer chip was Y2K-compliant. Would the supplier have been able to contract out the liability for death or injury caused by the machine? Or, less extremely, would the supplier have been able to contract out the cost to the hospital of having to buy a replacement dialysis machine because the old one was not Y2K-compliant? In the United Kingdom, the Unfair Contract Terms Act of 1977 would automatically have rendered similar exclusion clauses invalid and would render invalid other types of clause if they are considered to be unreasonable in the prevailing circumstances.

In South Africa most computer hardware is bought from dealers who exclude common-law warranties but make available a maintenance contract in their stead, either rendering this service themselves ('carry in' or 'on site') or making use of an outsourced third party specializing in computer maintenance. Care should be taken with this complex of contracting parties, bearing in mind that one is dealing with different parties in giving up and gaining rights. For instance, you give up your common-law rights as against the seller, who in turn offers you maintenance, which he again has to contract for with a third party on your behalf.

4.2.3 Software contracts

Again standard form contracts are used (often from overseas principals not willing to negotiate individual clauses) but now the type of contract changes. In stead of buying or leasing as in the case of hardware, software is mostly licensed. This originates from the days when copyright protection of software was reasonably uncertain and the software author decided rather to entrust his brainchild to the protection offered by the law of contract. According to Alheit, a licensing agreement is an innominate contract unknown to our common law.[47] This has the implication that it has no *naturalia* which will determine the scope of the agreement. A typical example might read as follows:

> 'Customer is granted a personal, non-transferable and non-exclusive license to use each X Disk Product. The license does not include the right to sublicence, assign, copy, reproduce, distribute, prepare derivative products of the X Disk Products, or alter the provided content on the flexible disk in any way.'

45 Project 47 of 1984.

46 Op cit 38.

47 Op cit 105.

'Non-exclusive' means that the product is also being licensed to other users and 'personal' and 'non-transferable' means that the user may not allow anyone else to use the program. To get around this severe restriction (legally) the so-called 'site-licensing' contract is used. This simply means a kind of mass-license which enables an entire institution (such as the University of South Africa) to buy one (very expensive) copy of a software package and then make it available over the network to as many users as the site-license provides for.

In a licensing agreement it will usually be important for the licensor to retain ownership of any back-up copies that the license may be allowed to be make. If ownership does pass, it may be stipulated that the extra copies have to be destroyed by the new 'owner' as soon as his or her license expires.

Otherwise than with the old mainframe computers, when purchasing a 'programmed computer' for the company was a major decision, solemnized with handshakes and photographs of the contracting parties, most modern software is sold over the counter or even electronically over the Internet. This is a result of so-called 'unbundling' in the sense that the customer no longer needs to buy the software and the hardware bundled together.

When sold over the counter two contracts are actually involved. The first is between the shopowner who receive the money and hands over the package between him or her and the customer the nature of the contract is still one of sale. However, a second type of contract comes into being shortly afterwards when the user wants to tear the cellophane off 'his' or 'her' software package but is cautioned by the following words.

> 'READ THIS PAGE CAREFULLY NOW, before opening the sealed diskette package. YOU AGREE THAT BY OPENING THE SEALED DISKETTE PACKAGE YOU HAVE SHOWN AGREEMENT TO THE LICENSE TERMS BY YOU AND ANY OTHER USER OF THIS SOFTWARE. (If you don't wish to enter this agreement, return this package with the sealed diskette package unopened to your dealer with your receipt for a full refund.)'

This is the so-called 'shrink-wrap'[48] agreement which sees the act of tearing the transparent cellophane wrapping off the software package as acceptance of the licensing terms. Michalson mentions that it is not clear whether this type of contract will be valid in South African law and then enters into an excursus on 'shrink-wrap license agreements'.[49] He points out that it is necessary to determine exactly who the contracting parties are.[50] It is clear that the customer constitutes

48 Named after the process which tightly stretches transparent cellophane over the box containing the software. It is also called 'box-top contract'.

49 Op cit in Appendix H at 128–9.

50 See my own remarks regarding hardware above.

one party but another party may also be involved — 'the manufacturer, the supplier, or both?' To these *dramatis personae* one could add the author of the program, his or her employer, the copyright holder, the master licensee (franchise holder), etc. In the end Michalson recommends that the ordinary paper-based rules with regard to contract should also be applied to the digital environment. This comes down to the fact that the purchaser had to know that the relevant writing existed on the package, and to know that this writing bore relation to his contract with the licensor. This bears the further implication that the person offering the document should have done what was reasonably sufficient to give the customer notice of these conditions.

Alheit draws an analogy with the United Kingdom 'ticket' cases where the customer receives a 'ticket', not supposed to be signed, which bears on its back the terms between the customer and seller. Here the customer is held liable even if the denies being aware of the terms printed on the back of the ticket. The equivalent problem on the Internet arises when a potential customer is presented with a screen full of legalese and has to indicate his assent to all conditions with a mouse-click (a so-called 'click-wrap' contract) in a certain spot, usually labelled 'I agree'. If he does not, the program does not proceed. This leaves one with the difficult legal situation where the customer has 'purchased' the package from the software seller but only afterwards learns about some licensing condition with which he or she cannot agree. What exactly would his or her legal position be in this case?

To understand the problem fully one has to appreciate, as mentioned above, that the typical software purchasing situation consists of two transactions.[51] The first is a contract of sale between the dealer and the customer, the second a licensing contract between the copyright holder and the customer. If the customer baulks at the licensing contract, he or she then also has to cancel the contract of sale by handing the package back to the dealer for a refund of the purchase price. The situation becomes problematical when he or she has taken the package home, installed it, and finds that he or she has to click on the screen to accept the licensing conditions. One suspects that the most users do this almost automatically as part of the installation procedure without applying their minds to the conditions, which might fill two or three screens with densely scrolling text. Even worse, the mouse click is often done by the friend or employee with computer expertise, who is doing the installation on behalf of the purchaser.

Another matter vital to licensing contracts is whether computer software should be seen as goods or services. This question will obviously affect the legal remedies of the contractants. As mentioned above, the sale of goods with latent defects

---

51 Also illustrated by the two stages in the purchase of the shrinkware package described above.

gives rise to the Aedilitian remedies under the proper circumstances, whereas the rendering of poor service can only lead to cancellation of the contract and a claim for damages. Alheit examines the situation in the United States and in the United Kingdom.[52] According to the United States law a program which is mass produced and marketed is likely to be classified as a 'product' and would therefore be covered by the phrase 'sale of goods' in art 2 of the UCC[53] and fall under that regime. On the other hand, a program which has been specially written (custom made) for one specific user would be classified as a 'service' rendered by the programmer and the legal situation would be covered by common law, since a 'sale of goods' did not take place. English courts, on the other hand, try to analyse the substance of the contract to see whether something which has been produced beforehand is sold or whether the contract calls for the future exercising of skill and labour. In the former case goods have been sold and in the latter services have been contracted for.

An interesting sub-theme is whether the fact that a program is fixed on a disk or other material medium can convert the object of the contract into goods and therefore into a contract of sale (and not services). It has been argued that because the value of the carrier medium (disks, tapes, etc) is so insignificant compared to the total value of the program, these media cannot affect the nature of the transaction. This argument is something along the lines of *De minimis non curat lex*. On the other hand, authors such as Tapper[54] and Reed.[55]

> 'find these arguments unconvincing and also irreconcilable with the treatment of books and works of art. A book is undisputably tangible property which constitutes 'goods' in legal terms, notwithstanding the fact that its major value lies in the writing, and not in the book. Therefore, software embodied in a physical medium is a good or product.'[56]

Closer to home, Michalson finds that software has not yet been formally categorized in terms of goods and services by our law and he suggests the following test. If software is delivered via a modem link, this might point to services as being the proper category since no physical 'container' or medium is ever delivered. (This actually shows up the *de minimis* argument made in the United Kingdom and discussed above.) On the other hand, Michalson suggests that shrink-wrapped software is more akin to goods, since 'it is a standard product which one can buy at a supplier'.[57] Bespoke software, specially written for a customer, would be

---

52 Op cit 110ff.

53 Acronym for uniform commercial code.

54 Colin Tappir *Computer Law* 4 ed (Longmans 1989) 181.

55 Chris Reed (ed) *Computer Law* (Blackstone Press 1996) 43.

56 Alheit op cit 114.

57 Op cit 45.

services. When a bundle of software and hardware is sold (a pre-programmed computer, for instance), Michalson argues that the totality, including the software, should be classified as goods.

These are interesting points, but to my mind simply illustrate that our law has not yet properly come to grips with intangible goods. Surely the method of delivery should not play such a major role in determining the very legal nature of something? The present writer would prefer a more principled differentiation between software which has already been created and is then sold (goods) and software which still has to be written on behalf of a customer (services).

Michalson also points out the practical significance of making the distinction between services and goods:

> '[I]n contracts for the provision of services (such as maintenance, facilities management, outsourcing, software development of Year 2000 solution provision) the law implies a warranty that the service provider must render his services in a proper and workmanlike manner. In a contact for the supply of goods, the law imposes far heavier obligations on the suppliers, namely those of 'merchantable quality' and 'fit for the purpose' for which they were supplied.'[58]

4.2.4 The different types of computer contract

The last quotation indicates that even with regard to one product (services) many different types of contract may obtain. The same applies to goods where acquisition may take a number of different forms. The following section will explore the ramifications of the different types of contract, measured by their very nature, not by the type of product which they govern (goods or services). It should also be borne in mind that each of these different types of contract may have different default terms implied *ex lege* and thus have different *naturalia* (see above).

(1) Contracts for the purchase and sale of goods or services

Here 'the seller undertakes to deliver possession of a thing in return for the purchaser's undertaking to pay a sum of money'.[59] *Essentialia* would therefore be agreement on the nature of the thing sold and agreement on the price. Otherwise than is the case with the law of things, the thing may be corporeal or incorporeal. The *naturalia* would include the liability of the seller for latent defects (as discussed above) and an implied warranty to the buyer against eviction. As mentioned above,, these *naturalia* constitute the default position and these consequences may be varied or excluded by means of *incidentalia* (special agreements

58 Ibid.

59 Alheit 125ff.

between the parties for this particular contract.) Software being what it is, no product will ever be completely free of bugs (latent program defects) but the courts have laid down that software need only be as functional as could reasonably be expected from such a product.[60] Alheit also deals with the liability of the seller (or supplier) as follows:

> 'Liability for consequential and other damage is almost always excluded by the seller because of the high risk of potentially large claims as a result of defective software. Liability of the supplier is also mostly limited to the remedying of defects or the replacement of defective software or the purchase price.'[61]

According to Alheit, the seller's main duty *ex lege* us to deliver the software in accordance with the stipulations of the contract (which used to include a long list of specifications and testing procedures in the old mainframe days.) If he or she has guaranteed the absence of defects or the presence of certain good qualities in the software and the software fails to live up to these warranties, a breach of contract (warranty) is committed and direct or consequential damages may be claimed with the *actio empti*.[62] A 'manufacturer' of the product (which in the case of software would be the developer) may incur liability in terms of the *actio empti* even if no warranties had been given and he or she was ignorant of the existence of the defects. A seller who is unaware of the defect will be liable 'where he publicly professes to have attributes of skill and expert knowledge in relation to the kind of goods sold'.[63] Most modern software shops such as 'The Incredible Connection' and 'The Computer Superstore' would probably qualify on this count.

In the case of delivery of something defective, without the seller having given any warranties or having made any representations of the nature described above, he or she may still be liable in terms of the Aedilitian actions, the *actio redhibitoria* and the *actio quanti minoris* mentioned above. The first gives the buyer the opportunity to resile from the contract and reclaim the purchase price, whereas the latter keeps the contract intact but makes provision for a reduction in purchase price. According to Alheit, this *ex lege* liability for latent defects may be excluded by agreement and the sale will then be *voetstoots* (or 'as is'). She cites the following requirements for the Aedilitian actions:

> '(i) a defect in the thing that renders it completely unfit or less fit for the purpose for which it was bought — the test is objective and the

60 *Holmdene Brickworks (Pty) Ltd v Roberts Construction Co* 1977 (3) SA 670 (A) at 683.

61 Op cit 126.

62 See J C De Wet & A H Van Wyk *Kontraktereg en Handelsreg* Volume 1 *Kontrakreg* 5 ed (Butterworths 1992) at 339 and the cases cited there.

63 *Kroonstad Westelike Boere Ko-operatiewe Vereniging Bpk v Botha & another* 1964 (3) SA 561 (A) at 571.

purpose for which it was bought can mean its normal use or a special use contemplated by the parties;

(ii) the defect must not be negligible;

(iii) the defect must not be apparent upon inspection by an average person — the test is objective;

(iv) the defect must have existed at the time of sale; and

(v) the purchaser must not have been aware of the defect — the onus of proof is on the purchaser.'[64]

Michalson adds a touch of practicality by applying the abstract principles of contract to the very real and practical problem of Y2K. He recommends[65] that buyers of software should try to obtain warranties and/or representations of Y2K-compliance from suppliers. On the other hand, the suppliers needing fixes should obtain the services of Y2K solution providers[66] and in turn try to obtain warranties and/or representations from these outside contractors.

Michalson also speaks of 'the implied guarantee of fitness for a particular purpose',[67] which remark one assumes he limits to the manufacturer or the person publicly professing skill and expert knowledge, since South Africa does not have the general guarantee of fitness or merchantability imposed statutorily on all sellers overseas. He also speaks of 'the common-law implied warranty against latent defects',[68] which is not correct. According to our common law, this action simply flows from the Roman edict of the *Aediles*, which has been extended by the courts to contracts in general, and should not be seen as based on an *ex lege* or fictional guarantee.[69] At any rate, Michalson argues that since more and more buyers are now insisting on specific Y2K-compliance, they would probably no longer be able to rely on the implied rights.

Michalson mentions that if the contract is subject to the provisions of the Credit Agreement Act,[70] s 6 (1)(*d*) of that Act prohibits the contactual exclusion by a vendor of these implied rights. He is also of the opinion that a lack of Y2K-compliance could clearly constitute a latent defect in goods 'in certain circumstances'. Unfortunately the Credit Agreement Act is not likely to apply, since hardware and software are not included in the regulations to the Act (which stipulate which categories are covered by the Act.)

---

64 Op cit 128–9.

65 Op cit 26.

66 ie outside contractors who undertake to help an organization become Y2K-compliant.

67 Op cit 35.

68 Op cit 34.

69 See De Wet & Van Wyk op cit 342–3.

70 Act 75 of 1980.

(2) Contracts for lease or rental

A contract of letting and hiring of things (lease) originates from the *locatio conductio rei* in Roman times. According to Alheit, it is 'an agreement whereby one party (the lessor) undertakes to grant the other party (the lessee) the temporary use and enjoyment of a thing in return for the latter's undertaking to pay the rent in money'. The *essentialia* are the above mentioned agreements with the *ius utendi fruendi*,[71] the rent and the temporary transfer of the rented thing. The *naturalia* coming from the common-law include protection against latent defects and a guarantee that the property will be enjoyed freely (*commodus usus*). The main duty of the lessor is to deliver the thing let to the lessee in the above manner and the main duty of the lessee is regular payment of the rent and care of the thing let.

With regard to lessors of computer software, Michalson mentions that a common-law obligation rests on a lessor of goods to keep the goods 'fit for the purpose for which they are leased'.[72] This could include an obligation to fix Y2K defects. As stated above, computer hardware and software probably do not fall under the Credit Agreements Act, but electrical appliances for domestic use, such as refrigerators, washing machines, high-fidelity systems and television sets do. As a result of embedded processors the whole machine may fail, which again brings into question the possible obligation of the lessor to fix Y2K defects. The extent of the Y2K problem is generally underestimated by people who assume that it will be limited to computers. These people do not understand the interdependencies of our modern computerized society, which might lead to even a lack of electricity and clean water if the computers of local authorities prove to be the weakest link in the chain.

(3) Contracts with regard to the provision of services

This is a contract for the letting and hiring of work, originating from the *locatio conductio operis* in Roman times. (This has to be distinguished from the normal contract of employment,[73] where the employee works permanently in the service of the employer.) The *essentialia* of the *locatio conductio operis* are that a piece of work is let out by the lessor to the lessee who agrees to the work in return for remuneration. The remuneration is usually calculated in money but does not necessarily have to be in this format.[74] To pay this and to see that the lessee is not out of pocket are the main obligations of the employer. On the other hand, the main obligation of the employee is to finish the piecework which he has been

71 Literally 'the right of using and enjoying'.

72 Op cit 36.

73 Known in Roman law as *locatio conductio operarum*.

74 It may be a share in the profits of a company or the produce of a farm — see De Wet & Van Wyk op cit 384.

contracted to do. Bespoke or custom-made software usually falls under this heading. According to Alheit, the *locatio conductio operis* carries an implied warranty that the work will be done in a proper manner and that the materials used will be of good quality and suitable for the particular purposes.[75] The common-law liability for the latent defects may be validly excluded, as with a contract for purchase and sale.

A broad range of the agreements discussed by Michalson would fall under either this or the following heading. These include software development agreements, software maintenance agreements, facilities management agreements (where the contractor operates software and hardware belonging to the user — a kind of 'insourcing'), and proper outsourcing agreements (where the contractor, using his or her own software and hardware, would take care of all the user's computing requirements). In all these cases Michalson advises that responsibility for Y2K-compliance should be clearly contracted for.

(4) Contracts for professional services

Related to the previous topic is that of professional liability. This may arise from delict of contract and only the latter is dealt with here. It refers to the liability which could be incurred by a person engaged in a profession, trade or calling which demands special knowledge and skill.[76] Negligence is therefore judged according to higher standard because more can be expected from an expert than from a lay person. The *ex lege* duties imposed by this kind of conract (categorized by Alheit as one of mandate) on the professional are to perform the task, to obey instructions, to exercise care and diligence, to advise and impart information, to account and to show good faith. If the professional does not meet the higher standards expected of a professional, he or she may be found negligent and the client could claim damages.

For Alheit, the exclusion of liability would not be invalid but the general rule is that professional persons of integrity should not resort to this mechanism.[77] What hurts the feelings of many computer programmers is that their field has not yet been seen as a truly professional area of endeavour. When this happens, it would also build in a degree of protection for the consumer.

(5) Licensing agreements

Many of the issues arising out this type of agreement have already been discussed above, for instance that it is an innominate contract with no applicable *naturalia* and that software is often obtained by a combination of a contract

---

75 Alheit op cit 128.

76 Alheit op cit 131 and the authorities quoted there.

77 Op cit 133 and the authorities quoted there.

of sale (between the dealer and the end-user) and a licensing contract (between the copyright holder and the end-user). Alheit[78] is of the opinion that the way in which software is transferred onto the user's computer system should not really make a difference to the nature of the transaction taking place (but see the contrary argument by Michalson above).

Alheit also refuses to accept the argument by Sieg Eiselen[79] and Maré[80] that licensing might serve as a contract of acquisition as well as the way of regulating the use of copyrighted material. The reader will recall her argument above that two contracts are usually involved in each transaction, namely one of sale by the dealer to the customer, and a licensing contract by the copyright holder licensing the use of the software to the customer. Alheit's argument runs as follows:

> 'To view the 'licensing' of software also as a manner of acquisition apart from sale, lease or the provision of services, is in my opinion, to negate the essence of the transaction taking place when software is acquired, which is that the user is put in the possession of a specific manifestation of the software as owner, lessor or the recipient of a service which includes the acquisition of the product, in exactly the same way as a book or tape or any other copyrighted product. Even the fact that software may be directly transferred electronically or installed on to the user's computer system, makes no difference to the nature of the transaction taking place. Depending on the nature of the transaction, the latter products are purchased, hired or acquired by way of a *locatio conductio operis*. To state in the case of a book for example that the purchaser of the book is no the owner thereof is absurd. The only difference between the latter products and software, to my mind, lies in the prescription of the use of the copyrighted material: in the case of software such use is much more narrowly defined than in the case of books and tapes, but the manifestation of the software remains the object of a sale or lease or whatever the case may be.[81]

Alheit then concedes that this matter has not yet been authoritatively decided by the courts and that licensing may still turn out to be a form of acquisition *sui generis*. The present author's view is that this is another example of the uneasy co-existence of traditional private law with the law of intellectual property. Before

---

78 Op cit 129.

79 'Computer Contracts' (unpublished memorandum, Potchefstroom University for Christian Higher Education 1996). It should be mentioned that many of the arguments by Alheit and Maré are based on this seminal work, which is not cited more widely in the present work because of its inaccessibility. It is to be hoped that Professor Eiselen will soon publish an article to publicize his findings.

80 E Maré *'Evaluering van kontraktipes by die verskaffing van rekenaarprogrammatuur'* (unpublished LLM thesis, Potchefstroom University for Christian Higher Education 1995).

81 Op cit 132.

information became such an important asset, these overlaps could be papered over, but now the strains are beginning to show. It also became manifest in chapter 2 Copyright above,[82] where the question of whether an independent right of use should still be catered for, even when unauthorized copying has been prohibited, raised equally intricate problems. While the process of copying remained an *a priori*[83] prerequisite to use (as with paper copies), the two fields could be kept distinct. Once the copying and the use took place simultaneously and inextricably bound up with each other (as with the use of the Internet) the border lines grow feint. Mention was made of Coenraad Visser's argument that copyright owners must be considered to have tacitly permitted reproduction if they allow their material to be placed on the Internet. One wonders whether this is an implied license to make a transient copy, an implied right to use, or both.

Michalson points out that it need not always be the copyright holder who grants the license for the software:

> 'The copyright owner may, for example, have authorized a third party, such as a distributor, to do so. It is therefore desireable for the potential customer to take any appropriate steps to ensure that the entity granting the license is entitled to do so. Of course, this is unlikely to be an issue if the licensor is the software house which wrote the program.'[84]

With mass-marketed software, however, the importance which software houses attach to the customer signing the 'warranty agreement' and sending it back to the United States would seem to indicate exactly where the real contracting party with regard to licensing is located. Licensing contracts usually specify that the law governing the contract will be that of one of the states of the United States of America,[85] which would be strange if both contracting parties were in South Africa.

4.2.5 Contracts — incidental matters

A matter which is of the utmost importance is proving the terms of a contract and that the contracting parties have agreed to all these terms. For purposes of proof it is obviously safer to have a contract in writing and signed by the contracting parties. In the days of word processors and e-mail this is becoming problematical, but technologies such as 'electronic signatures' should make electronic contracts possible. This matter is more fully explored in chapter 6 Evidence below. Good practice would be to create one printed-out 'original' which is to be signed physically by contracting parties and witnesses.

---

82 See section 2.3.4 above.

83 Something which has to take place in time before the subsequent event.

84 Op cit 24.

85 In fact, this usually works to the benefit of the (South African) customer, since consumers are much better protected by United States law!

Other matters such as all the different types of remedy and the type and quantum of damages are not that relevant to computer law specifically and a more specialized work on contract should be consulted in this regard. The same applies to specimen contracts — they would have filled a book of this nature and made it too expensive for its intended market. If one day, the present work gets onto the Web, there should be room for such additions.

4.3 COMPUTERS AND THE LAW OF DELICT

4.3.1 Introduction

As with the law of contract, the South African law of delict is based on Roman-Dutch law. According to most South African sources, a delict is defined as 'the wrongful and culpable act of a person which causes harm to another'.[86] Because these terms are very wide, it is obvious that the South African law is based more on general principle than the casuistic approach to 'tort law' in the United Sates and the United Kingdom. In line with this general approach and with the Roman law, the South African law of delict distinguishes between 'harm' to one's pocket for which patrimonial damages may be claimed and 'harm' to one's personality rights for which *solatio* ('solace') may be obtained in the form of money.[87] For the former the *actio legis Aquiliae* is available and for the latter the *actio iniuriarum*. Via the Roman-Dutch law, an action for pain and suffering of Germanic origin has also been introduced into South African law, by which non-patrimonial damages for pain and suffering may be claimed.

4.3.2 The elements of a delict

In terms of the above definition five delictual elements may be distinguished. These are:

(*a*) voluntary conduct;

(*b*) wrongfulness;

(*c*) fault;

(*d*) causation; and

(*e*) damage.

Each of these is now examined with a view to their applicability to computer law, and specifically with regard to the Y2K problem.

(*a*) *Conduct*

86 See Alheit op cit 140.

87 Alheit speaks of 'satisfaction or sentimental damages' op cit 141.

This has to consist of a voluntary human act or omission. A juristic person such as a company, a closed corporation or a software house may commit a delict through the conduct of one of its human members. Michalson mentions that in terms of the Y2K problem a typical example would be an omission on the part of the manufacturer or supplier to take reasonable steps to ensure that sold hardware or software is Y2K-complaint. If it is not, patrimonial damages would be claimable by means of the *actio legis Aquiliae*. The *actio iniuriarum*, on the other hand, would come into play where a person's right to privacy has been infringed by his or her employer reading his or her e-mail, for example, or where his or her feelings have been hurt in a 'flame war' in a discussion group.

(*b*) *Wrongfulness*

This could be seen as a very subjective test, so that both wrongdoer and victim could each feel himself or herself to be on the side of the angels in that he or she acted 'reasonably'. The courts therefore work with a general criterion of reasonableness, namely the *boni mores*,[88] also referred to as the legal convictions of the community. According to Alheit[89] the test is an objective *ex post facto*[90] process, said to be viewed by the courts from the perspective of the 'reasonable bystander'. The South African Constitution, and in particular the Bill of Rights, is also a factor to be taken into account in deciding whether particular conduct had been wrongful.

An important factor in testing for wrongfulness in a particular instance is to determine whether a ground of justification existed. There is no *numerus clausus* of these grounds, but typical examples could be self-defence, necessity, consent or authorization. In the last-mentioned case, the power of the state to authorize certain action would have to be tested against the protection which the Constitution provides to certain human rights. A typical example would be a request by the police to monitor the e-mail of a suspected criminal, which would have to be weighed against his or her right to privacy, which is guaranteed by the Constitution. This guarantee is not absolute, however, and may have to be limited if it is found by the court to be absolutely necessary in terms of the limitations clause.[91] (It is exactly this type of scenario which makes governments less enthusiastic about powerful encryption software in the hands of its subjects.)

According to Alheit,[92] wrongfulness could arise both from the infringement of a subjective right[93] or from the breach of a legal duty. The latter would occur

88 Literally the 'good customs' (of a community).

89 Op cit 149.

90 Literally 'from after the fact' — judging or acting on something after it has already happened.

91 Section 36 of the Constitution of South Africa Act 108 of 1996.

92 Op cit 153.

93 This has been dealt with above under the law of things.

in the case of liability for an omission or in the causing of pure economic loss. The *boni mores* test would again have to be applied in borderline cases. She warns that this legal duty (sometimes referred to as a 'duty of care') forms part of the element of wrongfulness and that it should not be confused with the test for negligence which is part of fault, the next element. The 'duty of care' doctrine with regard to negligence is an English doctrine used with reference to their specific tort of negligence and 'should be avoided as it causes confusion between the test for wrongfulness and the test for negligence'.[94]

(*c*) *Fault*

This might take the form of either intention or negligence. Michalson is of the opinion that Y2K liability will mostly sprout from negligence and this view probably holds good for most computer-related delicts. An exception might be deliberate sabotage by means of unlawful access to a computer system, for instance by spreading a lawful virus on the victim's network. This matter is more fully dealt with in chapter 5 Computer Crime below.

The test for negligence is take from *Kruger v Coetzee*[95] and goes as follows:

'For the purposes of liability *culpa* arises if—

(*a*) a *diligens paterfamilias*[96] in the position of the defendant—

  (i) would foresee the reasonable possibility of his conduct injuring another in his person or property and causing him patrimonial loss; and

  (ii) would take reasonable steps to guard against such occurrence; and

(*b*) the defendant failed to take such steps.'

This *diligens paterfamilias* (or *materfamilias*, one supposes) is supposed to be the reasonable man, the 'man on the Clapham omnibus', who is neither exceptionally bright or cautious nor dull-witted or reckless.[97] This test could turn out to be difficult to apply as far as computers are concerned: is the reasonable man or woman computer literate? If so, what does this standard really mean? Should everyone have taken Y2K precautions? Michalson fears that contractors may be held liable in that they should have foreseen this risk and should have guarded against it by taking reasonable steps to avoid this event, or at least by warning consumers of the situation before they purchase equipment.[98] (Of course, on this basis the entire software industry could be said to have been negligent by causing the whole Y2K problem!)

---

94 Alheit op cit 155.

95 1966 (2) SA 428 (A).

96 A diligent (male) head of the family who is presumed to be pretty responsible!

97 Alheit op cit 155.

98 Op cit 53.

Alheit again deals separately with professional negligence by professionals from whom one might have expected a higher standard of care. Many co-called Y2K consultants may turn out to be mere opportunists; but they should not be allowed to get away by hiding behind their real lack of expertise. According to the maxim *imperitia culpae adnumeratur*,[99] persons who undertake activities which require skill without possessing such skill will be held to be negligent at best, perhaps even fraudulent. Contributory negligence on the part of the claimant may, however, lessen the *quantum* (amount) of the claim. Michalson warns that loss of commercial data is likely to be much more expensive in damages than loss of domestic data.[100]

(*d*) *Causation*

Here one has to distinguish between factual and legal causation. Factual causation is tested according to the *condition sine qua non*[101] test. This means that 'but for' the causing factor the present result would not have occurred. Put negatively — if one thinks away the factor of causation, the present result should also fall away. This may, of course,, lead back to Adam and Eve causation, or to the primeval slime (depending on one's world view), so some limiting factor would have to be found. This is where legal causation comes in. In the past the theories of adequate causation, of direct consequences, of fault and of reasonable foreseeability have all had their day, but in *S v Mokgethi*[102] the Appellate Division opted for a 'flexible approach', meaning that no single criterion for legal causation can be applied to all factual situations.

The situation with regard to software is not clear. Michalson seems to work with reasonable foreseeability and states that the creators of chips that are later embedded in other products may be too remote in their causal connection with the end-user to be seen as having caused the unfortunate result.

(*e*) *Loss*

Alheit[103] states the damage caused by a delict is seen broadly as encompassing both patrimonial and non-patrimonial loss. both of these are compensated for by money in the form of 'damages' awarded by court. Pure economic loss refers to patrimonial loss not caused by injury to the plaintiff's person or property. Michalson cites the example of loss of profits as a result of a negligent misrepresentation. He also says

99 'Lack of skill is taken as negligence.'

100 Op cit 54.

101 Literally, the 'condition without which not'.

102 1990 (1) SA 32 (A).

103 Op cit 167.

> 'Use of a product in a foreseeable manner but in an unforeseeable context could produce far greater losses than the same product in a foreseeable manner and context.'[104]

Such use could be of a computer program which was functioning perfectly well in 1994 in a standalone computer, but which was 'part of an extremely intricate IT system involving many interfacing and mutually dependent products' by the time it failed. Hofman[105] is of the opinion that courts are cautious about allowing a delictual action for pure economic loss based on negligence. In the case of *Greenfield Engineering Works (Pty) Ltd v NKR Construction*[106] the difficulty of establishing the claim and the likelihood that similar actions will flood the courts were mentioned. Hofman feels that if there is Y2K computer failure on a wide scale, much of the loss is likely to be pure economic loss.

4.3.3 A typical cyber-delict — defamation on the Internet

Those of us who have spent some time 'surfing the Net' have probably joined a discussion group (usually called a 'list' for some reason) or have become involved in some kind of electronic discussion, that is, if you are not a 'lurker' (someone reading other people's opinions without ever contributing to the debate himself or herself). At any rate it becomes clear that when people disagree electronically[107] they sometimes do so vehemently and this often turns into a 'flame war' where feelings are not spared. For those readers who have not had the good fortune to be exposed to a flame war the following example taken off a real live 'list' will illustrate the point (keep in mind that capitals mean shouting on the Internet, so large capitals mean loud shouting):

>'ok, MR. <real name deleted>, WHOEVER THE HELL YOU ARE. THIS SETTLES IT. YOU ARE A SADIST

> *AND* AN IDIOT. I REFUSE TO BELIEVE THAT YOU CANNOT FIGURE OUT THAT YOUR

>E-MAIL ADDRESS HAS BEEN BOUNCING YOUR MESSAGES BACK TO ME FOR A MONTH.

>FURTHERMORE, IF YOU'RE THE LIST OWNER, YOU ARE ALSO A FOOL TAKE ME OFF

>THIS <expletive deleted> LIST.'

>

---

104 Op cit 57.

105 Hofman *Cyberlaw* 134.

106 1978 (4) SA 901 (N).

107 Psychologists should have a field day, telling us why people are so much more aggressive in the abstract than in person. Perhaps the absence of the possibility of a physical punch on the nose has something to do with it.

This raises the interesting possibility of defamation on the Internet. This topic has been explored locally in a recent article entitled 'Defamation on the Internet and other computer networks'.[108] After a comparison of laws the author also examines the South African situation, which differs appreciably because of the Roman-Dutch law still being in full flower locally. The definition of 'defamation' in South African law is as follows:

> 'The wrongful intentional publication of words or behaviour concerning another which has the tendency to undermine his status, good name or reputation.[109]

In her article, Nel remarks on the fact that even though there is no doubt that the person uttering such remarks on a public medium such as the Internet has complied with the above requirements, there is some doubt concerning a person who repeats, confirms or directs attention to these remarks.[110] She suggests that the liability of on-line service providers who exercise no editorial control over the messages on their bulletin boards should be compared to that of distributors or vendors (such as news agencies or bookshops) whose liability is based on negligence.[111] The typical Internet bugbear of jurisdiction again raises its head but Nel shows that, according to South African law, the plaintiff has the choice of either instituting action in the jurisdiction where the cause of action arose[112] or in the defendant's jurisdictional court. If the defendant remains physically absent, action would most likely have to be instituted in his or her home country, following that country's laws.

Unfortunately Nel does not treat the major defences to a defamation claim extensively, namely truth and public benefit, fair comment and qualified privilege. One would think that these defences should go a long way on a medium which is known to be free and unregulated. I would have been very surprised if Mr X, list owner in the above example had gone to court. Hofman[113] argues that the Internet might have developed its own community standards and because hyperbole and flaming are the norm, courts may find that such speech does not defame.

---

108 Sanette Nel (1997) 30 *CILSA* 154ff.

109 J Neethling, J M Potgieter & P J Visser *Neethling's Law of Personality* (Butterworths 1996) 140.

110 I may in fact have just committed defamation had I not deleted the name in the flame quotation above!

111 Op cit 168–9.

112 Would that be where the server is physically located, or the location of the computer on which the words were first typed?

113 Hofman *Cyberlaw* 127.

4.3.4 Some thoughts on privacy in a digital world

The foreign reader should by now have some idea of the South African law of delict. The defamation just dealt with is a typical example of a personality right being infringed and then compensated for by means of the modern version of the old Roman *actio iniuriarum*. Legally, privacy can be dealt with in the same way — our main problem nowadays is the changing situation of privacy in a world which has shrunk to a global village. The words of Marshall McLuhan have become truer than perhaps even he could see: 'As electrically contracted, the globe is no more than a village.'[114]

During June 1998 the United States Federal Trade Commission (FTC) released its long-awaited report on Internet privacy. It recommended that legislation be passed barring Web sites from collecting personal data from young children, but leaving the situation with regard to adults open. After about three years of studying more than 1 400 Web sites targeted at consumers, the agency fount that while 85% of the sites collect personal data from users, only 14% tell users what is happening. Only 2% of the sites provide a comprehensive privacy policy giving users details on how they will use the data. According to FTC chairman Robert Pitofsky, 'concerns about personal privacy are repeatedly cited as the most important reason not to get on the Internet'.[115]

There may be good reason for leaving the situation with regard to adults open. Ethan Katsh[116] points out that the individual whose privacy is at stake is no longer simply a victim but a collaborator: 'Personal information is no longer obtained surreptitiously or illegally, but is given away or sold.' For Katsh, the old nomenclature of 'one's home is one's castle' and 'zones of privacy' has a strong territorial connotation. (If this is so, it sounds like a throwback to the First Wave,[117] with its Agricultural Revolution, in which land was the currency of power and standing.) For him, the new concept of privacy should perhaps rather be of 'a condition that allows the individual freedom to choose when to establish a relationship and when not'. According to this test, it seems obvious that the surreptitious collection of personal data described in the previous paragraph should not be allowed, since it leaves the individual no choice with regard to his or her personality rights.

In South Africa the Constitution, very generally, guarantees every citizen a right to privacy, which includes the right not to have the privacy of their communi-

114 Marshall McLuhan *Understanding Media* (Abacus 1964) 12. McLuhan is also the originator of the popular marketing phrase 'The medium is the message.'

115 ZDNet 4 June 1998.

116 Ethan M Katsh *Law in a Digital World* (Oxford University Press 1995) 231.

117 See Alvin Toffler *The Third Wave* (Pan Books 1980). Toffler's metaphor has been used before in this work.

cations infringed.[118] Although the common law does protect privacy to a degree, it seems that some kind of specific legislation is required. The specific protection of privacy of communications would probably be covered by the Interception and Monitoring Prohibition Act[119] although some rumours of serious disagreement have been heard concerning possible amendments to this Act. Conversely, the Constitution guarantees every citizen access to information, whether held by the state or by another person, when this information is required for the exercise or protection of any rights. This time, the Constitution specifically requires legislation to give effect to this right.[120] An Open Democracy Bill has been waiting in the wings for a number of years now, but has not yet been enacted at the time of writing. A conundrum for the government is to provide reasonable access for citizen A to his or her personal data, while protecting citizen B's privacy against A's investigations. Even transparency has its limits.

In his treatment of the subject, Julien Hofman[121] distinguishes between 'Workplace Privacy' and 'Consumer Data Protection'. Under the first heading he ventures the opinion that an employee might take action against an employer for reading an employee's e-mail or monitoring his browsing patterns on his work computer. To the present writer it seems that this is something to be cleared out between management and the labour unions, obviously, but in this age of managerialism I find it unlikely that management would give up the right totally of monitoring computers for which they have paid, as well as their use during time which has also been paid for.[122]

Consumer data protection mostly has to do with credit bureaus building up consumer databases reflecting (upon) a consumer's buying habits and payment record and in this respect, South African consumers have much less protection than most of their overseas counterparts. After some comparative law research, Hofman suggests looking at the Canadian self-regulatory model (which are inadequate in certain respects, though), enforcing the common law properly (expensive and uncertain) or passing specific legislation in line with the European Union Directive on information privacy. This will ensure that South Africa is not cut off from participating in EU commerce. According to Hofman international cooperation on data privacy is also essential to prevent lawless 'data havens' from forming and also to avoid jurisdictional problems with regard to the physical location of internationally flowing data.

---

118 Section 14 of Act 108 of 1996.

119 Act 107 of 1992.

120 Section 32 of Act 108 of 1996, specifically s 32(2).

121 Hofman *Cyberlaw* 53.

122 Apparently two of the most popular destinations for on-the-job surfers are pornography sites and sites offering (other) employment.

In South Africa the right to privacy is protected by s 14 of the Constitution.[123] With constitutions working mostly vertically, this protection is aimed mainly against the state. At the moment the South African Law Commission is taking a fresh look at the Interception and Monitoring Prohibition Act,[124] certain of the recommendations of which have aroused a degree of controversy. The matter is nowhere near being finalized, however, and it is therefore not worthwhile commenting at this stage.

4.3.5 Conclusion

It is sad to say, but the present journey through the world of private law leaves one with a sense of a legal system which has not quite kept pace. Roman-Dutch law has always shown remarkable resilience in adapting to change, but now seems to have come to the end of the road. Particularly the law of things has left the field of immaterial things wide open to be (imperfectly) filled by branches of the law of intellectual property, such as copyright, competition law and trade secrets. The question of the commodification of information and digitized property should actually have been the domain of private law. Yet one has some sympathy with the following point of view:

> 'throughout the time I've been groping around cyberspace, an immense unsolved conundrum has remained at the root of nearly every legal, ethical, governmental, and social vexation to be found in the Virtual World. I refer to the problem of digitized property. The enigma is this: If our property can be infinitely reproduced and instantaneously distributed all over the planet without cost, without our knowledge, without it even leaving our possession, how can we protect it? How are we going to get paid for work we do with our minds? And if we can't get paid, what will assure the continued creation and distribution of such work?'[125]

Katsh provides the answer by pointing out that, in contrast to most corporeal possessions, the value of information diminishes rapidly when stored statically and is only really valuable if it is ploughed back in the information market. He cites Barlow's examples of sharks swimming, which are said to die of suffocation if they stop:

> 'The same is nearly true of information. Information that isn't moving ceases to exist as anything but potential ... at least until it is allowed to move again. For this reason, the practice of information hoarding, common in bureaucracies, is an especially wrong-headed artifact of physically based value systems.'

123 Act 108 of 1996.

124 Act 127 of 1992.

125 John Perry Barlow as cited by Katsh op cit 223.

(Again, this would seem to fit in with my personal definition of information as '(desired) items of knowledge, news'; whereas knowledge can be protected and hidden, information should be a public commodity, in whose waters any citizen can fish for personal knowledge.)

Katsh also cites Peter Drucker:

> 'Knowledge is power, which is why people who had it in the past often tried to make a secret of it. In post-capitalism, power comes from transmitting information to make it productive, not from hiding it.'[126]

Once the true nature and value of information has been addressed by private law, criminal law will breath a sigh of relief and the law of intellectual property can go back to protecting the tangible expression of ideas. Until that happy moment, all these fields of law will have to continue to develop *sui generis* and *quasi*-rules to patch up the law so that it can at least run, even though only firing on one cylinder and never knowing when it may break down completely. Not quite the vehicle with which to embark upon a rapid journey around the world!

126 Katsh op cit 224.

CHAPTER FIVE

COMPUTER CRIME

Horror stories abound and one is hard put to limit the number of examples that may be given.

COMPUTER CRIME

5.1 INTRODUCTION

Like the poor, crime has always been with us, and the first question in a chapter on computer crime should be whether the latter is any different from ordinary crime. In other words, do computers lead to new categories of specific offences and do they affect the general principles of criminal liability in a unique manner? Coupled with this is the question whether the legislature should intervene, as many state legislatures in the United States have done, or whether the Roman-Dutch common law of South Africa can cope adequately with space-age criminals. Otherwise than in the case of private law, dealt with in the previous chapter, the Roman-Dutch law principles of criminal law have not been preserved to the same pristine degree and a degree of British substantive law and procedure has been imported. For this reason, the comparative procedure used in the first few chapters of the present work will again be followed.

For purposes of the present chapter I shall mention only in passing the valuable role that computers play in the enforcement of law and order, also as far as non-computer crime is concerned, although the value of a national data bank containing particulars of criminals can be imagined and computers are also valuable in analysing technical evidence. It is interesting to note, however, that so-called computer matching and profiling may actually catch only less sophisticated violators, while giving professional criminals 'a license to steal'.[1] It is a feature of gang-related crime that the foot soldiers are caught and get themselves onto the databases while the big bosses live apparently blameless lives.

To return to the main theme, some commentators are of the opinion that computers are simply the latest tools of the criminal's trade and that nothing separates computer crime qualitatively from any other form of crime. In this vein Hugo Cornwall, author of *The Hacker's Handbook*,[2] quotes figures from the National Computing Centre to show that 90% of computer crime consists of putting false information into a computer, something that is not any different from conventional embezzlement:

> 'In such cases the computer simply carries out the fraud with more thoroughness than a human, and the print-out gives the accounts a spurious air of being correct.'

1 *Computing* SA 13 January 1984. Knowledge is still power and with the possibility of corruption in the South African Police Service a centralization of knowledge may also aid organized crime.

2 Hugo Cornwall *The Hacker's Handbook* (Century Communications 1985) 109.

One of the first local cases in point was the teller at the Permanent Building Society who defrauded his employers of nearly R1 million using a computer terminal.[3] The same type of fraud could have been perpetrated under manual accounting procedures, except that it would probably have been discovered earlier and therefore the amount would not have been so large. In the local case, all records, excluding the cheques, had been deleted by the perpetrator, so that the building society could only find the general disappearance of R853 409,97. With computers it is therefore easier to cover one's tracks, but again there does not seem to be a qualitative difference to other types of fraud.

None the less, as I shall attempt to show, the subject-matter of much computer crime, namely intangible property in the form of either abstract sums of money or information, has put severe strain on a criminal-law system which still defines the subject-matter of theft as 'tangible or corporeal movable property'.[4] This aspect has led to many unsatisfactory legal situations which has, in turn, led to a substantial amount of equally unsatisfactory legislation, caused in the main by a lack of clarity on the precise legal interests endangered by computer crime.

As has been explained above, in dealing with computer crime the comparative method used in most of the previous chapters has been adopted. The same countries are explored, with some 'guest appearances' by countries with particularly interesting developments. Special attention will be given to the use of computers in telecommunications, especially the Internet, because this area represents golden opportunities to a computer criminal. This is the preserve of the feared 'hacker', a word which formerly simply represented a computer enthusiast,[5] but which has recently taken on the connotation of a youthful trespasser in the files of authorized users. Although Cornwall tries to represent this type of activity as good, clean mischief, it is definitely illegal and material loss has been caused by those hackers not subscribing to Cornwall's voluntary code of hacker ethics, which he summarizes as follow:[6]

> 'Don't manipulate files unless you are sure a back-up exists; don't crash operating system; don't lock legitimate users out from access; watch who you give information to; if you really discover something confidential, keep it to yourself. Hackers should not be interested in fraud.'

Despite these exhortations, Scotland Yard's computer crime chief, Detective Inspector John Austen, has called for a ban on the sale of Cornwall's book.[7] In

3 *The Citizen* 10 August 1985.

4 See also chapter 4 Private Law above, particularly the law of things.

5 Enthusiasts (according to themselves, the 'true' hackers) have therefore tried to foist the name 'cracker' (criminal hacker) onto these electronic trespassers, but it has not yet really stuck.

6 Op cit 1.

7 *Your Computer* May 1985.

the same computer periodical, the book is advertised as desirable because 'it might help you break into the computers that store examination records'. It is also the consolation prize in a £600 competition 'for the best idea how to cheat in an exam or pull off a scam using a computer'. Even though the publishers may claim that this is simply in fun, the subtlety could be lost on some young minds who learn to accept that with computers 'anything goes'.

Some of our 'non-techie' readers could still be wondering if computer viruses, which are also part of the criminal scourges attacking computer users, have anything to do with the influenza which strikes down humans during winter. They are nothing of the sort, but constitute rogue computer programs which 'infect' computer systems, sometimes in a feeble attempt at a joke, but often causing damage and destruction and wasting hundreds of man-hours to clean up the mess. It is called a 'virus' because of its ability to replicate itself and to attach itself to healthy programs, but the process is logical, not biological. Most of these 'infections' rage for a few months until all system administrators and private users have found the cure, only to be confronted by a new 'strain'. Some of the earliest examples (1988) were the 'Italian virus',[8] where the symptoms were that a ball bounced across the computer screen wiping out the letters as it crossed them, and the 'Stoned virus', where the following message scrolled across the screen after the virus had struck: 'Your computer is now stoned — legalize marijuana.' Later examples included 'Michelangelo', which was supposed to re-create a picture of the master on your screen, and the 'time bomb', since it is triggered by the system clock. One time bomb bears the self-explanatory title of the 'Friday the 13th' virus. The Michelangelo virus scare was characterized by panicky predictions in 1992 that 5 million PCs would fail on 6 March, the artist's birthday, but in fact only a few hundred incidents were reported. South African legislation aimed at the hackers (crackers?) and the creators and disseminators of viruses is on the way and is discussed more fully in the South African section below.

The most recent scare has been the 1999 virus called 'Melissa'.[9] This virus sends itself to the first 50 people in the infected computer's address book. A worse variation called 'Papa' has also since been spawned — this one sends itself out to the first 60 people listed and also 'pings'[10] two Web sites, namely @Home and that of the anti-virus expert, Fred Cohen.[11] The creator of Melissa (one David Smith) has since been arrested and at the time of writing awaits trial on charges of interruption of, conspiracy to interrupt and attempt to interrupt public communication (second-degree crimes in the United States) as well as theft of and damage or wrongful access

8 Because it originated at Italian universities.

9 Allegedly named after a strip-tease artiste, it is also the name of Bill Gates's wife.

10 Meaning that it establishes contact with and sends to a destination address.

11 IT Web 1 April 1999, accessible at http://www.itweb.co.za

to computer services (third-degree crimes).[12] His virus has caused widespread damage — subjectively experienced when the University of Witwatersrand's constitutional law reports on the Internet were hit and subscribers had to wait a while for publication of an important case on the voting rights of prisoners.

5.2 THE UNITED STATES

5.2.1 Computer crime — a definition

The United States has not only been in the forefront of computer technology but has also (probably as an inescapable adjunct) been one of the foremost victims of computer crime. But what is computer crime? One of the foremost authorities on computer crime and prevention, Donn B Parker, started off 24 years ago with the following definition: 'Any intentional, malicious act associated with computers as objects, subjects, instruments, or symbols in which a victim suffered or may have suffered a loss and a perpetrator made, or may have made, a gain.' Later, he worked with an even wider definition for purposes of his research: 'An illegal act where perpetration, investigation, or prosecution requires a knowledge of computer technology.'[13] In my opinion the latter definition, though very wide, is preferable, because many of the hackers' exploits do not necessarily involve a gain or a loss and amount to no more than a kind of 'electronic trespassing'.

In the United States section of the excellent comparative work *Information Technology Crime — National Legislation and International Initiatives*,[14] Edward Wise also speculates on a proper definition. He points out that every state in the United States, save Vermont, now has a statute dealing specifically with computer crime. A very formal (and fairly useless) definition might therefore simply be 'the violation of one the states' computer crime statutes'! Wise also cites the OECD[15] definition of 'computer abuse' as 'any illegal, unethical or unauthorized behaviour relating to the automatic processing and the transmission of data' and the fivefold division of crime categories which would fit this definition. These are:

1. unauthorized access;
2. unauthorized use;
3. dishonest manipulation;
4. computer sabotage, and
5. theft of information.

---

12 IT Web 6 April 1999.

13 *Computerweek* 7 May 1985.

14 Ulrich Sieber (ed) *Information Technology Crime — National Legislation and International Initiatives*. (Carl Heymanns Verlag 1994). This work represents the preparatory reports, discussions and conclusions of three international conferences on computer crime.

15 Acronym for Organization for Economic Co-operation and Development.

Wise points out that this definition is 'under-inclusive' since it does not include theft of hardware (especially components such as chips). My own problem with the definition is the lack of certainty whether something such as 'theft of information' really exists and the fact that the creation of a virus is not so much 'dishonest manipulation' as it is 'illegal manipulation'.

Nancy Peter Finn start off an article on computer crime[16] by stating that there is no agreement among the experts as to exactly what computer crime might constitute. They then venture their own definition:

> 'Computer abuse, broadly defined, is any incident associated with computer technology in which a victim suffered, or could have suffered, loss and a perpetrator, by intention, profited or could have profited.'

The authors then identify five categories of computer abuse, namely financial crime, information crime, theft of property, theft of services and vandalism. This is a handy classification, especially the wide open category of 'information crime', which the authors see as involving the acquisition of valuable information via computer and rate as 'one of the least detected and most costly of computer crimes'. This lends support to the view, which will be propagated later that individualized information in the form of knowledge (whether as a form of intellectual property or not) should be one of the most important objects of protection by means of the criminal prohibition. In this regard, the Finns' classification also focuses more accurately on the legal interests involved than do the categories in the previous paragraph.

Unfortunately, the authors define theft of property as 'simply the taking of computer hardware for personal sale or use'. This excludes the many instances of theft of non-computer goods by means of computer, of which Paul Credo gives quite a few South African examples.[17] Also, their general definition of computer abuse is quite similar to Parker's older definition and therefore subject to the same criticism. For our purposes a modified version of Parker's later definition may be adopted, namely 'an illegal act where perpetration involved a computer'. I think it would be too wide to speak of 'computer crime' where a computer was involved only in the investigation or prosecution of a crime, which may have had nothing to do with computers themselves.

5.2.2 Examples of computer crime

Now that a working definition is available, what does computer crime look like in practice? Horror stories abound and one is hard put to limit the number of examples that may be given. In some crimes the use of a computer is necessary,

16 *Computer World* 17 December 1984.

17 P Credo & J-P Michels *Computer Crime in South Africa* (Data Time 1985).

but peripheral — as, for instance, the robbing of people who use an automatic teller on the sidewalk during late hours. Another example of a peripheral computer crime is the infamous insurance fraud case (the *Equity Funding* case). This was a simple case of selling forged insurance policies, for which the opportunity was created by a simulation exercise (by the real insurance company) of the effect of the sale of large numbers of insurance policies. This led to the creation of 64 000 simulated policies in computer-readable form which were fraudulently sold as real policies afterwards!

(1) Theft of property

An example of what the Finns would categorize as theft of property is constituted by the Georgia gang of 15- and 16-year-old thieves who specialized in computers and electronics. In one case they allegedly stole eight computer systems, valued with software and peripherals at $250 000, which they traded amongst themselves like supermarket coupons![18]

(2) Financial Crime

Most of the examples which make the headlines are these involving financial crime — 'the taking of funds via a computer', according to the Finns. The various techniques have been dealt with in detail by Donn B Parker[19] and are known by their amusing and descriptive computer jargon names. 'Data diddling' is probably the most common method used and involves changing data before, during or after its input into a computer.[20] The 'Trojan Horse' involves slipping an unauthorized instruction into an otherwise normally functioning program which may then later be triggered by the computer's built-in clock (the so-called 'time bomb') or by certain instructions being given (the so-called 'logic bomb'). According to a publication of the CSI (Computer Security Institute), entitled *Current and Future Danger*,[21] the planting of Trojan horses by insiders is a serious problem. It cites the examples of a Lithuanian power plant worker who placed a Trojan horse in the control system with the intention later to 'discover' it and be paid to remove it; and of an embittered Texas employee whose time bomb deleted 168 000 USPA[22] and IRS[23] brokerage records. It is interesting to note that the programming practices of *bona fide* but shortsighted programmers (by

18 *Computing SA* 2 July 1984.

19 Donn B Parker *Computer Security Management* (Reston Publishing 1989) at 229 (Appendix E: Computer-Related Crime Methods.)

20 This method is, of course, not limited to financial crime, but may also be used for vandalism or theft of property, for example.

21 *Current and Future Danger* 3 ed (Computer Security Institute 1998) 7.

22 United States Postal Authority.

23 United States Inland Revenue Service.

allowing only two digits for the year field) has now left us sitting on a gigantic Y2K time bomb, set to go off on 1 January 2000!

Also well publicized is the 'salami technique' which 'slices off' and transfers all fractions of cents in a number of doctored accounts to the perpetrator's private account. Because of the minute individual amounts, the victims are unlikely ever to discover that they are actually losing something, yet the total amount stolen may be very high, depending on the frequency of transactions in the accounts from which the slice is taken. 'Superzapping' involves the use by the criminal of a universal access program, built into the computer as an emergency repair device by the original designers. This device overrides all the normal safeguards. Parker likens this to a master key which is to be used only in emergencies when the normal keys, are lost or locked inside the enclosure they were meant to open.[24] Of course, this technique is supposed to be highly confidential, but unfortunately even computer programmers may be seduced by financial temptation. In the same vein, but used in software programs, the programmer may leave a 'trap door'[25] which gives him access to the program to eradicate program errors ('bugs'), which appear only when the program is in use. 'Piggy-backing' involves gaining access to a computer by 'riding in' on the password of an authorized user. There are many ways in which this can be done, one example being when the authorized person signs off improperly, leaving the computer open to further use by the unauthorized person. Another example would be simply to leave a switched-on computer unattended in an unlocked room!

In the view of Les Shone,[26] the prize for the most cost-effective fraud of the century should go to one Stanley Mark Rifkin, who managed to access the transfer room of the Security Pacific Bank of Los Angeles and to cable $10,2 million to a Swiss bank account. The theft was discovered only after eight days, in which time Rifkin had flown to Zurich and (foolishly) returned to the United States!

(3) Information crime

Two other techniques that would be especially handy in what the Finns call 'information crime', are 'scavenging' and 'wire-tapping'. The latter phrase is self-explanatory: it is interception of data by means of tapping the communication line between two computers. According to Parker, this may be done by means of equipment worth about $200 and available at computer stores. He places trust in encryption, or the secret encoding and decoding of data before and after transmission.[27] This method is likely to become more necessary as computers start

24 Op cit 239

25 Nowadays both techniques are mostly known as the 'trap door'.

26 *Die Suid-Afrikaanse Geoktroieerde Rekenmeester* February 1981.

27 D B Parker *Manager's Guide to Computer Security* (Reston Publishing 1981).

getting involved more and more with telecommunications. On the other hand, the illegal interception of microwave and satellite communications will be technically more difficult and financially out of the reach of many of the present hackers, although the number of privately owned 'bowls' or 'dishes' (signal receivers) is starting to grow. In a recent development, one of the major Internet service providers[28] in South Africa is actually offering the greater bandwidth of satellite to speed up online program downloads. Usually government telecoms are reluctant to give up their monopoly in providing telecommunication facilities and therefore this is a surprising but very welcome development. It may have been justified by the fact that the first connection and uploading still has to be made by modem over the existing earthbound telecommunications network.

'Scavenging' means either physically rummaging through the unshredded documents of a competitor, or anybody else with information that might have value to somebody, or, more technically, searching for residual data left in the computer after the previous user's job execution. More and more people are starting to realize that information may be a company's most important asset. Many state laws exist on the theft of trade secrets and this shows the growing importance which theft of information is starting to assume, despite the denial of many that something as intangible as information may be stolen. Another, quite practical, problem is that this type of crime is not immediately detected, since nothing is really physically lost. Nevertheless, the long-term cost to the victim of 'information theft' could be considerable, since the victim loses his or her competitive edge.

(4) Theft of services

There are many examples of what the Finns call 'theft of services', which is nothing other than the unauthorized use of a computer. William S Hopwood in *The Problem of Computer Fraud in American Business*[29] cites examples of employees who opened their own computer service bureau by using their employer's computer and of another five employees who also used their employer's computer during slack hours to operate their own data processing firm. He comments as follows: 'There probably isn't a corporation in the country that hasn't had its computer system appropriated for non-business use at some time.' This procedure is sometimes described as 'theft of time', for instance in the decision of *United States v Sampson*,[30] where the court found that the 'consumption of computer time' by using a government computer without permission was a transgression of a federal theft law.

---

28 The 'Siyanda' service introduced by pay-TV channel operator M-Web.

29 Unpublished MA thesis, University of Florida 1975.

30 6 Computer L Serv Rep (Callaghan) 879 (ND Cal 1978), quoted by M D Scott in *Computer Law* (Wiley 1984).

(5) Vandalism

The Finns' final example, that of 'vandalism', may be widened to include the teenage hacker who delights in accessing personal files with no other purpose than to delete or destroy them. A frightening manifestation of this was the article in *Newsweek* which had been critical of hackers and their methods.[31] After its publication the reporter who wrote the article was harassed by a number of hackers, who, amongst other things, caused him to be presented with a gigantic telephone account and also sabotaged his credit ratings!

Readers who are interested in hackers and their exploits are referred to the true confessions of Bill Landreth, alias 'The Hacker', who has made some money out of the tale of his exploits in a work which has been serialized in South African and overseas computer magazines.[32] Landreth was charged with, and convicted of, 'wire fraud', constituted by his unauthorized access to and use of the GTE Telemail network in the United Sates, and was placed on three years' probation.

Another legendary hacker of more recent vintage is the notorious Kevin Mitnick. Piecing together his exploits,[33] it seems that he started in 1981 at the age of 17 when he was convicted and placed on parole for stealing computer manuals from a Pacific Bell switching station. In 1982 he broke into the North American Air Defence Command computer, gained temporary control of three central telephone company offices in Manhattan and gained access to all the telephone switching centres in California. He was back in the news in 1984 for breaking into the NCSC's[34] Dockmaster computer by posing as a technician and phoning an authorized user with the news that he was issuing new passwords. In this way he obtained the gullible's user's proper password. In 1988 (and now 25 years of age) he secretly monitored the e-mail of MCI and Digital Equipment security officials. Digital Equipment charged him with causing $4 million worth of damage to computer operations and with stealing $1 million worth of software. Mitnick was convicted and received a one-year jail sentence at a low-security federal prison. In 1992 he was pursued by federal agents for parole violations but went underground and disappeared for a while. On Christmas Day 1994 he broke into Tsotumu Shimomura's system at the San Diego Supercomputer Centre. Egged on by racist slurs regarding his Japanese descent, Tsotumu conducted an electronic bounty hunt on Mitnick which has captured the public imagination and even made the pages of the *Reader's Digest*! The hunt culminated in Mitnick's arrest in January 1995.

---

31 See *Computer World* 17 December 1984.

32 Bill Landreth *Out of the Inner Circle* (Microsoft Press 1985).

33 I am indebted to the Computer Security Institute's publication *Current and Future Danger* for many of the details that follow.

34 Acronym for National Computer Security Centre.

In the court in Raleigh, North Carolina, Mitnick plea-bargained[35] for up to eight months on the local charges. However, the US Justice Department argued that the Mitnick case is multi-jurisdictional and termed the present plea-bargain 'only a partial disposition of the case'. In 1996 he pleaded guilty to one federal charge of cellular telephone fraud[36] and admitted violating probation on an earlier computer fraud conviction. In 1997 he was sentenced to nearly two years in prison for parole violations and using stolen cellular phone numbers to dial into computer databases. He was then still awaiting trial on 25 counts of computer and wire fraud, possessing unlawful access devices, damaging computers and intercepting electronic messages in an unrelated case. Later that year hackers broke into Yahoo!, one of the main 'portals' to the Internet, and left 'an ominous holiday greeting'. The group, identifying itself as PANTS/HAGIS claimed that it had planted a computer virus which would be activated on Christmas Day and cause widespread damage if Mitnick were freed. (This proved to be an empty threat, but Mitnick's incarceration remains a big issue for many hackers.)

The latest news in the Mitnick saga is that he has been sentenced to 46 months in a federal prison after pleading guilty to 'computer fraud and wire fraud for breaking into computers, intercepting communications and stealing proprietary software from several cellular phone companies'.[37] Because he has been in prison since 1995, he could be released after about a year, although he still faces charges in California.

Not to focus too much on one person, one could also mention other recent examples such as Jorge Adita's 1996 break-ins at certain sensitive sites, including Los Alamos National Library; Vladimir Levin's hack into Citibank in 1995; and the 1998 attacks on the US Defence Department, the Massachusetts Institute for Technology (MIT), the University of California and many other sensitive sites by 'the Analyzer' (in real life Ehud Tenebaum) described as 'a dyslexic 18-year old Israeli hacker'.[38] With two 'protégés' called 'Makaveli' and 'TooShort', he committed 'the most organized and systematic attack' the Pentagon has ever seen. During 1998 it was also reported on television that some Chinese hackers had been sentenced to death and executed for breaking into banks electronically in the People's Republic of China.

The most ominous manifestation of hacker activity up to now has probably been the first organized attack by the terrorist group on a target country's computer

35 A process in criminal procedure by which an accused person consents to plead guilty provided that certain other charges are dropped or he is assured of not receiving a harsh sentence.

36 Probably also the result of a plea-bargain.

37 *New York Times* 27 March 1999, as reported on Edupage.

38 *Current and Future Danger* 9.

systems.[39] A group called the 'Internet Black Tigers' launched a bid to swamp Sri Lankan embassies with e-mail — or 'suicide e-mail bombing', as the group called it. Although not much harm was caused, it is an indication of the scale to which cybercrime can easily escalate.

5.2.3 Reaction to crime

The establishment has reacted to the threat of computer crime both formally and informally. Informally, people hire computer security consultants, encrypt their messages and found organizations such as the International Association of Computer Crime Investigators (IACCI). Based in San Francisco, the idea behind the organization is to liaise with police departments all over the world and to develop a database of the methods used by a criminal as well as of the criminals themselves. A network of competent data processing experts will be set up in as many Western nations as possible, with an international membership directory of all involved. The organization will then be able to assist the police in finding sufficient evidence for successful prosecution of computer crimes.[40] Another such organization is CSI in San Francisco which, as mentioned earlier, has published *Current and Future Danger*, to which reference will be made again below. Encryption and other technical means of protection do not appear to have been too successful, since they slow up software and may steal valuable memory. In the United States persons such as Michael Brown[41] and Robert T Mcquaid have made fortunes selling programs which break copylocks and the latter boasts that no lock has been made that cannot be broken.[42]

Formally, state legislatures have charged upon the scene with legislative guns blazing against the 'computer criminals', although the Federal legislature has been more cautious. It is not possible in a work of this scope even to attempt a complete overview of American legislation on this point, but there appears to have been two stages. Seeing that trade secrets[43] was a fairly familiar field, an attempt was made at first to solve certain computer crime problems by creating the crime of 'theft of trade secrets'. Tapper[44] refers to some of the United States legislation of the late Sixties. He asks a logical question: 'The law of theft provides the normal remedy against misappropriation of property. Why should it not protect trade secrets?'[45]

39 'first cyberterrorist attack reported' ZDNet 5 May 1998 at http://www.zdnn.com.

40 *Computer Week* 23 April 1984.

41 Author of 'CopyII', a bit-copying program much used in the 'olden days'.

42 *Wall Street Journal* 7 February 1986.

43 See chapter 3 Trade Secrets above.

44 Tapper *Computer Law* 4 ed 301.

45 Ibid.

Instead of attempting to answer this central question (which turns on the proprietary nature of trade secrets and/or information and other intellectual 'property'), many American state legislatures rushed into a second, more general, type of computer crime legislation. The problem in both cases was that a completely new type of legal interest had to be protected, namely two categories of immaterial property, the first one being electronic money or credit or an abstract sum of money, the second being simply information, whether it be in the shape of trade secrets, know-how, military classified information, or data collected and systematized in a certain way. In the light of this, the justification for legislation ran, one should not be surprised to find that old definitions and general principles formulated at a time when money was mostly tangible and information had no or little commercial value, failed to cope adequately with computer crimes. Wise[46] explains that the effect of this kind of provision is 'to create a protected property interest in information *per se*'. He also cites the case of *People v Johnson*,[47] where knowledge of a telephone access code (which the defendants offered to let others use) was found to be 'possession' of stolen property.

To illustrate the nature of this type of legislation, I should like to refer to the Colorado Computer Crime Act of 1973,[48] which defines 'property' as 'financial instruments, information, including electronically produced data, and computer software and programs in either machine or human readable form, and any other tangible or intangible item of value'. While the inclusion of data as property should be commended, 'any other tangible of intangible item of value' goes too far, in that it includes even the air we breathe and the sunlight that ripens our crops! Surely the values requiring protection can be defined more narrowly than this? Another section of the same Act places a duty on a corporation to report a reasonably suspect computer crime to the authorities. It is interesting to learn that this legislation was the direct result of a Colorado court's holding that hospital record information was not a thing of value and could therefore not be stolen.[49]

Other statutes punish a person who 'maliciously accesses, alters, deletes, damages or destroys any computer system, computer network, computer program or data'.[50] This is to be welcomed, in that a type of electronic trespassing and an electronic form of malicious damage to property are created.

In the mid-Eighties two federal statutes were passed to combat on-line computer-related crime where federal interests were involved, namely the

46 Sieber *Information Technology Crime — National Legislation and International Initiatures* 522.

47 148 Misc 2d 103 (NY City Crim Ct 1990).

48 Article 5.5, title 18, Colorado Revised Statutes 1973.

49 January/February 1985 *Computer Law and Practice* 81.

50 Section 502 of the Californian Penal Code.

Counterfeit Access Device and Computer Fraud and Abuse Act (CFAA)[51] and the Electronic Communications Privacy Act (ECPA).[52] The only prosecution under the 1984 version of the first Act was that of a Los Angeles hacker, Philip Gonzales Fadriquela, who used his home computer to break into the computers of the Department of Agriculture. After plea-bargaining, charges were reduced to three misdemeanours for wire fraud (apparently an alternative charge) for which Fadriquela was sentenced to three years' probation, fined $3 000 and was required to do 200 hours of community work.

Insightful commentary on the Computer Fraud and Abuse Act is given in an article by Glenn D Barker entitled 'Trespassers will be prosecuted: Computer Crime in the 1990's'.[53] He explains that there had been criticism of the 1984 version of the Computer Crime Act (Fadriquela had not been convicted on any of these counts) and that these difficulties led to the passing of the Computer Fraud and Abuse Act of 1986.[54]

The 1986 Act added three new offences, namely (1) theft of property by the use of a computer as part of a scheme to defraud, (2) 'malicious damage' felony (which penalizes illegal access of a federal interest computer and altering, damaging or destroying information on it); or (3) preventing the authorized use of a computer. The third offence was aimed squarely at hackers who set up pirate bulletin boards on other people's servers and at people trafficking in passwords relevant to interstate commerce, or which are used by the United States government. Barker gives an overview of the cases and prosecutions which followed, inter alia of Mitnick (dealt with above) and Morris (dealt with below).

In 1991 the CFAA was used successfully to prosecute Robert Morris, a Cornell graduate student, who had created a 'worm'[55] which he then released onto the Internet and which had infected thousands of computers within a matter of hours. The cost of dealing with the worm at each installation ranged from $200 to more than $53 000. Even though Morris claimed that he had intended merely to create a program which would explore the Internet and gather information about computer security and that it had all gone horribly wrong, he was convicted in terms of s103(*a*)(5) of the CFAA and sentenced to three years' probation, coupled with the condition that he has to perform 400 hours of community service.

In 1996 President Clinton passed the Communications Decency Act (CDA) in order to try to curb obscenity or indecency by means of a 'telecommunications

51 18 USC § 130 (1984).

52 18 USC §§ 2510–711 (1986).

53 (1993) XII *Computer Law Journal* 61ff.

54 Codified as amended at 18 USC § 130.

55 A self-replicating computer program.

device'. The Act has since been declared to be unconstitutional in the case of *Reno v American Civil Liberties Union*[56] since the court felt that the Act, taken as a whole, would impinge upon the constitutional principle of freedom of speech.

According to Christopher J Millard's book *Legal Protection of Computer Programs and Data*,[57] there are three ways in which computer programs and data may be brought under the criminal law. One of these, 'the creation by statute of offences specifically related to unauthorised interference with software or date', has been discussed above. Another way is to attach penal sanctions to general statutes dealing with a field of intellectual property such as copyright. The third, and most controversial, has been to interpret 'property' so widely that it becomes susceptible to theft. The last alternative is probably also the most attractive (although not without its own problems) and we shall return again to this point when dealing with Great Britain, Canada and South Africa. In the United States, the case which has been perhaps the most striking example of this third approach is *Carpenter v US*,[58] which turned on advance information of the contents of stock market columns appearing in the *Wall Street Journal*. The judge held that the *Journal* had a 'property right' in keeping secret and exclusive the contents of the article. For this reason the *Carpenter* case has often been interpreted as holding that information *per se* is property.[59]

I shall let Robert Bigelow have the last word in this section:

> 'The problem with specific computer crime legislation is (as it has been since the first statutes in the field were passed) defining the abuse narrowly enough to solve the problem, broadly enough to encompass developing technology and not so broadly that the law covers things like watches and microwave ovens.'[60]

5.3 THE UNITED KINGDOM

5.3.1 Taking of funds via computer

In the previous edition of the present work I quoted the words of Meirion Jones[61] which still seem to hold good in 1999:

> 'Computer criminals will steal at least £1 billion in Britain this year—that's a Great Train Robbery every day in 1985. But unlike the train robbers, most

56 929 F Supp 824.

57 Christopher J Millard *Legal Protection of Computer Programs* (Sweet & Maxwell 1985).

58 108 S Ct 316 (1987).

59 See, for instance, Donald Pragoff in Sieber *Information Technology Crime* 113.

60 Letter to *Computer World* 21 January 1985.

61 *Your Computer* (May 1985) at 48.

> of the electronic thieves will get away with it and even if they are caught, financial institutions are unwilling to prosecute because public confidence in them might collapse if people knew how easy it had been to breach their security.'

In a more recent work,[62] the authors[63] refer to the definition of the Council of Europe in its report on computer crime:[64]

> 'The input, alteration, erasure or suppression of computer data or computer programmes, or other interference with the course of data processing, that influences the result of data processing thereby causing economic loss or possessory loss of property of another person, or with the intent of procuring an unlawful economic gain for himself or for another person.'[65]

The authors admit that this definition is very wide, including even 'a person who wrongfully uses another party's cash dispensing card to withdraw funds from a bank account'. Nevertheless, they feel that the emphasis correctly falls on the objective of unlawful economic gain. They also use a quotation from the ex- head of Scotland Yard's Computer Crime Unit to emphasize that prevention is much better than cure:

> 'The prevention of crime here is important. No, it's not important it's vital. These days money is not the pound in your pocket, it's the $234 billion worth of transactions which go out from the City of London and back every day. All that money really amounts to is electronic digits travelling down wires. That's real money.'[66]

In the interesting case of *R v Schifreen; R v Gold*,[67] which dealt with two hackers who had gained unauthorized (and unpaid) access to the Prestel system (equivalent to South African Beltel), the question arose whether the hackers had committed 'fraud' by using a false password. They had been charged in terms of the Forgery and Counterfeiting Act (1991), which was supposed to have been framed to 'take account of technological developments'.[68] The prosecution had based their case on the argument that the 'user segment', which acted as a repository for the password files, had been the 'false instrument'. The court rejected the argument as follows:

---

62 Chris Reed (ed) *Computer Law* (Blackstone Press 1996).

63 Ian J Lloyd and Moira J Simpson.

64 Recommendation No R (89) 9 adopted by the Council of Ministers on 13 September 1989.

65 At 245.

66 Op cit at 247.

67 [1988] AC 1063.

68 Reed op cit at 250.

> 'The Procrustean attempt to force these facts into the language of an Act not designed to fit them produced grave difficulties for both judge and jury, which we would not like to see repeated.'[69]

Unfortunately the prosecution missed an opportunity to focus on the question whether deception of a machine could constitute the common-law offence of 'obtaining property or services by deception', by making use of the 1991 statute instead.

5.3.2 Information crime

There have been dramatic examples of 'theft' of information in England. In one such event a sum of £42 million had been spent on developing software for a seat reservation system, which was then stolen, copied and sold to competitors at a fraction of the price. In another event in 1970, three computer operators were convicted of the theft of mailing lists worth £3 million from *Encyclopaedia Britannica.* The matter is explored further below.

The problematical nature of information and the uncertainty whether it can be subjected to theft has already been explored above. Reed quotes the American case of *Hancock v Texas*,[70] where computer disks were stolen but the matter was treated as a felony rather than a misdemeanour in the light of the informational value which has been created on the disks. In England, s 4 of the Theft Act of 1968 defines property as including incorporeal property but, as we shall see below, *Oxford v Moss*[71] has probably put an end to all that.

Mention has already been made of the committee work leading up to the Computer Misuse Act of 1990. After both the Scottish and the English Law Commissions brought out reports during the second half of the Eighties, their deliberations were capped by the Computer Misuse Act of 1990. This Act created three important new offences. The first is a 'basic hacking offence', which is a summary offence and triable only in magistrates' courts. In this regard s 1 provides:

> '(1) A person is guilty of an offence if —
>
> (*a*) he causes a computer to perform any function with intent to secure access to any program or data held in any computer;
>
> (*b*) the access he intends to secure is unauthorized; and
>
> (*c*) he knows that at the time when he causes the computer to perform the functions that that is the case.

69 *R v Schifreen; R v Gold* (supra) at 1071.

70 (1966) 402 SW 2d 906.

71 1978 48 Cr App R 183.

(2) The intent a person has to have to commit an offence under this section need not be directed at —

(*a*) any particular program or data;

(*b*) a program or data of any particular kind; or

(*c*) a program or data held in any particular computer.'

The latter subsection seems to introduce a kind of *dolus generalis*[72] which is useful in a networked computer context, where the hacker generally does not tackle any program or computer in isolation, but takes whatever constitutes a challenge. The section goes on to impose a maximum term of imprisonment of not exceeding six months, or to a fine 'not exceeding level 5 on the standard scale', or to both.

Section 2 of the same Act creates the so-called 'ulterior hacking offence'. It is ulterior in the sense that the hacker commits the offence described in s 1 above with the intent to commit the type of offence described in s 2 or to facilitate such offence. These offences are defined in subsec 2(2) as offences:

'(*a*) for which the sentence is fixed by law;

(*b*) for which a person of twenty-one years of age or over (not previously convicted) may be sentenced to imprisonment for a term of five years ....'

This would seem to limit the offence intended (by means of the hacking) to only fairly serious instances. Upon summary conviction (of the ulterior hacking offence itself) he or she might be sentenced in the magistrate's court to imprisonment not exceeding six months or to a fine not exceeding the statutory maximum[73] or to both. After trial upon indictment in the Crown court he or she may be sentenced to imprisonment not exceeding five years or to a fine, or both.

The third offence is really targeted at the people creating and distributing virus programs. It is titled 'unauthorized modification of computer material'. Section 3 of the Act provides that:

'(1) A person is guilty of an offence if

(*a*) he does an act which causes an unauthorized modification of the contents of any computer; and

(*b*) at the time when he does the act he has the requisite intent and the requisite knowledge.'

The 'requisite intent' is in turn defined as 'an intent to cause a modification of the contents of any computer and by so doing

72 Meaning 'general intent'.

73 One assumes that this refers to the limit of jurisdiction of the magistrate's court?

(*a*) to impair the operation of any computer;

(*b*) to prevent or hinder access to any program or data held in any computer, or

(*c*) to impair the operation of any such program or the reliability of any such data.'

The latter part is comfortably wide enough to include the damage that viruses may do. The same section also specifically excludes any 'damage' to incorporeal data from the ambit of the Criminal Damages Act of 1971 (thus nullifying the effect of the *Whitely* case which is dealt with below).

In his commentary on the above Act, Martin Wasik[74] cites the case of *R v Cropp*[75] where the accused amended a computer at a sales desk to make it appear that he was entitled to a 70% discount on the item that he was purchasing, while, in fact, he was not. He was at first charged under s 3 of the Computer Misuse Act (changing data), but the charge was then amended to s 1 (simple hacking). He was acquitted by the Crown Court judge on the amazing grounds that at least two computers have to be involved for the statutory crime of hacking to take place. Fortunately the court of appeal has since reversed this aberration.

A major complaint about the Computer Misuse Act also seems to be that not sufficient procedural and evidential aids were provided to aid the police in proving these very incorporeal offences. The Act will probably serve as model for draft legislation being prepared at the time of writing by the South African Law Commission and it is hoped to introduce some procedural measures in this regard which will, at the same time, comply with constitutional requirements. The matter is dealt with further in the section on South Africa below.

5.3.3 Vandalism

Mention has already been made of *The Hacker's Handbook* by Hugo Cornwall (who is really a British computer security specialist) and the fact that Britain's Prestel videotex service has been raided by hackers on numerous occasions. The very first demonstration on television of one of these services, Telecom Gold, was disrupted by the appearance of a hacker's message on the screen. Another hacker broke into Britain's Prince Philip's Prestel account and had the time of his life sending messages, including one to the manager of Prestel, stating: 'The household is very impressed with your work.' Prestel once found its main index corrupted to read 'IDNEX'. Such a change could theoretically have been made only by a Prestel employee with the highest internal security clearance. Some hackers claim to have altered the information pages of the news providers of the service. All

---

74 Sieber *Information Technology Crime* 505.

75 Unfortunately not formally reported.

this is also relevant to South Africa, where BELTEL operates in a mode analogous to Prestel.

The authors in Reed[76] opine that this kind of damage, if done intentionally, could amount to 'electronic vandalism'. They refer to the Scottish case of *Her Majesty's Advocate v Wilson*,[77] where an employee of an electricity company maliciously pressed the 'Emergency Stop' button which stopped the generation of electricity for 72 hours and cost the power station owners some £147 000. On appeal it was held that the causing of pure economic loss could amount to malicious mischief (the original charge):

> 'If the malicious intention improperly to stop the production of electricity is established and the achievement of that had the effect that of rendering inoperative a machine which should have been operating productively and profitably, then in my view that is just as must damage to the employer's property as would be the case in any of the more physical acts of sabotage.'[78]

(This would seem to open an interesting line of analogies with other incorporeal objects, but the matter is probably now moot as a result of the Computer Misuse Act of 1990.)

An equivalent English case was that of *Cox v Riley*,[79] where Cox was employed to operate a powered saw which was controlled by means of the insertion of a printed circuit containing a number of computer programs. He deliberately used a program cancellation facility to erase a number of programs, which made the saw unusable until reprogrammed. This would have cost the owner 'time and effort of a more than minimal nature' (much the same test as applies to the crime of malicious damage to property in South Africa). By focusing on the hardware instead of the program, the court managed to convict Cox of a contravention of s 1(1) of the Criminal Damage Act 1971.

Not quite happy with this result, the English Law Commission started the work which would lead to the Computer Misuse Act of 1990. Ironically, this Act was followed by the case of *R v Whitely*,[80] where it was decided that the offence of criminal damage *would* be committed if damage was done to computer data alone. By focusing on the magnetic particles themselves, Lord Lane CJ found that 'an impairment of the value or usefulness of the disk to the owner' could have taken place and that this could constitute damage in terms of the Criminal Damage Act of 1971.

---

76 Op cit 253.
77 (1984) SLT 116.
78 Supra 119.
79 (1986) 83 Cr App R 54.
80 (1991) 95 Cr App R 25.

5.3.4 Other reaction to computer crime

As in the United States, the arsenal of offences to charge these electronic criminals with, seems slightly outdated. The crime of theft seems to have been taken a step in the right direction in its 1968 amendment, which provides that 'property' includes 'money and all other property, real or personal, including things in action and other intangible property'.[81] This would seem to address the new type of commercial interest in credit and information which was emphasized above. Unfortunately s 1(1) requires that the property should be taken with an intention to deprive permanently, something which is obviously not done when information is simply copied. Tapper[82] has pointed out that a possible solution could lie in s 6(1) which provides that:

> 'A person appropriating property belonging to another without meaning the other permanently to lose the thing itself is nevertheless regarded as having the intention of permanently depriving the other of it if his intention is to treat the thing as his own to dispose of regardless of the other's rights.'

Tapper's original view was that this would seem to limit the applicability of the section to someone who wants to market copied programs and not someone who intends to use it himself. Also, he had doubts concerning the applicability of the section to something such as a trade secret:

> 'The difficulty is that the section clearly contemplates a situation where there is temporary deprivation of a tangible object rather than the permanent appropriation of an intangible object which is retained drained of its value.'[83]

The present writer's reaction upon reading Tapper's views, then, was that his argument indicated quite clearly that a theft of some intangible may have taken place, even though the tangible incorporation of it still remains, seemingly unaltered, in the owner's hands. Since Tapper did not foresee any trouble with the element of appropriation as far as computers are concerned, it did not seem that any further legislative efforts would be needed to cope with this aspect of computer crime.

Unfortunately, a series of decisions seems to show a trend of courts' abdicating their responsibility to develop the law of theft, preferring to leave software theft

81 Theft Act 1968, 1.

82 This was Tapper's opinion in the first edition of his work. In the third, he mentions that his 'optimistic construction' seems to have been rejected in *Oxford v Moss* (1978) Cr App R 183, where intangible property in the form of the proof copy of an examination paper was held not to constitute "property" in terms of s 4 of the Theft Act (1990). See below and Tapper op cit 279–80.

83 Tapper *Computer Law* 1 ed 107.

problems to further efforts by the legislature. In *Oxford v Moss*[84] it was decided that confidential information in the shape of the proof of an exam paper, illegally obtained by a student, did not constitute 'property' for purposes of the English Theft Act. Another problem with this Act is the question whether one could ever use the phrase 'deception' with regard to a machine.[85] There even seems to be some doubt whether trade secrets may be stolen. In the case of *Rand Film Distributors v Video Information Centre*[86] it was decided that copyright infringement could not be seen as a theft of the copyright. Hopes were finally dashed by the case of *R v Lloyd*[87] where the Court took a restrictive view of s 6 by limiting it to outright takings and not to takings where there has only been a diminution of value (thus neatly destroying my argument above). The court actually went so far as to state that it

> 'would try to interpret the section in such a way that nothing is construed as an intention permanently to deprive which would not prior to the Act of 1968 have been so construed'.[88]

Technical protection does not seem to be doing much better here than in other countries; in fact, a lecturer at the Thames Polytechnic encouraged his students to break computer locks as an exam test!

A final word before leaving the United Kingdom: Martin Wasik is concerned about a problem of which the present author has also become aware in South Africa:

> 'Finally there has been continuing publicity about the problem of "phantom withdrawals" from cash dispensers.[89] The banks steadfastly maintain that their systems are secure and that phantom withdrawals do not exist, but a Liverpool solicitor is to bring a civil action on behalf of some 20 individuals who claim to have suffered from phantom withdrawals against certain of the banks. Developments are awaited'.[90]

---

84 (1978) 68 Cr App R 183.

85 See the position in South African law, where the same problem has arisen with regard to the element of misrepresentation with fraud.

86 [1981] 2 All ER 76.

87 [1985] QB 829 (CA).

88 Supra at 836.

89 The equivalent of ATMs (automatic teller machines) in South Africa.

90 Unfortunately I am also unaware of the final outcome.

5.4 OTHER COUNTRIES AND GROUPINGS

5.4.1 Canada

Of countries which have criminal-law systems broadly related to the Anglo-American systems, Canada seems to have had the most experience with law relating to computer crime. In the previous edition of this work the present author quoted R Bigelow on what he (then) considered to be the only computer crime case to have been considered by the highest court of a nation, *Queen v McLaughlin.*[91] Here students made unauthorized use of the central processing unit of the mainframe computer at the University of Alberta by means of remote terminals on the campus. The highest court of the land supported the appeal court's reversal of the trial judge's finding that a computer was a telecommunications facility and that therefore s 287 of the Canadian Criminal Code (the penalizing provision) would be applicable. In *Queen v Marine Resource Analysts, Ltd*[92] programs were removed by individuals who had terminated their relationship with the owner of the computer system and they would have got away scot-free if they had not charged the government $827,30 for the computing costs. This enabled a conviction of an attempted fraud of the government.

This was followed by some interesting cases on the question whether information can be stolen. In the first *R v Stewart*,[93] the matter turned on the interpretation of s 283(1) of the Canadian Criminal Code which holds that 'anything whether animate or inanimate' is capable of being stolen. According to Millard, this phrase had previously been interpreted broadly enough to include theft of a bank credit.[94] Although a minority felt that the matter should be left to Parliament to act upon, the majority felt that s 283 was broad enough to include the theft of information, though recognizing that their decision was out of step with the British case of *Oxford v Moss*.[95] The matter is well summarized by Cory JA:

> 'If questioned, a businessman would unhesitatingly state that the confidential lists were the property of his firm. If they were surreptitiously copied by a competitor or outsider, he would consider his confidential data to have been stolen. The importance of confidential information will increase with the growth of the high-technology industry. Its protection will be of paramount concern to members of industry and the public as a whole'.[96]

91 2 Can S Crt 331, 7 CSLR 1420 (1980).

92 7 CSLR 1411 (Nova Scotia Distr Appeal 1980).

93 (1983) 5 CCC (3rd) 481.

94 Op cit 158. See the position in South Africa, where the theft of money in the form of credit is leading the law along the same route.

95 (1978) 68 Cr App R 183.

96 This decision, is discussed in 1984 *Law Quarterly Review* 252 by R G Hammond, who criticizes it on grounds of policy.

In the second *R v Stewart*[97] it was held that, whatever the legal classification might be for purposes of the civil law, information was not property for purposes of the criminal law. According to Donald Piragoff,[98] the court also held that even if information could have been considered property for the purposes of criminal law, it would still not fit in with the other elements of theft, such as asportation (by the thief) and deprivation (of the owner). Although Piragoff agrees with the decision, he feels that the court should have explored the possibility of recognizing a property or interest in information (for example, the right to confidentiality and exclusive use), as was done in the *Carpenter* case in the United States[99]. Personally the present author does not think very much of having one concept of 'property' for civil law and another for criminal law.

5.4.2 Germany

In the previous edition of the present work some examples of German hacking activity were cited. A simple one was the case of the German printer operator who pressed the repeat button when his own pay cheque was being printed, with the result that he received two hundred copies. According to Tapper,[100] he was arrested while cashing the 37th cheque for the identical amount at the same branch of the same bank! Tapper also reports a more sophisticated salami fraud in Hamburg, where the perpetrator netted nearly half a million Deutschmark before he was caught out. Cornwall reports that West German hackers have actually formed a Chaos Computer Club in Hamburg and obtained the password of the Hamburger Sparkasse, one of the information providers on *Bildschirmtext*, the German equivalent of the British Prestel or the South African BELTEL. The hackers then accessed the pages of the bank more than 13 000 times during one weekend in November 1984, by means of a special program, and ran up a bill of DM135 000 in access charges. However, since the bank's password was used and an information provider could not be billed for looking at its own pages, the only cost was embarrassment![101] Readers who are interested in learning of the further activities of the Chaos Computer Club (and who are able to read German) are referred to *Das Chaos Computer Buch*[102] for some good essays on hackers and hacker ethics.

Ulrich Sieber mentions that 'computer misuse' is a better term that 'computer crime', but points out that the latter term has a greater warning function, which

---

97 [1988] 1 SCR 963; 41 CCC (3d) 481; 63 CR 3d 305.

98 Op cit 114.

99 *Carpenter v US* 108 S. Crt. 316 (1987).

100 Tapper *Computer Law* 1 ed 126.

101 Cornwall *The Hacker's Handbook* 109.

102 The Chaos Computer Club & Jurgen Wieckmann *Das Chaos Computer Buch* (Wunderlich 1988).

may be useful at the present moment in order to persuade sleepy computer users to take the same precautions that they would against other crimes![103] Another word coming into vogue internationally seems to be 'computer-related crime'. In the section on Germany (in the already much-quoted *Information Technology Crime*[104]) Manfred Möhrenshlager mentions that the Police Working Group have agreed upon the following definition for dealing with (and classifying) computer crime:

> 'Computer crime covers all sets of circumstances where electronic data processing forms the means for the commission and/or the object of an offence and represents the basis for the suspicion that an offence has been committed.'

Nor has the German legislature been backward in the area of computer crime legislation. During 1986 the German Criminal Code (or StGB)[105] was amended to provide for different forms of computer crime. For instance, s 202a now criminalizes data espionage, s 263a computer fraud, s 269 computer forgery, and s 303a–b data alteration and computer sabotage.

5.4.3 International developments

Sieber's much-quoted work, *Information Technology Crime,* also contains some valuable essays on the activities of the Council of Europe,[106] the European Commission[107] and the United Nations.[108] It is difficult in a book of this nature (which attempts to focus on Africa) to give a comprehensive account of international activities. It may make sense to focus on the activities of the United Nations, including the Draft United Nations Manual on Prosecution and Prevention of Computer Crime.

Canada, with 20 co-sponsors, has sponsored a resolution for adoption by the 8th United Nations Congress on the Prevention of Crime and the Treatment of Offenders in 1990. The resolution was adopted unanimously and urged member states to combat computer crime by

'(1) Modernizing national criminal laws, including the institution of measures to

(*a*) ensure that existing laws adequately apply to the commission of offences when committed within the computer environment;

---

103 *Computerkriminalität und Strafrecht* (Carl Heymans 1980). He actually uses the terms '*Computermissbrauch*' and '*Computerkriminalität*'.

104 Sieber op cit 198.

105 '*StrafGezetzBuch*.'

106 Op cit 575ff.

107 Op cit 585ff.

108 Op cit 603ff.

(*b*) create new offences where required;

(*c*) ensure that laws apply adequately to the investigation and prosecution of existing and new offences; and,

(*d*) increase the effectiveness of procedures for preventing, investigating and prosecuting computer-related crimes;

(2) Improving computer security and prevention measures;

(3) Adopting adequate training measures for officials and agencies responsible for the prevention, investigation and prosecution of economic and computer-related crime;

(4) Teaching of computer ethics as part of the curricula of courses in informatics;

(5) Adopting policies towards the victims of computer-related crimes; and

(6) Increasing international cooperation in order to combat these crimes.'

From this followed the manual drawn up by the Canadian Department of Justice. Final responsibility lay with Donald K Piragoff, with help from some more Canadians as well as Ulrich Sieber from Germany and Bart de Schutter from Belgium. (Obviously this manual is worth individual study and cannot be dealt with adequately in a book of this nature.) At the time the hope was expressed that member countries would structure their computer-related legislation around the guidelines as set out in the manual.

5.5 SOUTH AFRICA

5.5.1 Definition and extent of computer crime

Although some people may not think so, South Africa has not escaped the ravages of computer crime. We shall first try to arrive at a definition and then investigate the extent of computer crime in South Africa. One South African definition runs as follows:

> 'Computer abuse or computer crime encompasses the use of a computer as a tool in the perpetration of a crime as well as situations in which there has been unauthorised access to the victim's computer, or data.'[109]. (The age of the definition shows in the fact that computer viruses are not mentioned.)

The present author has ventured a definition in the previous edition of this book which runs thus: 'An illegal act where perpetration involved a computer.' In retrospect, this seems a bit wide, but this is probably necessary in order to encompass the different types of computer crime as we have categorized it in the United States and the United Kingdom. For the second edition, I have changed to the definition used by the German police:

109 Credo & Michels *Computer Crime in South Africa* 2.

> 'Computer crime covers all sets of circumstances where electronic data processing forms the means for the commission and/or the object of an offence and represents the basis for the suspicion that an offence has been committed.'

In a recent address to INFOSEC AFRICA 99,[110] Captain Beaunard Grobler of the Computer Crime and Support Unit of the South African Police Service made use of the following definition:

> 'Computer crime is any illegal act which involves a computer system whether the computer is an object of a crime, an instrument used to commit a crime or a repository of evidence related to a crime.'[111]

One could probably assume that this will also be the working definition which the South African Police Service will be using during their investigations. It resembles that of the current author, but differs from it in stating that even where a computer is merely used to store evidence relating to a crime, that crime then becomes a computer crime?! To my mind that goes too far, especially in giving part of procedural law such a say on the very nature of substantive law.

In the opinion of local computer security consultants, Paul Credo & Jean-Pierre Michels, computer crime also extends to physical attacks on the computer and/or related equipment, as well as to the illegal use of credit cards and violations of automatic teller machines, including electronic fund transfer thefts and the counterfeit of hardware and software.

Because of the reluctance of victims to report them, local computer crimes have been severely underreported in the daily or weekly press. Credo & Michels are of the opinion that less than 10% of computer crimes committed become public knowledge, because companies are afraid of 'egg on faces' situations in South Africa's relatively small business community. In this regard they did the forces of law and order as well as the cause of scientific investigation a lot of good by publishing a collection of case studies which they had learnt of in the course of their consultancy, many of these by private communication.

One of the first cases involved some 'data diddling' by two company executives of Field Industries' rubber division, who allegedly embezzled money by feeding false information into the company's computer. The case was due to be heard in September 1982 but the accused were let out on bail of R2 000 each and skipped the country.[112]

A rather sensational case occurred in 1983 when a thief pulled off the biggest jewellery theft in South African history by stealing some of the stock of Sterns,

---

110 A conference on computer crime and security issues held at Midrand on 2 February 1999.

111 'Case studies in cyber crime.'

112 *Computing SA* 24 September 1982.

the well-known jewellers. The firm had been building the computer stock files of the company over a few years, using an IBM mainframe computer with IBM software, when the financial director discovered a rather large shortage in the stock. The *modus operandi* was that in punching out stock transfer documents, three out of 16 items somehow did not appear on the computer screen, even though the last three items were in fact despatched—straight to the thief! When the receiving branch found that the three missing items appeared on their chart, they would send in a request that the items be deleted, since they had never received them. The firm has now apparently tightened up the follow-up checking, has installed new software which restricts access to the terminals and has also placed X-ray equipment in the foyer.[113]

On 2 May 1985 a senior systems analyst employed by the United Building Society was convicted on 74 counts of theft in which he manipulated R197 000 of UBS client accounts into his own savings account.[114] In August of the same year the assets of a teller of the Permanent Building Society were frozen after he had defrauded his employer of nearly R1 million. In a probe it had been discovered that he had withdrawn various amounts via his terminal and transferred them to his own or to an accomplice's account.[115]

In spite of the paucity of reported cases, the Institute of Internal Auditors has estimated that computer crime cost South Africa's business community between R100 and R200 million during 1985. Colonel Hume, then head of the Commercial Branch of the South African Police, told delegates to a conference that he didn't think the seriousness of the computer crime situation had filtered through. He called for legislation on this point and appealed to victims not to conceal these crimes for fear of adverse publicity: 'This attitude is wrong and it should be realised by top management that, as in other types of corporate fraud, this type of crime cannot, and should not, be condoned.'[116] The colonel also pointed out that if these crimes are not exposed it may be unfair to any future employer of the perpetrator. One wonders, though, whether the South African Police are fully ready to handle a greater volume of computer crime complainants. In the United States some 200 FBI agents have already been trained in this area and the Metropolitan police of London also has a special computer crime squad.[117]

During 1993 insurers began to wake up to their possible exposure to computer crime and therefore raised their insurance rates appreciably. According to PFV Group Broking Services director Brian Gillespie the losses occurring through

113 *Computing SA 19 August 1983* 2.

114 *The Star* 3 May 1985 and *Computing SA* 6 May 1985.

115 *The Citizen* 10 August 1985.

116 *Computing SA* 15 April 1985.

117 Tapper op cit (3 ed) 219n4.

physical damage to computer systems or loss of data is 'peanuts' compared with the hundreds of millions of rands lost through fraudulent misuse of computers. He also stated that most of these cases are never reported to the police, even though cases examined by PFV showed losses ranging between R500 000 and R24 million! He cautioned that most policies do not include protection against third-party fraud as part of their standard cover, yet the risks were becoming higher:

> 'With electronic data interchange (EDI) and electronic funds transfer (EFT) coming to the fore, companies will not survive unless they introduce very tight security controls. South Africa is definitely a First World computer-literate country, but our attitude to computer security often borders on the Third World.'

Gillespie expects that insurance companies would eventually be forced to require greater disclosure of operating procedures from clients, before providing cover against computer fraud.

In the speech[118] referred to above, Captain Beaunard Grobler (head of the Computer Crime and Support Unit of the South African Police Service), gave some (scarce) recent South African statistics concerning the work that he and six colleagues had done during 1998. Note that these numbers relate only to the computers investigated forensically — a prosecution did not necessarily follow. The team had received 87 requests for assistance during 1998 (75 for 1997). The number of computers involved was 567 (233 in 1997). A further breakdown of statistics runs as follows:

> 1,4% — child pornography; 0,7% — child pornography and abduction; 1,4% — copyright; 2,3% — corruption; 0,7% — corruption and fraud; 5,3% — corruption and theft; 0,4% — illegal firearms; 0,4% — drug trafficking; 24,4% — fraud alone; 4,8% — fraud and theft; 1,2% — importing illegal tire casings; 0,2% — income tax; 1,4 % — computers themselves were stolen; 1,4 — offences in terms of the Police Services Act; 1,4% — theft alone;

He also categorized criminals in the following groups; the 'embezzler', the 'Data diddler', the 'real criminal', the 'hacker', the 'savehead' and the 'midnight entrepeneur'.[119]

Auditors have perhaps also not always kept up with the latest developments and sometimes try to audit 'around the computer', sticking to hard copy which is printed out by the computer instead of following transactions right through the computer, at least by making it run test programs and data. Perhaps as a result of this, some American research has shown that while auditors uncovered five

118 To 'INFOSEC '99", a conference on computer security held at Midrand on 2 February 1999.

119 Op cit 3.

percent of all computer crime, jilted lovers who turned in their partners were responsible for six percent of the crimes that were discovered! Harsh words were spoken about the auditors in the Sterns case discussed above, yet Lindsay Madden, a lecturer in accounting at the University of Cape Town, rallies to their defence:

> 'Often management has depended on the external auditor but it is especially unfair to rely on them in this regard. Equipped with only a green pen, calculator and a two-day course on "EDP Concepts and Controls", it is unlikely that the average South African auditor would detect a computer fraud within two years, let alone understand it.'[120]

An aspect which should be worrying to auditors is whether they can he held delictually liable by the client or third parties (such as shareholders), for not picking up a computer fiddle in time.[121]

5.5.2 Types of computer crime

In the Credo & Michels work, *Computer Crime in South Africa,*[122] the authors systematize the different crimes encountered in terms of the legal interests protected. Thus there are categories of theft of money, theft of information, theft of goods, sabotage of hardware and/or software, theft of software and 'other computer crimes'. These categories would seem to be a vindication for my view that theft of intangibles such as credit and information should be possible, but on closer analysis it appears that the authors did not explore the legal implications of these cases, confining themselves in the category 'Action and/or Penalty' to reporting the mere fact of prosecution, conviction or sentence. Add to this the fact that they did not try to draw any juridical distinctions and it is clear that the authors used the term 'theft' in a loose, layman's sense, without trying to make any dogmatically correct, substantive criminal-law pronouncements.

(1) Theft of money

In the first category, theft of money, only five of the 20 cases led to a prosecution and effective imprisonment of from two to seven years was imposed in those cases that led to a conviction. A favourite method seems to be the writing off of 'bad debts' on the computer and then collecting these with manual receipts. Most of the cases involve simple data diddling and would, in my opinion, amount to theft of intangible amounts of money or electronic credits, something which many dogmatic legal purists are not yet prepared to grace with the title of 'theft'. At any rate, all these 'thefts' also amount to fraud because of the forgiving fraud requirement of only 'potential prejudice', which is easily met. The only problem with

---

120 *New Scientist* 7 July 1983.

121 See the sources cited in 1983 *Obiter* 128.

122 Op cit (1985).

fraud seems to be the requirement of a misrepresentation leading to the prejudice. In the case of automatic teller machines (ATMs), the question could arise whether any kind of representation can be made to a machine!

It should be noted from the report of increasing insurance rates for computer crime above, that the theft (or fraudulent obtaining) of money by means of computer eclipses the other categories of computer crime in terms of financial damage. (Of course, the *quantum* of stolen money is also easier to measure in the short term. Information which has been compromised might have more deleterious long-term effects.)

(2) Theft of information

The second category, theft of information, did not lead to any legal sanction in any of the ten cases discussed. The worst thing that happened to any of the perpetrators was a reprimand! Most of the cases involved unauthorized users looking at information or authorized users later on making use of information in unauthorized ways. All these cases seem to me to illustrate that information is an exceedingly valuable asset and that it would be a defect in the criminal law to deny dogmatically the possibility of the theft of information or even to try and force all such cases into the mould of theft of trade secrets.

As explained previously, the present writer believes that one should differentiate between information which is '(desired) items of knowledge, news' and knowledge, which represents information that has been made part of an individual's range of knowledge. Thus the authorized users in the previous paragraph would actually be making use of their *knowledge* in unauthorized ways later on.

A recent example of information crime where data was the express target has been reported as 'Intruders hack into Medscheme records'.[123] The facts were that intruders had broken into the building and into the computers of South Africa's largest medical aid administrator in order to get at data which profiled medical aid fraudsters. Medscheme uses a so-called data warehouse to analyse 4,5 million claim lines per month, using sophisticated software to identify practices worth investigating. A spokesman for Medscheme ascribed the break-in to either medical care providers under investigation or to industrial espionage by other medical schemes. (It is interesting to note that the unauthorized access to data would have been criminal had South Africa's pending computer legislation been passed.)

123 *Business Day* 29 March 1998; also in electronic format at http://www.bday.co.za.

(3) Theft of goods

The third category, theft of goods, is rightly not confined to theft of computer goods,[124] as the Finns would have it in their classification of American law; but it does include the theft of any goods as long as a computer was involved somewhere in the process. In only one of the nine cases were charges laid and the authors were unable to discover if any criminal penalty was imposed. The weak link with most of the victims seems to have been a failure regularly to reconcile their stock physically with the stock on hand shown by the computer, as in the *Sterns* case mentioned above. It is interesting to note that the share value of one of the victim companies has been halved since the discovery of the fraud (probably as a result of a lack of credibility with the public, say Credo & Michels[125]). These cases all seem to meet the definitions of ordinary theft and fraud, the computer being simply a tool making execution of the crime easier, often by the deliberate creation of confusion.

(4) Sabotage of hardware or software

In the six cases of sabotage mentioned, not one was brought before court, even though the damage in some of the cases amounted to tens of thousands of rands. Paul Williams[126] mentions a lesser known incident during the Zimbabwean war of independence, when a night-time guerrilla attack was aimed specifically at a computer installation in Bulawayo. No great damage was done, since the guerrillas blew up data capture equipment adjacent to the main computer.

The planting of a virus program could be seen as 'sabotage of software' (it is called 'vandalism' in some of the other countries we have dealt with in this work). This would definitely have amounted to malicious damage to property if that (common law) crime did not require that a corporeal, tangible object had to be damaged. For this reason, the present Law Commission project in this regard proposes criminalizing the creation and distribution of virus programs.

It is not clear where Michels would have classified 'hacking', but it is probably closest to the present category. During 1995, Unisa was visited by a young hacker calling himself 'Koki', who actually turned out to be one Kriek Jooste, a schoolboy in the small Free State town of Harrismith. Buying up the blackened remains of a computer after a local ANC office had been firebombed, he had built up a system from which not only Unisa, but also major South African financial institutions suffered. Koki's motive was not to enrich himself but rather to show up vulnerabilities in computer systems. He became a brief celebrity in South Africa

124 An example of this is the theft from the University of Cape Town of a laboratory microcomputer; see *Computing SA* 27 May 1983.

125 Op cit 39.

126 *Computing SA* 27 May 1985.

after appearing on M-Net's *Carte Blanche* programme (an investigative journalism programme) and was featured in articles with such snappy titles as 'Teenager's sneaky antics set him up for exciting career'[127] (as security consultant) and 'Zen, or the Art of Installing Backdoors'.[128]

(5) Theft of software

What is really meant by this phrase is usually simply infringement of copyright in the software. This is dealt with under the chapter on copyright above. If software is really stolen from the rightful owner or licensee, the thief could probably be charged only with the value of the physical medium, which oftentimes would be '*de minimis non curat lex*'![129]

(6) Extortion and unauthorized use

In Credo & Michels' final category, a case of extortion, some cases of unauthorized use (so-called theft of computer time) and some interesting cases of fraud are dealt with (the latter seemingly overlapping with category (1) above). In one of the latter cases — computer-assisted forging and uttering of thousands of rands worth of bus tickets — the 'charges'[130] were very light, according to Credo & Michels, because the accused were charged only with the theft of the special paper on which the tickets were printed. This would, again seem to illustrate a pathetic attachment to tangible objects and an ignoring of the tremendous value contained in the tickets, this intangible value forming the true legal interest in need of protection. Unfortunately there is again no record of any criminal penalties being imposed in any of the other cases mentioned by Credo & Michels.

In an interview with Michels after publication of the book, he warned of an increase in computer crime over the next five or six years, but thought that it would tail off because computers and their operating systems should then be technically secure. One wondered about this, though, when he mentioned the fact that criminals in Europe and the United States are at present learning computer science while serving jail sentences![131] With the wisdom of hindsight, we now know that this was a hopelessly optimistic prophecy — computer crime seems to be getting worse, in fact. This is only to be expected when one considers the value of goods being transmitted regularly over networks and even over the Internet, the latter a development which Michels obviously did not foresee.

---

127 *Sunday Times* 14 January 1996.

128 By Carsten Knoch in *Intelligence* December 1995.

129 'The law does not concern itself with trivialities.'

130 The authors probably mean 'sentence'.

131 *Computer Week* 4 November 1985.

Perhaps one could also bring under this heading the mysterious use of ATM cards by unauthorized person, already mentioned above in connection with the United Kingdom. There seem to be an increasing number of people in both countries who swear that no one could have got hold of their PIN[132] code but that money has still been drawn from their accounts with lost cards (often retained in the ATM itself). One such instance has been the case of the Randburg technician whose salary had just been paid into the bank and who then tried to withdraw R100 after-hours.[133] The machine gave him the money and a slip but then refused to return the card. That same night eight illicit withdrawals were made, the maximum being R400, to a total of R1 700. The bank denied responsibility:

> 'The additional transactions totalling were only possible by a person knowing the PIN which only you should know. We are aware that confidence tricksters are active by removing the owner's card after observing the person keying in the PIN and then distracting his attention.'[134]

I would have been sceptical of this explanation myself had I not recently seen a video recording made by a concealed camera of some of these 'procedures' around an ATM.

Much-increased use of networks, including the Internet, has brought with it the so-called 'hacker', a person who 'trespasses' upon another person's network or computer. One of the most recent examples has been the hacker who accessed the Web site of the Pretoria Municipality and changed 'Pretoria is 'n lekker plek' to 'Pretoria is 'n k*k plek'.[135] In a guest column on ITWeb,[136] Win Mostert warns that even though no relevant legislation has been passed yet, hackers could be made subject to an interdict, a claim for damages, a prosecution in terms of South Africa's (widely formulated) security legislation, a claim for infringement of privacy or defamation, a claim for damages because of unlawful competition of dismissal for having brought their employer into disrepute. He also mentions the case in The People's Republic of China in December 1998 where two hackers were sentenced to death for computer theft even after they had repaid the stolen money to the bank. (Surely a case of overkill?)

5.5.3 The response of South African law

Although most common-law crimes seem to have the potential to cope reasonably well with computers, some interesting problems may arise with such general

---

132 Acronym for Personal identification number.

133 Reported in the *Sunday Star* 16 April 1989 as 'Eddie's Help-Yourself Card'.

134 Ibid.

135 See *Die Burger* 5 January 1999: 'Webkraker haal toe die lekker uit Pretoria.' For overseas consumption, this means that 'Pretoria is a nice place' has been changed to 'Pretoria is a [expletive deleted] place'!

136 'Hack at your own risk' posted to http://www.itweb.co.za on 15 January 1999.

principles of criminal law as attempt, causality and participation. What makes computers different here, is the fact that manipulation of output might actually be accomplished at a point in time long before the output is actually used or produced. A crime which has very special problems of its own is theft, as the reader may have gathered.

In an article entitled 'Computers and Crime',[137] Skeen discusses the requirements of theft with reference to computers. In discussing the element of *contrectatio* (roughly translated as appropriation) Skeen acknowledges that physical control is no longer necessary and that with theft by means of computer manipulation, (virtual) control is present. Nevertheless, he still feels that this control is 'not in the sense that the common law envisaged'. Obviously the Roman-Dutch law did not foresee computers, but it also did not foresee many other modern developments which it has nevertheless managed to accommodate and adapt to. Once our common law has started moving away from the rigid and old-fashioned idea of a physical removal, there is no reason to stop this development arbitrarily at some point short of what thieves with computers do.

Skeen also deals with the element of 'property capable of being stolen' and correctly remarks that this gives rise to the most problems. Even overseas countries have difficulty in coping with the anachronistic requirement that only movable corporeals may be stolen. Skeen remarks that in the case of copying of a program or disk 'nothing has disappeared (either corporeal or incorporeal)'.[138] It can be argued, however, that the value of the program has diminished to the true owner, if not necessarily to the licensed possessor at the time of copying. Skeen seems to realize this when he states: 'certainly the exclusive economic value may be diminished but conceptually this is different from the theft of money'.[139] Traditionally this is true, but the main argument remaining is no longer where we are going, but whether the courts will take us there by developing the common law, or whether specific legislation will be necessary.[140]

In brief, in exploring the problems attendant to the theft of money in the form of credit by means of computers, as well as the theft of ideas embodied in computer hardware and software, it seems to the present author that the true culprit is not the criminal law, but the law of things. Even though the Roman and Roman-Dutch law provide sufficient grounds to argue that one could own

137 (1984) *South African Journal of Criminal Law and Criminology* 262.

138 Op cit 264.

139 Op cit 265.

140 I have explored the dogmatic background to this issue in an article which I do not have the space to repeat here comprehensively and to which I refer the interested reader for more details: 1984 *SACC* 129. See also the more comprehensive treatment in chapter 4 Private Law above, under the law of things.

res incorporales,[141] this view fell out of favour in the light of the theory of subjective rights. Coming from the German Pandectists, this theory is strongly subscribed to by many South African jurists and lays down that one can 'own' only a *corporeal* thing. If the South African criminal law were to accept the possibility of the theft of incorporeals it would mean that the expression 'ownership'[142] would have a variable content, depending on whether the criminal law or the law of things was applicable at the time. To avoid this problem, the present writer suggested that the criminal law should extend the category of things which may be stolen to include immaterial property rights, but that care should be taken not to use the concepts of 'ownership', 'possession' or 'thing', — at least not until the law of things has put its own house in order. It may seem necessary for the legislature to carry out such drastic developments, but when one looks at the transformation which the concept 'money' has undergone in this century, without much legislative intervention, the latter does not seem to be a foregone conclusion.

Skeen also discusses the mental element of the crime of theft, which he insists is the intention to deprive the owner of the full benefit of his ownership. As Skeen mentions, this requirement is borrowed from English law, where it has already caused grave problems as far as the theft of trade secrets is concerned.[143] There are some jurists who would rather define this element in South Africa as the intention to own ('toeëieningsgesindheid').[144] On this interpretation one would again run into problems with the South African law of things. It seems to the present writer that a perpetrator often does permanently arrogate to himself the intangible embodied in a tangible, although the latter remains in the hands of the owner, albeit with its value diminished. If our courts are of the same opinion, this element should not present insoluble difficulties.

There is no doubt that a practical need exists for the theft of incorporeals to be 'criminalized' in South Africa. Such a need arose in a case which came to the present writer's personal knowledge. A software developer who has had one of his programs copied by a pirate tried to lay a criminal charge at his local police station. With great prudence on the part of the desk sergeant he was advised to see an attorney to help frame the charge and the complainant was indignant enough to do so. Because some changes had been made to the program, it was doubtful whether the criminal charges under the Copyright Act would be applicable, however. The attorney consulted then made out a strong case for a prosecution for theft of intangibles in a letter to the Attorney-General, in order to have

141 Meaning 'immaterial goods'.

142 'Possession' and even 'thing' are in the same boat.

143 Op cit 265.

144 C R Snyman *Strafreg* (Butterworths 1992) 491.

a test case. In this instance the Attorney-General declined to prosecute but possibly further such requests will follow.

Before the law can develop, however, more computer criminals should be brought before the courts. The reluctance of victims to report these crimes in the first place, has been raised but a question also hangs over the ability of the machinery of justice to investigate and prosecute this type of crime. In a first article on the topic of computer crime,[145] The present writer recommended that a division of the Attorney-General's office should concentrate entirely on this type of crime and should attempt to obtain basic training in order to be able to match the new generation of computer criminals. Many of the problems encountered relate to the law of evidence and these are touched on again in the relevant chapter of this book.

A relatively new initiative in the field of computer crime legislation is the initiative by the South African Law Commission which has led to an issue paper as well as concept legislation. At the time of writing this may be accessed at www.lawcomm.co.za. It deals with the criminalization of illegal access to a computer, either by itself or with the intention to commit another crime. It is interesting to note that New Zealand has also recently passed legislation along these lines. The original model is the United Kingdom's Computer Misuse Act, enhanced by some procedural provisions which the original lacked. A major problem with procedural provisions is that they will have to comply with the provisions in the South African Constitution[146] which guarantee fair treatment to arrested persons and a fair trial once investigations have been completed. Because of the ease with which relevant evidence can be made to disappear (or made inaccessible by means of encryption), search and seizure can be tricky.

Part of the feedback engendered by publishing the issue paper mentioned above demanded that the legal status of information itself be protected. Because of the controversial nature of this topic, however, it was decided to concentrate on physical access to the computer, as the lawgiver in the United Kingdom has done.

Most other South African legislation on the protection of information is related to state interests, which is not the main focus of the present work (being more commercially orientated). In his doctoral thesis entitled 'Die Regsbeskerming van Inligting',[147] Geldenhuys deals with most of these statutes, for instance the Protection of Information Act,[148] after some excellent comparative analysis of

145 1983 *Obiter* 124 at 132.

146 Act 108 of 1996, s 35. Section 35(3)(1) also prohibits criminal charges for an act which was not criminally prohibited at the time of commision. This might inhibit the argument by anolagy mode in the previous paragraphs.

147 Tertius Geldenhuys 'The Legal Protection of Information' (unpublished LLD thesis, Unisa 1993).

148 Act 84 of 1982.

the law. Geldenhuys was also the author of the latest Police Services Act,[149] which is progressive in dealing with information as it affects the police. Another Act dealt with by Geldenhuys protects the privacy of the individual, namely the Interception and Monitoring Prohibition Act.[150]

5.5.4 Computer security

An informal way in which victims have been trying to help themselves, lies in the related field of computer security (prevention is better than cure!) Physical security means that access to the computer system or its terminals is physically prevented, but this comes from the old days of mainframe computers which were self-contained, or contained within the premises of its owner. With the Internet, physical security is almost impossible since one can access the Internet from any computer and modem all over the world.

Nowadays computer network administrators try to protect the sensitive internal data of a company connected to the Internet by means of a 'firewall'. This is usually a computer, separate from the internal network, which first screens all incoming data before allowing it to flow to the rest of the network. These firewalls often defeat their own purpose, since they then become targets of attacks by hackers all over the world who try to beat the security system in order to prove their own expertise!

In the case of data transmission, this field relies, inter alia, on the encryption of data which has to be sent from one computer to another. Many techniques are available, for instance the so-called substitution (A = 1), transposition (BACK = KCAB) and arithmetical transformation (A = A + 1, in other words A = 2) methods. One of the most popular standards used to be the Data Encryption Standard (DES) of the American National Bureau of Standards, which uses both substitution and transposition. A recent rival of this is the so-called key system, in which a public key is used to encode all messages sent, but decoding is possible only by means of a secret key, unique to its user. This technique is based on a complex arithmetical transformation. According to a local authority on computers, Professor S H von Solms of the Rand Afrikaans University (RAU), some very sophisticated coding and decoding algorithms already exist, which should make the electronic transmission of data reasonably safe.[151] This is borne out by Cornwall of *The Hacker's Handbook* fame, who mentions that encryption and decryption capabilities were left out of the older mainframe computers because

149 Act 68 of 1995.

150 Act 127 of 1992. Amendments to this Act are at present the subject of a project by the South African Law Commission.

151 *Rapport* 20 May 1985.

they tended to slow things down too much, but that the largest manufacturers now seem to have found a solution to the problem.[152]

Nowadays a whole hierarchy — called the public key infrastructure (PKI) — has been worked out with regard to the safeguarding and authenticity of keys. One of the most popular of such software packages, PGP,[153] used to be available only in 64-bit encryption strength, because of the United States prohibition on the exportation of powerful encryption. By all kinds of subterfuges, including publishing the source code in a book, PGP is now available in 128-bit encryption strength. It works by generating a public and a private key for each of the contracting parties, the public key being accessible to both. A then encodes a message using both his private key and B's public key, which B can then decode by making use of his own private key and A's public key.

Complicated, is it not? The matter is explored further in chapter 6 Evidence.

5.5.5 Conclusion

One of the questions which must be asked before any new criminal legislation is prepared, is whether new crimes are really necessary in an era of decriminalization. It is the opinion of the current writer that this chapter has shown that this is the only way out. Many hackers are not well-to-do (they are often schoolchildren), so the possibility of a civil suit against them is very slender. In the second place, information (turned into knowledge) is proving to be the most important asset of this century and probably the next one too. Although security serves an important preventative function, dealing strongly with those miscreants who do manage to slip through the security net is an important cornerstone to of successful security policy.

Despit my arguments above, Roman-Dutch law seems, sadly, to have come to the end of the road in terms of further development in this particular area and we probably need legislation. This should come, first, in the areas of access and vandalism, as with the British Computer Misuse Act[154] and the American federal statute.[155] Later on the nettle of protecting information and knowledge will have to be firmly grasped. There is no doubt that the currency of present times is constituted by information, and no longer by land, or by capital and labour.

152 H Cornwall *Data Theft* (Mandarin 1989) 313.

153 Pretty Good Privacy!

154 Computer Misuse Act (1990).

155 Computer Fraud and Abuse Act (1984).

CHAPTER SIX

When your house is not in order, do you put it in order, or do you change the law so as to define it as being in order?

EVIDENCE

6.1 INTRODUCTION

From the preceding chapters it should have become apparent that information plays a very important role in post-industrial society. In the right hands, and used properly, it can be a vital asset. Unfortunately the converse is also true. Like any potent object, such as a firearm, or chemical components, it may also be misused. This is also the age of disinformation and propaganda and unfortunately the computer is sometimes an aider and abettor in this process. People sometimes have a grossly misplaced trust in the veracity of any data that has been produced by computer.

The legal field where data can really be tested for veracity is the field of evidence. Unfortunately, like all other fields of law, it sometimes finds itself strained to adapt from a world where the emphasis had been on material things and on personal knowledge of affairs, to a new world where paper is being phased out of commercial transactions and to 'decreasing contact between human beings and the information needed to conduct business'.[1]

One author seeks the difference between records stored in a digital computer, and other conventional types of records, in the meaning of the term 'digital'. James A Sprowl[2] argues that the older forms of record-keeping such as the original copy of a check contains 'non-digitizable' information such as the shape of the signature, the condition of the safety paper and the spacing of the letters or numbers that guard the check's authenticity. Once this information has been digitized in order to keep it as a computerized record, later alterations can no longer be detected easily, as no tell-tale traces are left when one presses the 'DELETE' key of a computer and part or whole of the record concerned is instantaneously erased. Most evidential problems concerning computers have arisen in the following fields. Take, for instance, the traditional hearsay rule — since the computer cannot be cross-examined as to the truth of its printouts, may such printouts be treated as exceptions to the hearsay rule or should special statutory provision be made? Since all computer printouts are strictly speaking copies, what should one make of the best evidence rule? Can anything take the place of a manual signature as a guarantee of authenticity? Does digital storage comply with the record-keeping (archival) requirements of many South African statutes? How does the easy alteration and deletion of computer records affect the question of discovery of documents in civil litigation?

---

1 M E French 'The Admissibility of Computer Records in SA Law of Evidence — a comparative survey!' 1982–83 *Natal University Law Review* 112.

2 James A Sprowl & Peter B Maggs *Computer Applications in the Law* (West 1987) 4–5.

All these questions are examined by looking at the international position, where the United Nations has considered the problems and has had some research done, as well as at the United States, the United Kingdom and certain Commonwealth countries such as Australia, where the subject has received special attention.

6.2 THE UNITED STATES

Here, as in South Africa, efforts have been made to accommodate computers by means of common-law and statutory exceptions to the hearsay rule. The common-law exception is based on the shopbook rule[3] and admits hearsay evidence, provided that the record had been made in the ordinary course of business, at or near the time that the transaction occurred and provided that there had been no motive for the proponent to misrepresent the transaction. In addition, the declarant must have had personal knowledge of the transaction or must have made his or her declaration on the basis of the report of someone who had such knowledge.

In the view of Colin Tapper,[4] there has been a greater acceptance of the shopbook exception in the United States than in the United Kingdom because of local circumstances, but also because of 'the absorption in New York of the older Dutch civil-law attitude to the use of documentary evidence'. Even today, in Europe, much less agonizing is done over the *admissibility* of certain types of evidence and more emphasis is placed on gauging the *weight* of this evidence, once it has been admitted. This is mostly as a result of a lack of jury trials on the Continent, jury members being supposedly unable to attach the proper weight to certain types of evidence and therefore having to be shielded from this by strict rules of admissibility. Even though South Africa has done away with jury trials for many decades, these still cast their shadow over the present-day South African law of evidence, resulting in strict rules of admissibility.

Tapper mentions that there have been no fewer than five attempts in the United States to draft model statutes devoted to the admission of business records. These include the Model Act drafted by the Commonwealth Fund Committee; the Uniform Business Records as Evidence Act drafted by the Commissioners for Uniform State Laws; s 541 of the Model Code of Evidence drafted by the American Law Institute; rule 63(13) of the Uniform Rules of Evidence drafted by the Commissioners for Uniform State Laws; and rule 803(6) of the Federal Rules of Evidence promulgated by the Supreme Court of the United States and approved by the Judiciary Committee of both Houses of Congress.[5]

---

3 An exception to the hearsay rule in order to admit business records based mostly upon considerations of convenience.

4 Colin Tapper *Computer Law* 4 ed (Longman 1989) 380ff.

5 Op cit 381n55.

Tapper lauds the way in which courts have interpreted these statutes in order to ensure that the wheels of commerce keep turning and are not unduly held up by legal obfuscations. One of these case was *King v Mississippi ex relatione Murdock Acceptance Corporation*,[6] where computer records were accepted under this exception. Before doing so, however, the court satisfied itself that the following three conditions had been satisfied, namely:

1. that the electronic computing equipment was recognized as standard equipment; and
2. that the entries were made in the regular course of business at or reasonably near the time of the occurrence of the event recorded; and
3. that the court was satisfied by the foundation testimony that the sources of information and the time and method of preparation were such as to indicate its trustworthiness and to justify its admission.[7]

In the first edition of his work,[8] Tapper repeated the third consideration as boiling down to the fact that the court 'means to require credible testimony of the working of the system from someone knowledgeable enough to be cross-examined fruitfully'. This, to my mind, is the central *ratio* of the hearsay rule, and computer-related exceptions will have to bear this in mind.

In his fourth and most recent edition, Tapper expands as follows:

> 'The court explicitly recognized that the weight of the evidence was still disputable and could be attacked in exactly the same way as any other business entry. It may be noted that the evidence was eventually rejected because of the failure of the foundation testimony to show the accuracy of information.'[9]

This emphasis on weight rather than mere admissibility of evidence equates with the Continental emphasis explained above.

The Federal Rules of Evidence have been discussed in an informed article by Paula N Singer.[10] Although these contain no specific computer-orientated rules, the term 'data compilations' has been added to several rules. Singer discusses the rules under the headings of Authentication, Hearsay and Best Evidence, all areas where computers have caused the courts headaches. Singer believes that foundation testimony plays an important role in the area of authentication and criticizes the trend towards shifting the burden of persuasion to the opponent of the evidence to prove that it is inaccurate or untrustworthy, thus dispensing with foun-

6 222 So 2nd 393 (Miss 1969).

7 At 397.

8 Tapper *Computer Law* (1 ed) 156.

9 Tapper *Computer Law* (4 ed) 382.

10 (1979) *Rutgers Computer and Technology Law Journal* 157ff.

dation testimony. She is also not enamoured of the fact that rule 902 dispenses with authentication for public documents because 'the accuracy of those documents depends on the accuracy of the process which creates them'. Presumably computers in the employ of government function no differently from those in the private sector! She believes that testing a computer process with another program is more accurate than relying on the credibility of the testimony of the proponent of the evidence and she suggests a new rule 901(*c*) to aid in the authentication process:

> '(c) COMPUTER PROGRAM OR SYSTEM. Evidence describing a computer program or system of computer programs used to produce a result and showing, by a description of the computer hardware, programming method, stored data base, operation of the system, system security and specific application controls, that the program or system produces an accurate result, satisfies the authentication requirement for a computer programmer or system. Voluminous testimony should not be required to lay a foundation for the computer system or process. For instance, the explanation of the computer hardware need not be more than an overview by the manufacturer of the central processing unit and of the types of input/output devices used by the system.'

Besides the above, a statement that all the equipment was functioning reliably should be included. Even though I consider it doubtful that any one person will ever be in the position to give such a guarantee, at least the proposed article has the merit of attempting to provide sufficient technical information to enable the court (hopefully including a computer-literate assessor) independently to assess the reliability of the system.

With regard to hearsay evidence, Singer deals with the exceptions of records of 'regularly conducted activity and of public records'.[11] She supplies the following quotation to illustrate the element of unusual reliability of business records, which is provided

> 'by systematic checking, by regularity and continuity which produce habits of precision, by actual experience of business in relying upon them, or by a duty to make an accurate record as part of a continuing job or occupation'.[12]

To the above she adds the comment that with computers the above rationale applies only to the controlled, repetitious processing of the operational system and not to the human beings operating it:

> 'The fact that a computer system is relied on in the usual course of business should not be viewed as sufficient to meet the authentication requirement

11 Op cit 176.

12 Op cit 177.

> since it is possible that the system is susceptible to inaccurate records due to weaknesses in any of the abovementioned cases.'[13]

These weaknesses include the fact that human examination would be 'impossibly burdensome', and that merely looking at the materials would be useless without background on the input procedures, internal control and access to the system, as well as the controls, modifications and installation of the programs themselves.

The rationale for the public records exception is apparently based on 'necessity and assumed trustworthiness'.[14] Necessity has to do with the disruptive effect which the bringing of busy public officials to court would have had, and public records are regarded as trustworthy because a public official had been charged with a duty to keep the record. Singer shows convincingly that this rationale does not apply to public records which have a computer system as their source: 'The duty of a public official to keep accurate public records does not determine the skill and accuracy with which a computer system and the data which it processes are developed and maintained.'[15] In *United States v Farris*[16] computer data presented by the Internal Revenue Service (these guys never lose) was held admissible as a self-authenticating record, for which no foundation testimony was required. As far as the 'necessity' is concerned, Singer is of the opinion that the disruptive effect of bringing public officials to court is more than offset by the fact that the accuracy of a computer system and the records it produces cannot be presumed to be accurate, but that the burden of proving inaccuracy is now cast onto the other party.

Dealing with the best evidence rule, Singer points out that in many business operations computer-generated records are the best evidence since these form the only record of certain transactions. 'In addition, many computer-generated records have no underlying documents from which the information can be obtained since they are created by the computer system itself.' As far as bringing the evidence (which may only be visible on a display terminal) to court, Singer suggests that the original be treated as 'not obtainable', which would allow a witness who viewed the display to testify as to its contents or allow a photograph of the display itself, since this is the best secondary evidence.

The author summarizes this section (and, it would seem, the whole article) rather well by pointing out that too much attention has been focused on the form of the evidence presented and that too little attention has been paid to the safeguards taken to assure the accuracy of the information.

---

13 Op cit 173.

14 Singer op cit 182.

15 Op cit 182.

16 517 F 2d 226 (7th Cir).

More within the realm of civil procedure, Tapper also deals with the question of discovery in the United States and mentions the case of *Greyhound Computer Co v IBM*,[17] where the defendant literally deluged the applicant with paper by making available thousands of documents in four different locations, as well as six reels of magnetic tape, without any additional facilities to explain even the formatting of the documents — yet this was held to constitute sufficient discovery. Another problem with discovery seems to be that the applicant might gain access to the computer containing the litigation support system of the defendant and in this way get a sneak preview of the latter's litigation strategy (which forms part of his work product).

Michael D Scott[18] also discusses the latter problem and mentions that this is actually a doctrine developed by the courts. He suggests that the best way to preserve the attorney's work product from prying eyes is to leave the whole litigation strategy entirely up to the lawyers and to keep the client in ignorance about detail. Therefore the client's papers would be 'clean' and may be discovered.

Concerning the form in which discovery should take place, *US v Davey*[19] laid down that the tender of a 'hard copy' print-out did not absolve a party from also showing its machine-stored data:

> 'In this era of developing information-storage technology there is no conceivable reason to adopt a construction that would immunize companies with computer-based record-keeping systems from IRS scrutiny.'[20]

(Told you that those guys never lose!)

Probably one of the most controversial issues with regard to computer evidence recently is the question whether computer print-outs will be admitted in court as evidence of stored records. There are principles in the Federal Rules of Evidence which (with sympathetic interpretation by the courts) would admit these in evidence and leave the weight to be decided by the court in the final instance. Nevertheless, certain states have enacted their own legislation in this area, for instance Wisconsin, which has placed its state law on 'Optical Images'[21] on the Internet at www.archiveindex.com/law-wi.html. In Adm 12.08 they put forward a very useful ruling:

> '(1) Any state agency or country may utilize paper, microfilm, or optical imaging or combinations of the three for records or records storage. Any system of records shall be used consistently and shall be relied upon in the regular course of business as being accurate, reliable and trustworthy.'

---

17 Op cit (1989) 417ff.

18 Michael D Scott *Computer Law* (Wiley 1984) 10–11.

19 543 F 2d 996 (2nd Cir 1976) at 999.

20 Ibid.

21 Wisconsin Act 201 (1995) Senate Bill 639.

Overseas, one of the essential building blocks towards e-commerce, is the digital signature.[21a] The question of digital signatures has received much attention from lawgivers in Europe, the United States and Asia. In the United States, some states have passed specific digital signature legislation, for instance Utah and Illinois. The latest such piece of legislation is the Illinois Electronic Commerce Security Act, which was due to come into operation on 1 July 1999. The Act aims to remove existing legal barriers to e-commerce, facilitate the legal trustworthiness of electronic communications and specify the rules that apply to electronic commercial transactions. A copy of the Act as well as comment by the Illinois Commission on Electronic Commerce and Crime, the creators of the Act, is available on the Internet at www.mbc.com.

More specifically, the Illinois Act focuses on 'electronic records' and 'electronic signatures' and accomplishes four objectives. These are, first, to authorize the use of electronic records and electronic signatures, in order to remove any doubt as to their enforcability and admissibility. Secondly, the Act creates a new category of 'secure electronic records' and 'secure electronic signatures' that should enhance reliability in order to establish the TRUST required for e-commerce. Thirdly, the Act specifies the legal rules relating to a special type of electronic signature known as a 'digital signature' (see the discussion above). Finally, it specifically authorized all state agencies to conduct their business electronically.

Utah had thought of an original way to give digital signatures credibility: the governor of that state digitally signed a declaration proclaiming 19 November as 'Digital Signature Day' and encouraging secure e-commerce in that state. Earlier, Utah had become the first legal system *in the world* to pass a complete digital signature Act (in 1995).

6.3 The United Kingdom

6.3.1 Introduction

In the first edition of his book, [22] Tapper built the admissibility of computer-generated evidence around the hearsay rule and linked this with documentary evidence:

> 'Much of the history of the law of evidence, and particularly of the hearsay rule, over the last 100 years, has been one of painful and ponderous adaptation to the reception of documentary evidence.'[23]

21a A digital signature is simply a form of encryption which links a specific person to a certain (electronic) document and in this way authenticates the document.

22 Tapper *Computer Law* (1 ed) 149ff.

23 Ibid.

This ties in with the opinion of a South African expert[24] that the most dynamic area of development for the law of evidence of the future is likely to be in the field of documentary evidence.[25] Computers have something to do with this, of course. As has been pointed out above, the human element has been removed from record-keeping and it is therefore no longer realistic to expect any one person to be able to give evidence from his personal recollection as to what went into a certain document, or even as to the authenticity of the document. The whole process has been automated.

6.3.2 Legislation

Tapper mentions three ways in which the law of evidence may respond to this challenge, namely

- *(a)* by expanding the common-law rules;
- *(b)* by extending to computers the exceptions to the rules applicable to hearsay or best evidence, originally crafted to deal with ordinary documentary evidence; or
- (c) by creating a statutory solution drafted specifically with computers in mind.

In England the first course has not been as great a success as in the United States, where the exception was cast in the mould of the acceptance of business records. As Skeen has put it, the common law has 'petrified' in the United Kingdom on this point, as the last new common-law exception to the hearsay rule was allowed in 1876.[26]

As far as expansion of the general rule by statute is concerned, the legislative spider has woven a most tangled and complicated web. The most important pieces of legislation are the Evidence Act of 1938, the Criminal Evidence Act of 1965, the Civil Evidence Act of 1968, the Police and Criminal Evidence Act of 1984, the Criminal Justice Act of 1988 and the Civil Evidence Act of 1995. (The 1938 Act still applies indirectly in South Africa by means of the South African Civil Proceedings Evidence Act.)[27] The situation in the United Kingdom has been summed-up well by Tapper:[28] 'The unfortunate result is that England has three different statutory provisions for documentary hearsay, the Criminal Evidence Act 1965 for all criminal cases, the Civil Evidence Act for civil cases in the higher

---

24 Now living in New Zealand.

25 C Eckard in 1985 *De Jure* 384 at 390.

26 (1984) 101 *SALJ* 675 at 676.

27 Act 25 of 1965.

28 Op cit 1 ed 157. This statement was obviously made before the enactment of the Police and Criminal Evidence Act of 1984 and the Criminal Justice Act of 1988.

courts and the Evidence Act 1938 for civil cases in the lower courts.' The matter has been complicated even further by later legislation, as will be seen below.

The most serious drawback to the 1938 Act is the definition section which defines 'document' as including 'books, maps, plans, drawings and photographs', without any mention of computers. (All courts in South Africa are still struggling with this problem because the corresponding Act has never been brought up to date, although patchwork has been done by other South African statutes.)

This Act was followed by a specific computer provision in s 5 of the Civil Evidence Act (CEA) of 1968, which reads as follows:

> '5. (1) In any civil proceedings a statement contained in a document produced by a computer shall, subject to rules of court, be admissible as evidence of any fact stated therein of which direct oral evidence would be admissible, if it is shown that the conditions mentioned in subsection (2) below are satisfied in relation to the statement and computer in question.'

Subsection 5(2) then places great emphasis on the 'regular' use of the computer, the 'regular' supply of information to the computer 'in the ordinary course of activities' and the fact that the computer was operating 'properly' (see the next paragraph for more detail). According to English commentators,[29] these conditions are

> 'painfully complex and verbose, particularly insofar as they make special provision for cases in which two or more computers are used in combination. They manage, at the same time, both to include unnecessary restrictions on the admissibility of reliable evidence, and to omit any safeguards against the use of computer evidence derived from potentially inaccurate human input.'

Another commentator speaks of it in equally scathing terms:

> 'Not only does it lay down conditions for admissibility which are both totally unnecessary and of Byzantine complexity, but it fails to provide adequate rules for the authentication of this evidence.'[30]

Tapper[31] is especially critical of the statute, particularly of s 5. Whereas some might see the lack of reported cases on these provisions as an endorsement of their effectiveness, he prefers the explanation that the reason might lie in 'the unnecessary complexity of the relevant provisions'. He criticizes the too wide definition of computer as 'any device for storing and processing information' and argues that the word 'computer' is by now an ordinary word in the English language and no

29 I Carr & K Williams *Computers and Law* (Intellect 1994) 167.

30 Chris Reed in the periodical *Computers and Law* (1990–1) at 13 with an article entitled 'The Admissibility and Authentication of Computer Evidence — A Confusion of Issues'.

31 Tapper *Computer Law* (4 ed) 395ff.

longer in need of special definition. Tapper's criticism is especially vehement on the omission by s 5 to require the originator of information to be processed by the computer, to have had personal knowledge of the truth of the information. This is required by s 2 and 4 of the same Act. Section 5(2)(*b*) and (2)(*d*) require the information to be supplied in the ordinary course of activities and s 5(2)(*a*) and (2)(*c*) require the computer to be 'used regularly' for this kind of activity and to be 'operating properly' during the material part of the relevant period.

A later section relating specifically to the evidential value of computer documents is 69 of the Police and Criminal Evidence Act (PACE) of 1984, which provides as follows:

> '69. (1) In any proceedings, a statement in a document produced by a computer shall not be admissible as evidence of any fact stated therein unless it is shown
>
> (*a*) that there are no reasonable grounds for believing that the statement is inaccurate because of improper use of the computer;
>
> (*b*) that at all material times the computer was operating properly, or if not, that any respect in which it was not operating properly or if not, cut of operation was not such as to affect the production of the document or the accuracy of its contents;'

Subsections 69(1)(*c*) and (2) provide for rules of court in this regard.

The two subsections cited above, seem to deal respectively with human fraud or error and with electronic or mechanical malfunction. At first blush this effort seems to contain more safeguards than previous Acts, in the sense that the onus is on the proponent of the computer evidence to prove (*a*) and (*b*). However, one fears that the two statements will simply be given as a matter of routine evidence, without really investigating possible weak points in the computer system.

After recommendations by the Roskill Committee, s 68 of PACE was repealed in favour of a new Criminal Justice Act (CJA) of 1988. Section 24 of this Act provides that documents arising from trade, business, professional, occupational or official activities which record information supplied by a person who had personal knowledge of the matters recorded, would be admissible in criminal proceedings provided that the provisions of s 23(2) and s 24(4)(iii) are complied with. The former deals with absent witnesses and the second with a witness who cannot be reasonably be expected to remember the matters contained in the record. Even when the latter requirement has been complied with by a computer-stored document, the provisions of s 69(1) of PACE (described above) still have to be met. On the other hand, neither would the fact that a document has complied with PACE exempt it from the s 24 requirements of the CJA. According to the decision in of *R v Minors*[32] both statutes have to be complied with for admissibility.

In an article entitled 'The Admissibility and Authentication of Computer Evidence — A Confusion of Issues',[33] the writer argues that it is time for both s 5 of the CEA and s 69 of the PACE to be abolished:

> 'Special rules for the admissibility of computer-related evidence can no longer be justified, particularly where those rules are based on false exemptions about the technology. It is also time to legislate for authentication. Important questions need to be answered. Can an electronic document be 'signed', and if so what will constitute a signature?[34] Can the parties to a communications network agree authentication procedures which will then be authenticated by the courts? Is a system log adequate evidence of the changes made to a record, and if so, what should it contain? It is beyond the scope of this article (and indeed the competence of the author) to put forward a draft Bill at this stage, but the longer the work on this topic is delayed the worse the position will become.'

Another article entitled 'Proving Computer Crime'[35] by Peter Sommer, foresees the end of s 69 of the PCA and s 5 of the CEA, because of a final report of the British Law Commission: *Evidence in Criminal Proceedings: Hearsay and Related Topics*.[36] According to these recommendations, business documents will be automatically admissible, 'document' and 'copy' will be more widely defined and judges will gain a judicial discretion to exclude on the basis of reliability. (One wonders if computer-illiterate judges might not need some firmer legislative guidance than this.) Sommer also seems to be worried about this:

> 'How are the courts to be helped with unfamiliar raw material and technical terminology in arriving at judgments about weight? What are the criteria for reliability, can we produce general guidelines, can there be standardized procedures for computer-derived exhibits as there are for many other classes of forensic material? In fact, the concept of 'reliability' contains within it all sorts of other ideas. Can we link the exhibit to the circumstances of the case and the person who is supposed to be responsible for it? Can we describe accurately to a lay audience, the salient aspects of how a computer system operates? Was the original data upon which the computer relies correct? Was the internal processing correct? It is often assumed that mistakes of processing are usually manifest, but there are plenty of contrary

32 [1989] 2 All ER 208.

33 By Chris Reed in (1990–1) July-August *Computer Law and Security Report* 13ff.

34 Meanwhile 'electronic signatures' have become commonplace, thanks to encryption.

35 In (August–September 1997) *Computers and Law* 29.

36 Report Law Com No 243 published in June 1997.

> indications. Again, how was data collected for specific evidential purposes? Was evidence altered during collection and forensic processing?'[37]

In the end he closes with not much more consolation than saying that 'these are heady and challenging times for all involved ..."(!)[38]

The latest piece of United Kingdom legislation has been the new Evidence Act of 1995, which is applicable to civil cases. This has enabled a broader interpretation of 'document' and 'copy' but the courts will still have to interpret the term 'authenticity'. It also seems to have disposed of the hearsay problem, at least in civil cases.

6.3.3 Case law

Some British case law, even though not involving computers directly, nevertheless had serious implications for the reception of computer evidence. Thus in *R v Pettigrew*[39] the matter turned on proof that notes with certain serial numbers had been stolen in a burglary. The court refused, however, to admit a printout of the Bank of England's computer as to the serial numbers of the notes, because no person had knowledge of the information produced by the computer! In a discussion of this case, J C Smith argues that this was not really hearsay evidence, put in to prove the truth of its contents, but real or direct evidence. He draws an analogy with the *Statue of Liberty* case, which dealt with evidence supplied by a radar apparatus and finds such evidence perfectly acceptable: 'Hearsay invariably relates to information which has passed through a human mind. Thus [sic] information never did so.'[40] Still, Professor Smith concedes that legislation might not be altogether such a bad thing. Another horror story has been the case of *Myers v Director of Public Prosecutions*,[41] where a car manufacturer's records about the serial numbers of stolen cars were not admitted, since the court found it to be hearsay. It is said that the Criminal Evidence Act of 1965 was passed directly as a result of the unfortunate outcome of the *Myers* case.

As has been shown, even the new legislation does not really provide sufficient safeguards for admissibility. The legislature, as it proposes further rules, would do well to remember the advice of Kelman & Sizer in their well-written, witty, yet informative book *The Computer in Court*.[42] After describing a fictitious case in which all kinds of computer evidential horrors crop up, they close with 'Seven Statements' which the ideal affidavit accompanying computer evidence should

37 Ibid.

38 Op cit 36.

39 (1980) 71 Cr App R 39.

40 'The Admisibility of Satements by Computer' (1981) *Criminal Law Review* 387.

41 [1965] AC 1001.

42 Alistair Kelman & Richard Sizer *The Computer in Court* (Gower 1982).

contain. These deal, inter alia, with the qualifications and experience of the person in charge of the computer system; a description of the computer system itself, the quality of the individual components; the testing and documentation standards of hardware and software, the procedures for logging updates to the software and the qualifications of the subordinate staff involved with the system, the physical and electronic security features of the installation, and a description of how the particular computer printout came into existence and what it purports to show.

Certain English cases have followed the Smith doctrine explained above, namely treating computer print-outs as real evidence and avoiding the hearsay rule in this way. Examples of these are *R v Wood*[43] and *R v Ewing.*[44]In discussing these cases, C J Millard[45]finds that their *rationes*[46]

> 'suggest that the degree to which data are generated by a computer without human intervention will be determinative of whether a printout is admissible as real evidence, or alternatively is hearsay which must be brought within a statutory exception to be admissible.'

Tapper[47] also comments favourably on the case:

> 'The court explained that here the computer was being used only as a calculator, and did not purport to reproduce any human assertion which had been entered into it. Where it was so used the court held that its output was just as admissible, and with as little reliance on the hearsay rule as any calculation performed by a witness for the purposes of giving evidence, for example using a sliderule or a weighing machine.'

A House of Lords case turning on s 69 of the PACE Act was *R v Shepherd.*[48] The facts were that the appellant had been convicted of stealing food and clothing from a branch of Marks & Spencers.[49] She had been convicted in the court *a quo* largely on the evidence of a store detective who testified that the tills showed no sign of malfunction at the time of arrest, which malfunction might have explained the appellant's lack of a sales slip. Lord Griffiths upheld the conviction, mentioning that computer law cases varied and that one did not need an expert in every case. In *Sophocleus v Ringer*[50] it was held that s 69 would not apply if persons only used a computer in preparing for their oral evidence. The witness, a Home Office

43 (1983) Cr App R23.

44 [1983] 2 All ER 645.

45 Christopher J Millard *Legal Protection of Computer Programs and Data* (Sweet & Maxwell 1985) 166.

46 Plural of *ratio*, which means the main reason for deciding a case.

47 Op cit (1989) 376.

48 [1993] 1 All ER 225.

49 A large English department store.

50 [1988] RTR 52.

analyst, was accordingly permitted to refresh her memory from the printout of a computer which she had used, without bringing s 69 into play.[51] This case may, on the other hand, be explained by the fact that the computer had only performed numeric calculations and might therefore have been treated by the court as real evidence.[52] In *R v Spiby*[53] it was held clearly that s 69 would not apply to real evidence, as opposed to hearsay statements (printouts treated as documents).

6.3.4 The question of optical storage

Given the lack of storage space for documents, the possibility of misfiling and the difficulty of finding them, many companies have decided to store their documents optically on a WORM[54] or CD-ROM[55] system. Almost without exception, these companies are all very scared that the print-out may not be acceptable in court because it is not the original (best evidence) which is being tendered, and because it may be regarded as hearsay and as not having been properly authenticated.

In an article by Kenneth Toombs entitled 'The Legal Admissibility of Electronic documents — Five Years On'[56] the spectrum of English standards-related guidance is discussed. There is BS7768 (the BSI[57] standard), PD008 — the Code of Practice that accompanies BS 7768 and PD 009 — the Workbook that accompanies the Code. From personal interviews with judges confronted with the admissibility of the print-out of an electronically stored document, Toombs is convinced that judges need 'clear and unambiguous authentication' of the source of this type of document. He refers, inter alia, to the standards suggested by Kelman & Sizer (see above). He is also concerned as a result of a trend among major users of EDM[58] to try and work around PD008 because it slows them down too much and they lose the typical speed of processing documents which EDM brings. He warns these 'super-users' of the dangers of skirting proper procedure and legislators and also warns legislators 'that ever stricter and tighter conformance may, through people's perceptions, turn organizations away from the principles of BS7768 and back into the land of uncertainty that many have now left'.

51 See Karr & Williams *Computers and the Law*.

52 See Chris Reed's article at 13.

53 *The Times* 16 March 1990.

54 Acronym for write once read many (times).

55 Compact Disc Read Only Memory. (The term has become misleading because even compact disks have become rewritable and are therefore no longer 'read only'.)

56 In (1996/97) *Computers and Law* 30ff.

57 Acronym for *British Standards Institute*.

58 Acronym for Electronic Document Management.

6.4 OTHER COUNTRIES AND INTERNATIONAL AND SUPRANATIONAL LAW

6.4.1 Australia

Special mention must be made of Australia under this heading, because of its special treatment of computer evidence. Whereas the state of Victoria had simply re-enacted s 5 of the English Act described above, the state of South Australia has inserted a new part entitled 'Computer Evidence' into its Evidence Act. By Act 9 of 1979 these provisions were extended to criminal cases. According to the first edition of Tapper[59] any legislature wishing to enact similar legislation would do well to consider the provisions of the South Australian Evidence Act. He finds it far superior to the English provisions for the following reasons.

Whereas the English Civil Evidence Act defined computer too widely as 'any device for storing and processing information', the Australian Act picks out the special characteristics that distinguish computers from other machines in its definition of 'computer'as:

> 'a device that is by electronic, electro-mechanical, mechanical, or other means capable of recording and processing data according to mathematical and logical rules and of reproducing that data or mathematical or logical consequences thereof'.[60]

Tapper also prefers the Australian Act's definition of 'input' and 'output'. Whereas the English Act simply sees the former as 'information' the Australian Act prefers to speak of 'data'[61] which is defined as 'a statement or representation of fact that has been transcribed by methods, the accuracy of which is verifiable, into the form appropriate to the computer into which it is, or is to be, introduced'. The Australian Act defines 'output' as 'a statement or representation (whether in written, pictorial, graphical or other form) purporting to be a statement or representation of fact—(*a*) produced by computer; or (*b*) accurately translated from a statement or representation so produced'. Tapper sees the main advantage of the Australian definitions in the fact that 'it avoids entirely the language of documents and copies of documents',[62] a concept which the English statute had particular trouble defining.

---

59 See in general Tapper (1 ed) 168ff.

60 Section 59a of the Australian Act.

61 Kelman & Sizer op cit 22n6 argue that 'data' and 'information' are different from one another in that the former is tangible, the latter not. They quote as follows from the Report of the Data Protection Committee: 'Information is the knowledge conveyed to the mind by a statement of fact, and it is not therefore susceptible of ownership.' The matter is debated in the first chapter of the present work.

62 Op cit 169.

The gravest complaint which Tapper makes against the English statute is its 'total lack of control over the reliability of the information'.[63] As long as anyone[64] would have been able to give oral evidence as to the matters sought to be put in from the computer, the computer's evidence would be admissible. By contrast, the Australian statute requires the court to be satisfied 'that the data from which the output is produced by the computer is systematically prepared upon the basis of information that would normally be acceptable as evidence of the statements or representations contained in or constituted by the output'.[65] In other words, the data would have to be checked against someone's personal knowledge for accuracy before the court would accept the computer evidence.

It is interesting to note Tapper's feelings towards the South Australian legislation 11 years later. Having originally praised it as a triumph of drafting skill, he now has to concede that the track record of the statute has not been that great. In the last edition of his *Computers and Law*[66] he still lauds the legislation:

> 'these provisions seem to have been drafted by someone who had given careful consideration to section 5 of the English Civil Procedure Act, 1968, but had decided to re-draft them so as to address deficiencies both in relation to understanding computer methodology and terminology and in relation to legal adequacy.'

Nevertheless, he has to admit that notwithstanding the quality of the statute, the South Australian Supreme Court has twice found itself unable to admit print-outs under its provisions 'because of its lack of satisfaction in these matters'.

6.4.2 International developments

In the treatment of computer evidence in the first edition of the present work, the present author found that the Report of the Secretary-General of the United Nations Commission on International Trade Law (UNCITRAL)[67] gave valuable insights into the comparable evidential problems experienced by the civil-law systems.

The report first distinguishes between three types of transaction-orientated business records, namely:

(*a*) originals or copies of transaction documents;

---

63 Op cit 170.

64 In other words, someone not necessarily having personal knowledge of the facts he or she was deposing to.

65 Section 59*b*(2)(*b*).

66 Op cit (4 ed) 398.

67 Reported by Senior Legal Officer Eric E Bergsten in the July–August 1985 issue of *Computer Law and Practice* at 205.

(*b*) chronological records of transactions, such as a log of incoming communications; or

(*c*) summary records of transactions, such as an accounting ledger.

Whereas the latter two categories may also be important, the report sees the transaction documents themselves as having the ultimate legal significance.

A distinction is then made between paper-based documents and records and electronic ones. The former have the advantage of being durable and portable, but most important, also the security advantage that alterations of the documents or records may easily be detected and that the documents or records can be authenticated by signature or other means. This is the Achilles' heel of electronic documents and the area where one of their greatest advantages, the fact that they are easily updated and altered, count against them. These alterations may be made by unauthorized outsiders gaining access to the system or, even more difficult to detect, by the enterprise itself for unauthorized reasons such as tax evasion or fraud on its shareholders. Another supposed advantage, the fact that there are no requirements for storage space as there would be with paper documents, would be neutralized if the enterprise were to keep all its paper records anyhow as a forensic backup.

Keeping these problems in mind, the report then deals with criteria for the admissibility and credibility of computer records. After comparing the civil- and common-law systems of the law of evidence, the report concludes that there is no need for a unification of the rules of evidence regarding the use of computer records in international trade. According to the report, there are traditional differences in the bases of adjudication, to which the rules of evidence are closely tied, and these differences.have caused no noticeable harm to the development of international trade. Even though the common-law countries have problems with the hearsay rule and the rule of best evidence, most such countries have adopted or are adopting special laws providing that computer records may be admitted if certain conditions are fulfilled. 'As a result of these developments, there are no remaining theoretical or philosophical objections to the use of computer records as evidence in common-law jurisdictions.'[68] The problems with reliability of the evidence are the same in both systems and may be addressed by keeping original paper-based documents for limited periods, say for two years. The report also had high hopes of future technology, such as optical disks, which can store data in unalterable form (this was written before the day of the re-writable CD-ROMs). The best evidence rule is dealt with by a recommendation that the rules of evidence be amended to provide that a printout could be considered an original record.

68 Op cit 210.

What bothered the commission most were outdated requirements that certain documents had to be in writing or had to be authenticated by handwritten signature and it accordingly recommended to governments to take these measures under review.

Nowadays most development in the rules on electronic evidence takes place as a result of the perceived increase in e-commerce that is going to take place 'real soon now. The authentication problem is taken care of by an 'electronic signature', which is brought about by encryption. Most international developments are tracked by Patrick van Eecke in a *Memorie van Toeligting*[69] in which he points out two new European initiatives in this regard, namely one dealing specifically with e-commerce[70] as well as one dealing with the safety of, and trust in, electronic communications.[71] He also mentions some UNCITRAL initiatives, for instance a model law on e-commerce. In s 7 of the model law new techniques of authentication are explored, for instance, passwords, biometric recognition and cryptography. The last is manifested in digital signatures, which seem to be the most useful model since they most closely approximate the functionality of manual signatures. The whole system of a Public Key Infrastructure (PKI), which supports the digital signatures is explored by Jos Dumortier & Patrick van Eecke in an article entitled 'Naar een juridische regeling van de digitale handtekening in België'.[72]

The matter of e-commerce is more completely explored in the section on e-commerce in the final chapter of this book, whereas the question of digital signatures is expanded upon in the South African section below.

6.5 SOUTH AFRICA

6.5.1 The Civil Proceedings and Evidence Act

The centrepiece of the South African law of computer evidence has been, and still is, the Computer Evidence Act.[73] In adopting specific computer legislation, South Africa has surpassed a few more 'senior' countries such as the United Kingdom, and the legislation has already attracted attention in internationally known works such as Tapper's *Computer Law*. Nevertheless the new law has caused considerable controversy, to say the least, and some people believe that the difficulties attendant on its application are making it quite useless. The Computer

69 Roughly translated as 'a protocol of information'; unpublished: communicated to the author personally.

70 Com (97) 157.

71 Com (97) 503.

72 Roughly translated as 'Towards a juridical regulation of the digital signature in Belgium' in *Computerrecht* (1997) 154–9.

73 Act 57 of 1983.

Evidence Act also does not apply to criminal cases, so that an overview of the South African position before the Act may also be in order.

After a particularly 'hard case',[74] in which the respondent sought to lead evidence about the results of a search which one of its officials had made of a government department's records but the evidence was still excluded as hearsay, the position was finally alleviated by Part VI of the (then) new Civil Proceedings and Evidence Act.[75] This brought about a substantial exception to the hearsay rule as the following provision illustrates:

'34. Admissibility of documentary evidence as to facts in issue

(1) In any civil proceedings where direct oral evidence of a fact would be admissible, any statement made by a person in a document and tending to establish that fact shall on production of the original document be admissible as evidence of that fact, provided—

(a) the person who made the statement either—

(i) has personal knowledge of the matters dealt with in the statement; or

(ii) where the document in question is or forms part of a record purporting to be a continuous record, made the statement (in so far as the matters dealt with therein are not within his personal knowledge) in the performance of a duty to record information supplied to him by a person who had or might reasonably be supposed to have personal knowledge of those matters; and

(b) the person who made the statement is called as a witness in the proceedings unless he is dead or unfit by reason of his bodily or mental condition to attend as a witness or is outside the Republic, and it is not reasonably practical to secure his attendance or all reasonable efforts to find him have been made without success.'

Subsection 34(2) gives the presiding officer an overriding discretion still to admit the above-mentioned statement, notwithstanding the fact that the person who made the statement was available and yet was not called as a witness, or that only a copy of the original document was tendered, if 'he is satisfied that undue delay or expense would otherwise be caused'.

74 The saying goes that 'hard cases make bad law'. The case in question was *Vulcan Rubber Works (Pty) Ltd) v SAR and H* 1958 (3) SA 285 (A).

75 Act 25 of 1965. This Act was broadly based on the English Evidence Act of 1938, which means it was rather out of date to start with. See the section on the United Kingdom above.

In s 33 'document' is defined as including 'any book, map, plan, drawing or photograph'. The whole Act was obviously inspired by the old English Evidence Act of 1938 and suffers from the same primary defect pointed out in my discussion of English law above, namely that the definition of 'document' is not wide enough to include computers. As M E French has put it: 'It is submitted that the Civil Proceedings and Evidence Act cannot include computer-generated evidence although the Act caters well for the traditional record-keeping process.'[76] The limitations of this Act for computer-held evidence were well exposed in *Narlis v South African Bank of Athens*[77] and pressure as a result of this decision led to the adoption of the controversial Computer Evidence Act of 1983.

Before the latter Act, which applies only in civil matters, is discussed, mention must be made of the situation in criminal trials as far as computer evidence is concerned. The situation is governed by ss 221 and 222 of the Criminal Procedure act.[78] Although also based on the English model, it has managed to avoid many of the computer-related pitfalls which has laid low the South African Civil Proceedings Evidence Act. To start off with, the definition of 'document' seems wide enough to encompass computers and their storage devices, viz 'any device by means of which information is recorded or stored'.[79] Even though it might have been better to do as the Australians have done, and do away with the idea of 'documents' altogether, the present definition does not rule out computers immediately.

In the second place s 221(1) speaks of 'any statement contained in a document' instead of the Civil Proceedings Evidence Act's corresponding 'any statement *made by a person*[80]contained in a document', thus neatly avoiding the fatal objection in the *Narlis* case that a computer is not a person.

Finally, s 221 is confined to business records, but s 222 makes the relevant sections of the Civil Proceedings Evidence Act *mutatis mutandis* applicable to criminal proceedings, for what it might be worth. Probably not much as far as computers are concerned!

As far as business records are concerned, therefore, we have an overlap, but s 221 seems to contain more promise for computers. The situation is bleak in criminal cases where non-business computer records are sought to be admitted, since the *Narlis* case has already exposed the shortcomings of the civil provisions which s 222 imports into the Criminal Procedure Act. French is of the opinion that even s 221 is wholly unsuited to the problems of computer-based litigation and that it will not help to counter the growing upsurge in computer crime. He

76 1982/83 *Natal University Law Review* 112 at 121.

77 1976 (2) SA 573 (A).

78 Act 51 of 1977.

79 Section 221(5) of Act 51 of 1977.

80 My emphasis.

is all in favour of legislation specially tailored to accommodate computers. It might be mentioned in passing that the South African criminal procedure sections discussed above are based on s 1 of the English Criminal Evidence Act of 1965, which has in the meanwhile been supplanted by the Police and Criminal Evidence Act of 1984, which latter Act has been discussed in the section on the United Kingdom above. Even the 1984 Act is not completely suitable and could be on its way out, which shows how far behind we really are in South Africa.

6.5.2 The Computer Evidence Act

We come, then, to the Computer Evidence Act. There is little doubt that its genesis lay in the decision of *Narlis v South African Bank of Athens.*[81] In this case the bank sought to put in evidence extracted from its computerized records to show that the respondent had an overdraft with them. The bank was unable to utilize s 28 of the Civil Proceedings Evidence Act (which makes specific provision for entries in bankers' books to be admitted in evidence) because of s 33 of the same Act which precludes this possibility, if the bank is one of the parties to the litigation in which the evidence is sought to be used. The bank therefore tried to avail itself of s 34, which has already been discussed above. As explained, there the section is applicable only to 'any statement made by a person' and, as Holmes JA remarked: 'Well, a computer, perhaps fortunately, is not a person.' Although this effectively disposed of the case, he proceeded to show other dangers inherent in accepting the bank's evidence.

There was, for instance, no evidence as to how the computer operated, who operated it, and who fed information into it. The personal surveillance of the witness with regard to the matters he was deposing to was minimal and he did not say that he had checked the opening debits of the computerized accounts, the correctness of the interest charged or the rate charged. the other debits shown on the computerized accounts or the correctness of certain other figures.

The outcome of the case caused great unhappiness and uncertainty in the banking community, most of whom make extensive use of computers for record-keeping purposes, and the Clearing Banker's Association instructed a South African judge, Justice Didcott (as he then was), to prepare a report and draft bill on their behalf. This was presented to the South African Law Commission, which in turn presented a 'Report on the Admissibility in Civil Proceedings of Evidence Generated by Computers'[82] to the Minister of Justice. Finally, the Computer Evidence Act 57 of 1983 came into force during 1983. Tapper[83] gives an interesting outsider's perspective on the genesis of the Act at the hands of Justice Didcott:

81 Supra.

82 Project 6, dated April 1983.

83 Op cit (4 ed) 400.

> 'He first considered the possibility of following the American model, and essentially leaving it to the judiciary to develop a suitable exception to the hearsay rule. He rejected this solution, partly because there was, in South Africa, no firmly established shopbook exception upon which to build, and partly because of the more conservative approach of the judiciary in South Africa. He went on to assess the relative merits of generic and specific legislation, coming down in favour of specific legislation, largely because he took the view that a very sharp distinction existed between computer-derived records and those of different provenance.'

Tapper also understood Didcott J to favour expanding admissibility but leaving the assessment of weight to the judges, 'with as little interference from the legislature as possible'.[84]

The preamble to the 1982 report contains some interesting remarks concerning the background to the legislation. The commission found s 34 of Act 25 of 1965 to be unsuitable for computerized records because it prescribes personal knowledge of the matters dealt with in the statement, the Act ruled out statements not made in the ordinary course of business (which ruled out statements specially prepared for litigation), and as a general rule the maker had to be called as a witness, if available. The latter consideration is perhaps not quite as pertinent as the others—s 34(2) does give the presiding officer a discretion to dispense with the calling of the witness if he or she was satisfied that undue delay or expense would otherwise be caused.

The commission also did not feel disposed to extend the applicability of the new Act to criminal proceedings because unrepresented accused would not be able to give an informed consent to, or be able to oppose effectively, computer evidence put in against them. Also, the consequences of criminal proceedings are far more serious, because the liberty of the individual might be at stake. Another interesting point made was that criminal proceedings do not provide for the discovery and inspection of documents, something which is pretty controversial even in civil proceedings, as the furore around Anton Piller orders has shown! The latter seems to be a typical computer remedy[85] and one should therefore welcome the latest Appellate Division decision[86] that has given these orders the green light, provided adequate precautions are taken against abuse.

Although the commission was aware of the need for safeguards, as 'computers are the object of deep public suspicion', it felt that overseas efforts in this regard have simply given rise to complicated legislation without really achieving their

---

84 Ibid.

85 Speed and secrecy are needed because the evidence can be deleted so quickly!

86 *Universal City Studios v Network Video* 1986 (2) SA 623 (A).

object.[87] At any rate, the commission felt that these objections also applied to conventional records and that this was 'in any event not a matter that ought to be regulated by the law of evidence'.[88] This lack of safeguards is the downfall of the legislation — a point that will be returned to later.

Finally, the commission justified the exemption of public records from the stringency of the criteria of admissibility, because of inconvenience to the public service and the unlikelihood that the latter would attempt a fraud on the public. My problem with this argument is that most computer errors are caused by negligent human error or by computer malfunction and state computers are no more immune to this than private computers. Perhaps the commission should have considered the provisions of s 34(2) of Act 25 of 1965 and have given the presiding officer a discretion to dispense with the calling as a witness of a public servant if 'undue delay or expense' would be involved.

The mechanism of the Act works as follows. Section 3 provides that in civil proceedings 'an authenticated computer print-out shall be admissible on its production as evidence of any fact recorded in it of which direct oral evidence would be admissible'. Section 2 sets out the procedure by which such a printout may be authenticated and this also contains the safeguards as to the accuracy of the facts to which the printout deposes. Great reliance is placed on an affidavit by a person

> 'qualified to give the testimony it contains by reason of—
>
> (*a*) his knowledge and experience of computers and of the particular system by which the computer in question was operated at all relevant times; and
>
> (*a*) his examination of all relevant records and facts which are to be had concerning the operation of the computer and the data and instructions supplied to it'.

The deponent should be suitably awed by the provisions of s 5, which makes him or her guilty of an offence if he or she gives evidence in the affidavit which is false or misleading in any material respect. Negligence appears to be sufficient *mens rea* for the offence which carries a penalty of a fine not exceeding R4 000, or imprisonment for a period not exceeding two years, or to both. Section 1 contains a few interesting definitions such as those of 'computer', which corresponds with the definition in the South Australian Act quoted above, except for a few minor changes, and 'computer print-out', which means 'the documentary form in which information is produced by a computer or a copy or reproduction of it, and includes, whenever any information needs to be transcribed, translated

87 Project 6 4.10.

88 Ibid.

or interpreted after its production by the computer in order that it may take a documentary form and be intelligible to the court, a transcription, translation or interpretation of it which is calculated to have that effect'. The latter definition is quite important as the 'print-out' seems to be considered the only form in which computer-held evidence can be admitted to court.

6.5.3 Reaction to the Computer Evidence Act

Reaction to the new legislation has been varied, although no cases have been reported on it as yet — after 13 years! Even though Staniland questions whether any one person will have sufficient knowledge of all the various subsystems and their controls in a computer of any size or complexity and therefore be really qualified to make the required affidavit, he feels that the Act 'has, at last it seems, brought South African law abreast of the needs and practices of the business community' and 'that it is a vast improvement on the previous situation is without doubt'.[89] French has the same doubts: 'Furthermore, it can be said, that as computer security is tightened, fewer persons will comprehend the whole operation of the computer, and it may be difficult to find a person who will qualify to make the 'authenticating affidavit".[90] Nevertheless he feels that the courts will be able to get around these problems and that 'such defects are relatively minor in the face of the possible strides made by this long overdue legislation'.[91]

Skeen[92] also concentrates on the contents of the affidavit as prescribed by s 2 of the Act, and mentions that errors in the output of a computer can develop in a number of ways and may be caused by unrelated factors such as faulty air-conditioning and changes in voltage.[93] Some faults may develop only when particular software is interacting with particular hardware.[94] This could make it impossible for anyone to certify that 'the computer was unaffected by any malfunction, interference, disturbance or interruption which might have had a bearing on such information or its reliability' as is required by s 2(1)(*d*)(ii), especially when the guarantee has to cover a fair span of time. Seeing that the identity of the computer operator might also be unknown it would be impossible to evaluate his reliability, motives to misrepresent 'and other human variables that may affect the correct and competent handling of the computer'.[95] Nevertheless, Skeen also feels that the "Act is to be welcomed despite the possible dangers discussed above'.[96]

89 (1985) September/October *Computer Law and Practice* 21 at 24.

90 1982–83 *Natal University Law Review* 112 at 123.

91 Ibid.

92 At St Q Skeen 686.

93 The dreaded electronic 'spike'.

94 The feared 'fatal embrace'.

95 'Evidence and Computers' (1984) 101 *South African Law Journal* at 675.

96 Op cit 688.

In the 1983 *South African Law Journal* commentary is less positive. Steele is sceptical about the commissioners' 'understanding of matters computing'. He feels that, whereas it might be appropriate for the physical printout to be merely identified by means of affidavit, 'it certainly seems inappropriate for the accuracy and reliability of its contents to he authenticated by this means'.[97] He then suggests that the latter task may be undertaken only by a chief executive officer.

In the 1983 *Obiter* the criticism is even harsher. Delport analyses the Act with a fine-tooth comb and finds confusion. Many of his problems are caused by a human 'transcription, translation or interpretation' of a print-out, which products will, strictly speaking, not be admissible in terms of s 2, which requires that the print-out must have been produced by a computer.[98] This situation is not likely to be very common in practice as a computer can usually do all the translating and printing (transcription) that is necessary. Nevertheless, his point is well made that the legislator should have concentrated on the authenticity of the *information* contained in the affidavit, rather than to have cast everything in the strait-jacket of a technically interpreted 'print-out', which is the only way to get the evidence before court.[99] Subsections (4) and (5) s 2 add to the confusion with their requirement that the deponent has to 'verify' the records and facts concerning the operation of the computer and the data and instructions supplied to it. As Delport points out, the idea was probably to verify *his examination* of these records. Although a sympathetic court might be able to bridge some of the gaps with an interpretation *ut res magis valeat quam pereat*,[100] these deficiencies are unlikely to inspire much confidence in the Act among prospective litigants. The fact that there have as yet been no reported cases on the Act may be an ominous sign that banks are bypassing the provisions of the Act by having their computer records informally accepted by contracting for it.

Still, I find the most cogent criticism of the Act to be that of a computer scientist, Ebden, who asks:

> 'When your house is not in order, do you put it in order, or do you change the law so as to define it as being in order? It is remarkable that the draftsmen of the new legislation appear to have ignored an avalanche of evidence that the house of computing is not necessarily in order.'[101]

He points out that the requirement could have been set that books should have been audited, expresses the fear that some opinion evidence may come out of

---

97 J T Steel 'Computer-produced Print-out Reliable as Evidence' (1983) 100 *SALJ* 510.

98 J T Delport 'Die Wet op Rekenaargetuienis' 1983 *Obiter* 140.

99 Delport op cit 142ff.

100 Literally, 'that the matter may be strong, rather than that it should perish' — in other words, a translation in favour of validity.

101 A J Eben 'Computer Evidence in Court' (1985) 102 *SALJ* 687 at 688.

the computer looking like factual evidence and echoes the fears of the previous authors mentioned, that it would be virtually impossible for anyone to authenticate an affidavit, as meant in s 2, with any degree of confidence. He is also sceptical about the solution of Smith, mentioned in the section on the United Kingdom, that this type of evidence can be treated as real evidence, like evidence from a radar speed trap, for example. The computer is much more complex because it has to perform a variety of functions instead of one and he finds this 'in itself a significant difference', which he then illustrates with some practical examples.[102]

In closing, Ebden suggests some improvements, with the 'seven statements' of Kelman & Sizer as a good starting point.[103] (See the section on the United Kingdom above.) To this he adds the possible creation of categories of acceptability based on the reliability of the data concerned. Only the most reliable categories should then be acceptable in criminal cases. He also suggests that only disinterested deponents should be used. The Act itself and commentator Steele[104] suggest that an employee of the firm concerned should be used, but this could lead to a massive conflict of interest—Ebden would prefer independent auditors to be used. He also feels that public computers are as error-prone as private computers[105] and should therefore not be partially exempted, that it should be specified what computer controls were in operation at the particular installation, that original documents should be kept in certain cases, and that the source of important information be recorded to enable non-expert opinion to be recognized for what it is.

One of the latest works on evidence in South Africa, by Schwikkard, Skeen & Van der Merwe,[106] tabulates the problems they see arising out of the Computer Evidence Act. These are a lack of sufficient supervision by the data-processing manager (who has to certify that the computer-stored evidence is correct), the multiple causes of error in a computer system and the difficulty of identifying and evaluating the 'computer operator in question'.[107] As to the question of concentrating on the weight of the evidence rather than on its admissibility (as Didcott J suggested), the authors are not very optimistic: 'Suspicions may be swept under

102 Op cit 693.

103 Op cit 694.

104 (1983) 100 *SALJ* 505 at 510.

105 See my argument above.

106 P J Schwikkard, A St Q Skeen & S E van der Merwe *Principles of Evidence* (Juta 1997) 270–1.

107 The last statement seems slightly naive in the light of present practice, where almost all computers in an enterprise are connected to each other by means of a local area network (LAN) to which each user has access. Does this make each of them a 'computer operator'? If so, at least the network manager should be able to keep tabs on each user logged onto the network.

the carpet by a bland and reassuring affidavit made by someone who cannot possibly speak on all the surrounding circumstances.'[108]

6.5.4 Life outside the Computer Evidence Act

In this section some attention will be given to the situation in criminal law, to which the Computer Evidence Act has never applied, and some attempt will be made to look at the way forward after the possible repeal of the Computer Evidence Act.

In the case of *S v Harper & another*[109] the prosecution tried to prove certain documents of account relating to a company's affairs, which documents had been partly stored on computer. The accountant who had been dealing with the books was overseas and it would have been very difficult to call her as a witness. Milne J considered the definition of 'document' in s 221 (5) of the Criminal Procedure Act[110] and found that this definition (as a device which stores or records evidence) would not accommodate a computer, since it also sorts and collates evidence. Hoffmann & Zeffertt[111] therefore deduce from this case that 'a computer printout produced by a computer that sorted and collated information would not be admissible'.[112]

The authors' statement was tested in the case of *S v De Villiers*,[113] which, although decided in Namibia, was decided in terms of principles equally valid in South Africa. Here O'Linn J found that Hoffmann & Zeffertt's conclusion was based on an incomplete assessment of the *Harper* case. Even though Milne J had found in *Harper* that the s 221(5) definition of 'document' was not applicable, s 221(1) simply speaks of 'a document', and it was held in *Harper* that this 'ordinary' definition was wide enough to include a computer printout (even one where the information has been sorted and collated) and that this would be admissible provided that the other requirements of s 221 had been satisfied. These were roughly that direct or oral evidence of a fact be admissible, that a statement is contained in a document, that the statement tends to establish that fact, that the document is produced, that the document forms part of a record relating to any trade or business, that it was compiled in the course of that trade or business from information supplied by persons with personal knowledge of the matters concerned. Finally, that the person concerned (who supplied the information contained in the statement) is dead, or outside the Republic or unfit by reason

---

108 Op cit at 24.

109 1981 (1) SA 88 (D).

110 Act 51 of 1977.

111 L H Hoffmann & D T Zeffertt *The South African Law of Evidence* 4 ed by D T Zeffertt (Juta 1988) 142.

112 Ibid.

113 1993 (1) SACR 574 (Nm).

of mental of physical condition to attend, or cannot (with reasonable diligence) be identified or found, or cannot now be expected to have any recollection of the matters dealt with in the information he supplied then. Given this state of the law, O'Linn J applied it to the facts and found computer print-outs to be 'duplicate originals' and therefore admissible.[114]

The position with regard to criminal law therefore seems to be reasonably clear, provided that a computer print-out complies with the prerequisites set out by Milne J in the *Harper* case.

6.5.5 Optical storage

Another field leading to complications has already been raised above in connection with the United Kingdom, namely that of optical storage. This was one of the problems raised with the South African Law Commission's attempt to redraft the Computer Evidence Act towards the end of December 1995. The present writer indicated in representations to the Law Commission that their attempt to introduce a version of the shopbook rule to replace the present Computer Evidence Act would not clarify the position of computer-imaged documents in optical storage, nor provide for future developments such as the Internet. It would therefore be out of date almost before it is promulgated. I was joined in my representations by Mark Heyink, who prepared certain memoranda for submission to the Law Commission. The gist of both our submissions was that the proposed changes did not consider the most recent developments in technology whereas this was a golden opportunity to do so:

> 'In reading through the recommendations, however, the words "imaging", "video" and "voice recording" are not even mentioned while "EDI" is referred to briefly in half a page of the document which is approximately 150 pages long.'[115]

The matter was then referred by the South African Law Commission to the South African Rules Board, to find out if the matter could not conveniently be disposed of there. Heyink and I had a meeting with Zulman J, the head of the Rules Board, on 5 December 1996 to voice again our concerns. It was pointed out that the Rules Board was probably not the ideal body to work with these matters since the matters raised were too complex. First, admissibility of computer documents was not the only concern, but how the weight of these could be gauged accurately by presiding officers who might be computer illiterate. Secondly there were a number of statutes which require records and documents to be kept for a determinate time and also required these documents to be kept in a certain format (which often did not provide for computer-stored documents.) This required a review of South African

114 Supra at 579.

115 Letter from Mark Heyink to the SA Law Commission dated 3 May 1996.

statute law, which was not really the task of the Rules Board. Zulman J agreed and the matter was referred back to the South African Law Commission, where it still lingers, although the present commission on computer crime will need to look at evidential matters, at least in criminal cases.

6.5.6 Digital signatures

One of the greatest problems in handling computer-stored documents is the question of authentication. Presiding officers now have a discretion to admit hearsay evidence and one could probably work around the best evidence rule in some way, but the matter which is most critical is whether we can duplicate the authentication (and other) functions of a plain old signature at the bottom of a document.

Human (or holographic) signatures have served to ensure integrity, authentication and non-repudiation with regard to documents to which they have been affixed. Integrity means that the document has not been changed since signing; authentication means that the source (author) of the document is clear and non-repudiation means that the person signing expresses a commitment to honour the undertakings preceding his signature in the document.

The most feasible way in which these functions can be replicated electronically (for documents transported via the Internet or other computer networks) is by means of a so-called "electronic signature". This is a form of encryption where the whole plaintext document is changed into unreadable ciphered text and "signed" by using a special cryptographic key. Symmetric encryption means that both the transmitting and receiving partners have to be in possession of a common secret key in order that the one can encode and the other decode. There are several problems attached to this procedure. In the first place it is very difficult to exchange these keys without the risk of third parties becoming privy to the key and thus becoming a security risk which could compromise the digital signature. It also works better between two parties who regularly contract with each other than in the case of one party which has to stay in contact with a multitude of other net users.

In the latter instance, asymmetric encryption may prove to be a better solution. Here the transmitting party has two cryptographic keys, a public key and a private key. The private key is known only to the transmitter and he uses this to encrypt his message and then to digitally 'sign' it. His public key is mathematically related to the private key although the one cannot be discovered from the other. The public key may be published to third parties (on the Internet, for instance) and may then be used by the third parties to decode the message and to ascertain that it was, in fact, signed by the holder of the private key. The whole topic is much more complex than this, but it should be clear from this brief explanation that the old functions of the human signature can be performed even better by the digital signature. It also includes some unexpected benefits, such as protection of privacy, which a postcard or a steamed-open envelope could never guarantee.

The question now arises: will the South African law accept digital signatures in the place of human signatures? In order to reach a conclusion, a review of South African legislation and case law with regard to the role of a signature might be appropriate.

Ordinance 15 of 1845 of the Cape dealt with the formalities with regard to wills and required the following for a valid will, namely that it:

> '... be executed in the manner hereinafter mentioned; that is to say it shall be or shall have been signed at the foot or end thereof in a will or other testamentary writing by the testator or by some other person in his presence or by his direction ... and such signature shall be or shall have been made or acknowledged by the testator ... in the presence of two or more competent witnesses present at the same time, and such witnesses shall attest and subscribe and shall have attested and subscribed the will in the presence of the person executing the same; and where the instrument shall be or shall have been written upon more leaves than one, the party executing the same and also the witnesses shall sign or shall have signed their names upon at least once side of every leaf upon which the instrument shall or shall have been written'.

In the corresponding Ordinances in Natal, the Transvaal and the Orange Free State, however, provision was also made for the testator to sign by way of a 'mark'. From the Free State Ordinance, 11 of 1904, it becomes obvious that this provision was probably intended to cover persons who could not write (and therefore sign their own names), since it provided that the mark be 'made in the presence of and attested by a justice of the peace and two witnesses', (This could count against electronic encryption or even a mouse-click being seen as a 'mark' and therefore acceptable in law as a 'signature'.)

One of the first cases which judicially considered these statutory provisions was that of *Van Vuuren v Van Vuuren*,[116] where the majority of the court held a will to be invalid where the testator and one of the two witnesses simply initialled the first page but signed fully on the second page of a will. Bell J wrote a lengthy minority dissenting judgment in which he found that the Cape statute was similar to British legislation (which had been interpreted to be satisfied with initials or any other mark made with the intention of signing). He therefore found that a

116 2 Searle 116.

cross or a mark would be an adequate signature, particularly in the case of an illiterate or disabled person, and that if a mark was sufficient, so would initials be. (According to this more liberal interpretation, even an electronic signature could be held to be equivalent to 'any other mark', and therefore acceptable in law.)

The more liberal tradition in interpreting 'signature' triumphed later on in the case of *In re Trollip*,[117] decided in 1895, in which the majority judgment in *Van Vuuren* was overruled. It was held that the initials of a testatrix and of witnesses on the first page of a will which was duly signed at the end thereof were sufficient and adequate. However, in 1953, the Wills Act,[118] came into force and again (like the old Cape Ordinance) made no provision for marks. The omission by the legislature was held by the court in *Dempers v The Master(1)*[119] to overrule the more liberal approach in the *Trollip* case. Hart AJP looked at definitions in dictionaries, for instance:

> "Sign' bears the following meanings: "To attest or confirm by adding one's own signature; to affix one's name to a document etc; to affix one's signature to; to write or inscribe one's name as a signature"'.[120]

'Signature' was defined as follows in the same dictionary:

> 'The name or special mark of a person written with his or her own hand as an authentication of some document or writing; the action of signing one's name or of authenticating a document by doing so.'

(Here the requirement of an "own hand" would tend to militate against electronic signatures.)

In *Webster's Dictionary* the following definitions were found.

> 'Sign — to affix a signature to; to subscribe in one's own handwriting.'
>
> 'Signature — the name of any person written with his own hand on a document.'

The liberal approach won through yet again in the case of *Ex Parte Singh*,[121] where Vermooten J looked in greater detail at the treatment of the word 'sign' in the *Trollip* case:

> 'The requirement is that the testator and witnesses shall "sign", not write, their names. What is the original meaning of the term "sign"? It is a "mark", from the Latin *signum*. To sign one's name, as distinguished from writing one's name in full, is to make such a mark as will represent the name of the person

117 (1985)12 SC 243.

118 Act 7 of 1953.

119 1977 (4) SA 44 (SWA).

120 *The Concise Oxford Dictionary*.

121 1981 (1) SA 793 (W).

> signing the document. For that purpose it is no more necessary to write one's surname in full than it is to write one's Christian names in full.'[122]

(To 'make such a mark as will represent the name of the person signing' would seem to draw closer to the idea of a digital signature again, except for the fact that a physical mark is not made, but some electronic changes are wrought. Also, the legislator probably had in mind just a physical mark by illiterates.)

Vermooten J also looked at the case of *Jhajbay v Master & another*,[123] where the court adopted an even more liberal criterion for 'signature', focussing entirely on the intention of the person signing:

> 'In my view, in the Wills Act 7 of 1953, "sign" includes the accustomed mode of signature of a witness, as well as any other mode adopted by him (not being a mark) to write or sign his name. It may or may not be his full name. The intention of the witness in writing or signing is the criterion. If he intends his mode of writing or signing his name to represent his signature, it is effective as such.'[124]

(This subjective test for the 'intention of the witness' is most encouraging step towards the legal acceptance of digital signatures, where the person encrypting by means of his public or private key obviously intends affixing an 'electronic signature' in the sense that he identifies the document with himself.)

Vermooten J thus overruled the *Dempers* case and found that merely initialling the will complied with the requirements of a signature in terms of the Wills Act 7 of 1953, provided that the person signing intended it to be his signature. This view is also supported by Sonnekus.[125]

This would seem to be the state of play at the moment as far as the South African courts are concerned. Even though there are some promising leads towards accepting a digital signature as sufficient (if it works for wills it should also be acceptable for other documents such as contracts and certifications) the matter is not settled at all. If judges concentrate on the intention of the signatory all should be well. If, on the other hand, they require a physical mark or sign, everything goes back to the drawing board (and the legislature) as far as the acceptability of digital signatures are concerned.

In South Africa, some noises are being made by, for instance, the Department of Communications and the Department of Trade and Industry, to start talks which might pave the way for legislation in the light of overseas developments. It may be a good thing for the South African private sector also to get involved. In this

122 Supra 796.

123 1971 (2) SA 370 (D).

124 Supra 372.

125 J C Sonnekus 'Dempers and others v The Master and others' (1978) 2 *Tydskrif vir Suid-Afrikaanse Reg* 175.

regard the foundation of ECASA[126] has to be welcomed, and it is to be hoped that they will be able to form a pressure group of the nature of the Illinois Commission on Electronic Commerce and Crime (mentioned in the section on the United States above).

One of the urgent matters which ECASA will have to concider is the question of certification authorities (those entities that guarantee the authenticity of the public keys published for purposes of e-commerce.) In Belgium, a draft Act (according to European Union guidelines) has been circulated, which gives one an idea of the niceties which have to be dealt with. The draft defines 'digital signature' as follows:

> *'digitale handtekening: het resultaat van de omzetting van een digitale gegevensverzameling met behulp van een private sleutel, derwijze dat de identiteit van de titularis van de private sleutel en de integriteit van de digitale gegevens nagegaan kunnen worden met behulp van een overeenkomstige publieke sleutel vergezeld van het certificaat van een certificatie-autoriteit;'*[127]

and defines 'certificate' as follows:

> *'certificaat: een bevestiging, verzekerd door de digitale handtekening van een certificatie- autoriteit, van een of meer informatiegegevens die door haar zijn vastgesteld, onder meer van het verband tussen een natuurlijke persoon, een privaat- of publiekrechtelijke rechtspersoon, een overheidsbestuur of een feitelijke vereniging en de publieke sleutel ervan.'*[128]

and 'certification authority' as follows:

> *'certificatie-autoriteit: een natuurlijke persoon of een rechtspersoon die de certificaten opmaakt, aflevert en beheert.'*[129]

According to s 4 of the draft Act, the Belgian Government decides on the conditions according to which a certification authority will obtain its authority, what guarantees it will have to supply, what the minimum conditions of liability would be, etc. An interesting condition (4k) relates to the minimum standards of secrecy and integrity which the certification authority will have to comply with. Section 9 provides that the certification authority would have to keep an electronic registry

---

126 Acronym for the Electronic Commerce Association of South Africa.

127 Translated as: 'the result of the conversion of a digital collection of data with the aid of a private key, in such a way that the identity of the title-holder to the private key and the integrity of the digital data may be checked with the help of a corresponding public key accompanied by the certificate of a certification authority.'

128 Translated as: 'a confirmation, guaranteed by the digital signature of a certification authority, of certain information established by that authority, among other things of the relationship between a natural person, a private or public law legal person, a governmental authority or an association and the public key thereof.'

129 Translated as: 'a natural or legal person which makes up the certificates, delivers and controls them.'

which is accessible to all electronically, but is also not susceptible to change by outside parties (sounds like quite a challenge to hackers!). Section 14 provides for the revocation of certificates and determines that such revocation should immediately be entered into the registry. Section 17 provides that a certificate delivered by an overseas certification authority would be given the same force as the certificate from a local certification authority, provided that the overseas certificate comes from a European Union member country, or from a country which has signed the '*Verdrag voor Europese Economische Ruimte*'. Section 19 deals with the possible liability of a certification authority.

The topic of digital signatures is also thoroughly explored by Julien Hofman.[130] He distinguishes between a true digital signature and an 'electronic signature', the latter being simply an electronical bitmap picture which can be transmitted as a whole.[131] He also (correctly) distinguishes a digital signature as 'a process not a mark'.

Readers who are interested in the deeper technical aspects of digital signatures would find Hofman's work well worth reading. From a legal perspective, even more interesting is his explanation of the Public Key Infrastructure (PKI),[132] which structure contains some deep- reaching legal implications. Since e-commerce also has to work on a global level the PKI should be acceptable internationally.

Some mention has been made in the Belgian concept legislation, treated above, of 'Certification Authorities' (CA's) which have to authenticate the public keys which authenticate, in turn, the signature of the user of the public key. These CA's might be some of the big players in the computer business, such as Netscape, Microsoft or IBM. It might also be a dedicated cerfication agency such as Verisign, of which the South African Certification Agency (SACA) is the local agent, or a smaller local outfit such as Thawte, in Cape Town. Some banks act as their own certification authority, which leads to sceptical messages from your browser complaining about an 'unknown certificate'.

Hoffmann distinguishes between very hierarchical CA's, for instance those making use of the International Telecommunication Union's X509 standard, and more astructural 'flatter' systems, for instance the PGP[133]-standard. Both standards

130 Julian Hofman *Cyberlaw* (Ampersand Press 1999) 69ff.

131 In other words, it is not reducible to individual characters, as would happen as a result of the optical character recognition (OCR) process. Even though an electronic signature might look convincing it has none of guarantees of reliability and authenticity that are built into a digital signature. A typical example is the 'signature' at the bottom of a fax document which might easily be scanned in from a separate piece of paper.

132 From 71ff.

133 An acronym denoting 'Pretty Good Privacy'.

have problems with revoking certificates which have expired for some reason. Uniquely X509 has no on-line system for doing this[134] and relies on published lists. X509 also necessitates a lot of administration and huge databases having to be maintained. On the other hand, PGP simply links to an e-mail address and its 'trust' model might also have limitations because different people define 'trust' differently. Thus the fact that B trusts C might not be sufficient warrant for A to trust C, even though she trusts B.[135]

Further problems which still have to be resolved with the PKI is the question of anonymity as well as the considerable legal liability which CA's might be saddled with.

Until we have new legislation in place, South Africa will continue to rely on the common law, existing statutes and case law to provide a framework for e-commerce. None of these has envisaged anything like e-commerce or signing electronic documents that are never reduced to hard copy. Even the South African Computer Evidence Act, 57 of 1983, is geared towards making print-outs from computers acceptable as documentary evidence, obviously not meeting e-commerce needs with regard to 'virtual' documents. Nevertheless, an encouraging trend has emerged in our case-law when interpreting the concept of 'signature'. If the more liberal interpretation of making the intention of the signatory predominant gains favour, there might be a case for treating electronic signatures as being an intended "signature" for purposes of relevant statutes and common law. It would remain a calculated risk, however.

6.5.7 Conclusion

It sems clear that the common law (South Africa follows English, not Roman-Dutch, common-law in the field of evidence) is no longer able to cope with the challenges of the computer age. One of the few examples of South African computer-law legislation, namely the Computer Evidence Act, has also proved to be less than satisfactory and therefore leaves the field open for systematized reformation. Unfortunately, it also seems that the South African Law Commission has its hands so full at the present moment that this is unlikely to happen very soon. One of the other commission activities, namely the creation of a first statute on computer crime, could impact on this need indirectly, since the police will obviously need to be able to prove their case against computer criminals.

---

134 It had been conceived before the Internet made ubiquitous telecommunication possible.

135 Hofman op cit 72.

The whole question of e-commerce, which has been mooted a few times so far in this book, relies on the necessary legal and regulatory infrastructure and it seems clear that South Africa is still a long way away from the latter. The one advantage that we do have, however, is an ability to look at developments in other countries and to try to avoid making the same mistakes.[136] The very international nature upon which e-commerce is grounded led to intractable jurisdictional and international private law issues, and some of these are explored in the next chapter.

136 As the early American saying has it: 'The pioneers are the guys with the arrows in their backs!'

CHAPTER SEVEN

Some Mercantile-Law Issues; Issues of Internationality; Legal Informatics

The Internationality of computer law has posed challenges to which the legal system has responded with varied success.

SOME MERCANTILE-LAW ISSUES; ISSUES OF INTERNATIONALITY; LEGAL INFORMATICS

At the beginning of the present work the reader was promised coverage of a subject that was omitted from the previous edition, namely legal informatics (or the way in which computers can be useful to the legal world). This does not justify an entire chapter, however, and the topic has been tagged onto the back of the present chapter, which deals first with one or two mercantile-law issues relating to computers and/or the Internet followed by a discussion of the issues arising from internationality. By the latter is meant problems of jurisdiction, choice of law, international private and public law and all other fields of law (for instance, civil and criminal procedure) which try to cope with the international nature of the Internet and the e-commerce it has spawned.

7.1 SOME MERCANTILE LAW ISSUES

7.1.1 Introduction

Mercantile law ('Handelsreg') has established its own niche in the academic world, fully separated from its mother, private law. Making use of the principles from especially the law of contract, mercantile law has become a sort of 'applied' private law. It focuses specifically on areas such as company law, the law of negotiable instruments, competition law, insurance law, labour law, insolvency law and the law of intellectual property. The last-mentioned branch has undergone convulsive upheavals as a result of the computer and thus justified a separate chapter in the present work. Other areas where the computer is starting to play a significant role are aspects of company law (especially trading shares on the Stock Exchange) and competition law. These disciplines therefore also receive some attention in the present work, together with a more general new phenomenon, namely e-commerce. Even though 'e-commerce' involves other areas such as the law of evidence and the law of contract, its heart is with mercantile law and therefore it should resort under the present chapter. Also in this chapter will be found the new 'Dematerialization of Share Certificates' project as well as new legislation on insider trading. For reasons of convenience, competition law is treated in chapter 3 on Trade Secrets (also an aspect of mercantile law).

7.1.2 E-commerce

The term 'e-commerce' has rapidly become a buzzword and should be explained right at the outset.[1] Most readers should be familiar with the concept of the

1 Although some people speak of a wider concept of 'e-business' which would include electronic commerce.

Internet, the so-called 'network of networks'. The Internet spans the globe, connected by all kinds of communications technology: from satellite (expensive but fast), through cellular and microwave transmission and even by means of plain old copper telephone cabling (inexpensive but slow). E-commerce roughly boils down to selling things 'electronically' by means of the Internet. Since there are no paper-based contracts and transactions are carried out electronically, this phenomenon has obvious implications for the law of contract and the law of evidence, to mention but two. A related phenomenon, which has been kicking around for a number of years, is 'Electronic Data Interchange' (EDI). This describes the electronic interchange of commercial trade documents (such as invoices and bills of lading), which speeds up the process of (especially international) trade.[2] E-commerce may be distinguished from EDI by the fact that the latter is usually between two known partners who have previously agreed to do business in this way by means of a so-called 'EDI agreement'. By contrast, e-commerce is carried on with the whole wide world as customer, necessitating a high degree of up-front security. It is hoped that this will be accomplished by forms of encryption (such as the 'digital signature', which is more fully discussed in the chapter 6 Evidence). More than mere encryption is needed, however. Unless the whole legal and regulatory infrastructure is changed or modified to accommodate this new way of doing business, it will always remain a bit of a legal gamble. Businessmen will simply not know what legal effect courts will render their contracts and other e-commerce dealings.

E-commerce is a reality in South Africa and the law can no longer afford to ignore it. M-Web, the Internet service and content provider, offers its services as an Internet service provider in a so-called 'Big Black Box'.[3]

Internet trading in South Africa is conservatively projected to be worth more than R30 billion per year by the year 2000. Internationally, Internet-based commerce (including EDI transactions placed over the Internet) could reach $3,2 billion by the year 2003. This would represent nearly 5% of global sales.[4]

One of the success stories overseas has been the electronic bookstore at www.amazon.com. Because these booksellers do not physically have to keep their

2 See in this regard the article on EDI by Sieg Eiselen in (1992) *THRHR* 204. *THRHR* is the abbreviation for *Tydskrif vir Hedendaagse Romeins-Hollandse Reg* (*Journal of Contemporary Roman-Dutch Law*).

3 This simply contains a modem and the necessary software to make connection with the Internet possible. The firm has recently also started offering for sale the 'Big Business Box', which it advertises with the slogan 'Shop from your desktop 24 hours per day!'. Although the accompanying blurb reassures potential customers that they need have no worries concerning technological or security aspects, the firm is remarkably reticent concerning the legal infrastructure for its advertised e-commerce. Here I believe that legal certainty is as important as technological security to make e-commerce successful in South Africa.

4 'The Switch to E-Commerce' *Financial Mail* 15th January 1999.

books for sale on the shelf, they are able to provide a much greater range. Their success has spurred traditional booksellers such as Bertelsmann also to enter the electronic market.[5] Other products which seem to sell well on the electronic market are computer software and hardware as well as music and video products.

Most of the legal issues underlying e-commerce relate to the question of contracting on-line, which has been dealt with in chapter 4 on Private Law, and the question of authenticating transactions, which has been dealt with in chapter 6 Evidence. The non-legal field of security, including encryption, is also of the greatest importance. Although it is dealt with in passing in chapter 6 Evidence, readers should consult specialized (and up-to-date) books on the subject.[6]

In the United Kingdom the Department of Trade and Industry has recently published a consultation paper to act as a guide in the process of transformation to an information economy. Called 'Building Confidence in Electronic Commerce', it states the government is not planning to increase wiretapping powers or to make use of 'key escrow'. The latter is a scheme by which government agencies, armed with a search warrant, would have 'trapdoor' access to scrambled private communications. A related scheme, known in the United States as the "Clipper Chip' program, has met such determined opposition there that the Clinton Administration has not yet been able to force it through. Under the United Kingdom plan, the police will be given the power to access private encryption 'keys' with a warrant. (What will be done about a conveniently 'lost' private key, or 'forgotten' passwords, one is not so sure.) It is reported that the government was holding talks with the country's largest computer companies to help find workable alternatives to key escrow.[7]

The United Nations Commission on International Trade Law (UNCITRAL) has released a 'Model Law an Electronic Commerce'[8] which provides guidance on aspects such as digital signatures and the Public Key Infrastructure (PK1).[9] The fact that e-commerce needs to work internationally makes an initiative by the United Nations very valuable.

Mention has already been made of a similar initiative from certain government departments, including Justice and Trade and Industry, to help set up the necessary regulatory infrastructure for e-commerce in South Africa. This is echoed by a similar initiative from the private sector, where an organization called ECASA[10] has been

5 Although bibliophiles might wonder if a picture on a computer screen can ever match the tactile pleasures of leafing through a new book.

6 See for instance Julian Hofman's *Cyberlaw* (Ampersand Press 1999) 66ff.

7 'To hold in escrow' means to keep safely, as a trusted intermediary, on behalf of someone else until some condition has been met.

8 UN Doc A/51/17 (1996).

9 See digital signatures in chapter 6 on Evidence above.

10 Electronic Commerce Association of South Africa.

formed with roughly the same goals. At the time of writing, these two initiatives have not yet been harmonized, nor hax a joint meeting of the two organizations been held.

7.1.3 The dematerialisation of share certificates

In what has become known as the STRATE project,[11] a battery of new legislation will introduce a new system of share trading in South Africa during the course of 1999. At a *Current Commercial Law Workshop*[12] one session was devoted to this topic. Chaired by the Legal Advisor of the Johannesburg Stock Exchange (JSE), Nicky Newton King, Maria Vermaas of the University of South Africa (Unisa) explained that the new developments would kick in by means of the insertion of a new s 91A into the Companies Act,[13] a new Custody and Administration of Securities Act and a new Uncertificated Shares Act.

Vermaas explained that the present system was cumbersome, where a Transfer Secretary has to deal with thousands of share certificates. The new system would work electronically by means of a Central Securities Depository (CSD). During question time the matter of 'tainted script' was raised in connection with the authentication problems which any system of electronic trading brings with it. Apparently there has been a great rush to get the JSE rules finalized and the matter of authentication has been skirted around. When the security aspects have been finally sorted out, a Directive in this regard will be issued.

The outside (computer-literate) observer cannot help but be uneasy that a matter which has been considered so central to successful e-commerce, namely a good marriage between security and law, has been assumed as a given in a major undertaking such as the present. An electronic stock exchange would seem to be the ideal target for hackers for the same reason that Jesse James robbed banks: 'That's where the money is!'

During the recent demutualization of South African mutual insurance giant SANLAM,[14] the new STRATE system was touted as one of the advantages of shareholding in the company, because of the ease and speed with which shares can be traded. Unfortunately many shareholders sold immediately and, with the new systems not yet in place, considerable delays occurred. (Probably in a roundabout way an advertisement for the new system, in the end!) An allegation has also been made[15]

---

11 Acronym for 'Share Transactions Totally Electronic'.

12 Organized by Juta and the Centre for Business Law, University of South Africa, and held at Midrand on 11 March 1999. It has now been published in (1999) 11 *SA Mercantile Law Journal* 119ff.

13 Act 61 of 1973.

14 South African National Life Assurance Company ('Maatskappy' in Afrikaans.)

15 'South Africa's banks are at it again.' The 'David Gleason column' in *The Weekly Mail and Guardian,* 18 to 24 June 1999.

that South African banks are deliberately frustrating the STRATE process. The report states that the extent of 'tainted scrip' as a result of present maladministration (which will be revealed) might prove to be an embarassing moment for the banks. (Another possibility might be fears that the computers can also lose some scrip!)

7.1.4 Insider trading

This subject also deserves a mention in the present work because it is an excellent example of how that protean concept, information,[16] still requires piecemeal treatment for the lack of a principled stance. The increasing need is indicated by a new specialized Insider Trading Act.[17] At the same *Current Commercial Law Workshop* mentioned above, S Luiz (also of Unisa) spoke on this topic.[18] The Act criminally prohibits three types of conduct, namely:

(*a*) for any individual who knows that he or she has insider information to deal, directly or indirectly, for his own account or for any other person, in securities or financial instruments to which such information relates or which are likely to be affected by it;[19]

(*b*) for any individual who knows that he or she has inside information to encourage or to discourage another to deal in securities or financial instruments to which the information relates or which are likely to be affected by it;[20]

(*c*) for any individual who knows that he or she has inside information to disclose that information to another person.[21]

There are a number of defences to these offences and a number of definitions. 'Insider information', for instance, must be specific or precise information, must not have been made public, must have been obtained or learned[22] as an insider and has to be information which if made public, would be likely to have a material effect on the price or value of any securities or financial instruments.[23]

The Financial Services Board (FSB) has also been given a piece of the action. Besides reserving the common law rights to civil action by persons affected by such insider trading, the new Act also gives a derivative civil action which may

---

16 Or in this case, advance knowledge.

17 Act 135 of 1998.

18 S Luiz 'The Insider Trading Act 135 of 1998'. Now published in (1999) 11 *SA Mercantile Law Journal* 136ff.

19 Section 2(1)(*a*).

20 Section 2(1)(*b*).

21 Section 2(2).

22 To me, bringing this information within a particular person's range of information makes it 'knowledge' according to the *Concise Oxford Dictionary's* definition.

23 Section 1(vii).

be instituted by the FSB.[24] If successful, the defendant may be ordered to pay an amount not exceeding three times the profit made or loss avoided together with any commissions or considerations received in that respect. These amounts will be kept in trust by the FSB, and after charges have been deducted, the balance must be distributed to claimants according to statutory prescription.[25]

Another interesting development is the power given to the FSB to regulate insider trading. In this respect an Insider Trading Directorate had been established as a committee of the FSB. The reader will recall that in chapter 1 above it was decided to abide by the *Concise Oxford Dictionary* definition of information as '(desired) items of knowledge'.The value of information (once it has become knowledge) as an asset is well illustrated, to my mind, by the fact that the value of one type of information[26] has to be dealt with in a statute utilizing criminal law, private law and administrative law.

7.2 INTERNATIONALITY

7.2.1 Criminal jurisdiction

In criminal cases not as much thought seems to have been given to the deeper complexities of jurisdiction as has happened in civil cases. Hiemstra's *Suid-Afrikaanse Strafproses*[27] simply distinguishes between substantive jurisdiction as to crime (for instance, ordinary magistrates' courts cannot try murder), jurisdiction as to punishment (for instance, ordinary magistrates' courts cannot impose life imprisonment) and territorial jurisdiction. This discussion centres on territorial jurisdiction, since this is where the problems which arise with implementation in cases of Internet and computer law usually resort. Section 110 of the South African Criminal Procedure Act[28] deals with submission to jurisdiction, which makes it unnecessary to consider any other grounds:

'110. Accused brought before court which has no jurisdiction

(1) Where an accused does not plead that the court has no jurisdiction and it at any stage—

(*a*) after the accused has pleaded a plea of guilty or of not guilty; or

(*b*) where the accused has pleader any other plea and the court has determined such plea against the accused, appears that the court in question

24 Section 6(1).

25 Section 6(7).

26 Inside information or, more accurately, 'inside knowledge' in this instance.

27 V G Hiemstra *Suid-Afrikaanse Strafproses* 5 ed by Johann Kriegler (Butterworths 1993) 277ff.

28 Act 51 of 1977.

> does not have jurisdiction, the court shall for the purposes of this Act be deemed to have jurisdiction in respect of the offence in question.'

According to Hiemstra's commentary on the South African Criminal Procedure Act, the normal principle obtaining in territorial jurisdiction is that a crime is justiciable only by courts of the country where the crime has been committed.[29] However, there are certain Acts where South Africa has legislated for extra-territorial jurisdiction. Some of these are Acts extending jurisdiction to criminal acts in South African territorial waters or airspace. Examples of such Acts are the Act on Mercantile Shipping,[30] the Act on Territorial Waters[31] and the Aviation Act.[32] The Protection of Information Act[33] provides that a South African citizen or someone domiciled in the Republic who commits one of the proscribed acts outside the Republic may also be held liable. The South African Police Services Act,[34] which is one of the more information-wise South African Acts, also provides for extra-territorial jurisdiction in s 71(5):

> '5) Any act or event for which proof is required for a conviction of an offence in terms of this section which was committed or took place outside the Republic shall be deemed to have been committed or have taken place in the Republic: provided that—
>
> (*a*) the accused was in the Republic at the time he or she performed the act or any part thereof by means of which he or she gained or attempted to gain unauthorised access to the computer, caused the computer to perform a function or modified or attempted to modify its contents;
>
> (*b*) the computer, by means of or with regard to which the offence was committed, was in the Republic at the time the accused performed the act or any part thereof by means of which he or she gained or attempted to gain unauthorised access to it, caused it to perform a function or modified or attempted to modify its contents; or
>
> (*c*) the accused was a South African citizen at the time of the commission of the offence.'

Therefore if either the operator or his computer was in the Republic (or he himself was a South African citizen) it would not matter that parts of the computer-initiated chain of events took part outside the country. This is a far-sighted way of legis-

29 Citing the Roman-Dutch law writer Voet 5.1.67.

30 Act 57 of 1951.

31 Act 87 of 1963.

32 Act 74 of 1962.

33 Act 84 of 1982.

34 Act 68 of 1995.

lating which keeps in mind that even the sending of an e-mail message to the girl next door may entail 'packets' of information going via a detour to the United States!

A more general provision, and one which could also prove handy for dealing with Internet situations, is the common-law rule[35] that if any necessary element of a crime started outside the Republic is committed within the Republic, the state will have jurisdiction. The prime example is the firing of a shot outside the border which then hits someone within. This happened in the British case of *R v Coombes*[36] and the result was accepted as correct in *R v Holm*.[37] The facts in *Holm* seem analogous to the Internet situation. The accused had been a propagandist for the Nazis, broadcasting to South Africa from Germany. Even though the broadcasts originated in Berlin, it had its effect in South Africa and the court held that it had territorial jurisdiction. The same argument could obviously be applied to the Internet — the only problem could be to get hold of the criminal 'broadcaster' if his or her servers are situated in a country which is not very concerned to comply with international norms.

The question of extradition depends on specific treaties (whether bilateral or multilateral) between the country where the crime has had its effect and the crime where the alleged perpetrator resides. At the time of writing the courts in the United Kingdom are dealing with the thorny question whether the ex-dictator, Pinochet, should be extradited to Chile. The case is controversial because one of the judges involved at a previous juncture, Lord Hoffmann, is a life member of one of the organizations demanding extradition, namely Amnesty International.

7.2.2 Civil jurisdiction

(1) Introduction

According to *LAWSA*:[38]

> 'The scope of the conflict of laws, whose purpose is to assist the forum in deciding a case which contains a foreign element, is reflected in three areas: (1) the jurisdiction of the forum in the sense of its competence to hear and determine a case; (2) the selection of the appropriate rules of a system of law (the forum's or foreign substantive law) which it should apply to resolve the dispute over which it has jurisdiction and the extent to which the chosen *lex causae* should be applied; and (3) the recognition and enforcement of judgments rendered by foreign courts or awards of foreign arbitrations.'

In the following discussion we will deal first with the selection of the legal system applicable to resolve the dispute (point (2) above.) This is the area of international

---

35 Voet 5.1.67.

36 1 Leach 38.

37 *R v Holm, R v Pienaar* 1948 (1) SA 925 (A) at 929.

38 W A Joubert (ed) *The Law of South Africa* vol 2, 'Conflict of Laws' (Butterworths first re-issue, 1993) §§ 461, 464–9.

private law or conflict of laws (in the narrower sense) which is a complicated subject and really deserves a book by itself. The legal system which governs a contract is of course a matter which may be negotiated for and many hardware and software contracts provide that the law of a federal state in the United States will apply. (This could actually be in favour of an unwitting contractor since the American laws are usually more protective of the consumer than South African law!). Most of the rest of this section deals with jurisdiction in the sense of competence, including attachments to found, or confirm, jurisdiction, which means dealing with point (1) in the *LAWSA* quotation above. At the end of the section a few words will be said concerning the enforcement of foreign judgments— point (3) above.

(2) Conflict of laws

In his work *International Transactions and the International Law Merchant*,[39] Hercules Booysen traces the relationship between conflict of laws and the *lex mercatoria* and distinguishes between them as follows:

> 'The conflict of laws aims to solve conflicts resulting from the existence of different legal systems and jurisdictions. This is done by referring the legal relationship between individuals from different legal systems to the national legal system with which it has the closest contacts as the governing law. The purpose of the international *lex mercatoria* is not to solve a conflict between different national legal systems aiming at governing a particular legal relationship, but rather to avoid such conflict by providing substantive legal rules, capable of governing that relationship directly.'

Thus, instead of trying to pick one of two possible domestic systems, why not concede that as far as international commerce is concerned, we need a new substantive *international* set of rules! This seems to be a very promising idea, especially in the sense that totally new rules might be better equipped to deal with the world of e-commerce than trying to put new wine in old skins, in the words of the Bible. One of the problems might be practically to give effect to these principles, especially when an urgent court order (an interdict or an Anton Piller order, for example) is applied for. Will the local enforcement mechanisms give effect to something as abstract as the *lex mercatoria*?

In an address to the *Current Commercial Law Workshop* already mentioned above, Coenraad Visser specifically singled out conflict-of-laws problems on the Internet, which is the ideal breeding place for this kind of mischief.[40] He mentioned the example of a book on the life of former President Mitterand of France which

39 Hercules Booysen *International Transactions and the International Law Merchant* (Interlegal 1995) 13. See also Hofman *Cyberlaw* 148ff.

40 'Choice of Law in Internet Copyright Dispute'. Now published in (1999) 11 *SA Mercantile Law Journal* 268ff under the title of 'Choice of Law in Internet Copyright Disputes'.

was held in France to infringe post-mortem copyright.[41] Although the physical book was then taken off the shelves, a copy had been scanned and appeared on the Web site of a French Internet firm in Besançon. Hardly had the copyright owners started to take action than the information also appeared on Web sites in the United States and Canada. These countries might have a different view to France as to the role which the personality rights play in copyright. Which legal system should apply?

Visser then discusses these problems in the light of three International Copyright Conventions, the TRIPS[42] agreement, the Berne Convention[43] and the WIPO[44] conference at the end of 1996. In his opinion, the TRIPS agreement is a bit of a "cop-out" since it merely makes the Berne Convention applicable with one or two additions. WIPO brings Berne into the Internet world and determines, for instance, that one needs the author's permission to put his writings onto the Internet.

In order to solve the tricky choice-of-law issues in the French example above, one first has to see whether the particular copyrighted work can be brought within the purview (points of attachment) of the Berne Convention. According to Article 3 of that convention, this may depend on nationality (which includes habitual residency)[45] or time and place of first or simultaneous (which includes within 30 days)[46] publication.

The courts will therefore often have to determine where 'publication' had taken place. According to the Berne Convention, this consists of making available copies of the work (whatever their means of manufacture) in such a way as to satisfy the reasonable demands of the public. This raises the question whether the ephemeral copy made in the RAM[47] of a computer, and which is necessary merely to receive or view the work, would constitute a 'copy' in terms of the Berne Convention. Visser quotes some authority pro[48] and contra[49] this view,

41 In many European countries the right to personality is very much part of copyright.

42 Acronym for Trade Related Intellectual Property issues.

43 South Africa and most of our trading partners are members of the Berne Convention, an international agreement whose signatoris undertake to honour the copyright in published works.

44 Acronym World Intellectual Property Organization.

45 Article 3(2) of the Berne Convention.

46 Article 3(4) of the Berne Convention.

47 Random Access Memory, explained in chapter 1.

48 Mihály Fiscor 'Copyright for the Digital Era: The WIPO Internet Treaties' (1997) 21 *Columbia-Villanova Journal of Law and the Arts* 197 at 203ff.

49 D P van der Merwe 'Copyright and Computers, with Special Reference to the Internet: "From Penmanship to Peepshow"' (1998) 115 *SALJ* 180 at 182–3; and Thomas C Vinje 'The New WIPO Copyright Treaty: A Happy Result in Geneva' (1997) 5 *EIPR* 230 at 233–4.

but adds that since the copy may be stored, whether on magnetic medium or by printing it out, this puts the matter of publication beyond any doubt.[50] Assuming that making a work available through the Internet does amount to publication, Visser then asks some questions germane to conflict of laws. Where a work is disseminated by means of the Internet, where is it published? If it is to be the country from which the work is uploaded onto a Web site, Visser sees two disadvantages:[51]

> 'First, that country may only have a tenuous connection to the work, as the author may post the work from anywhere in the world (including from countries through which the author is merely travelling).[52] Secondly, the work is not available to the public until it arrives at the website to which members of the public will have access.'

He also rejects the possibility of the country where the Web site host server is located because this location might perhaps be unknown to the author and mentions the further possibility of the country where the Internet user has downloaded the work. (The latter would make as important a concept as 'publication' dependent upon the whims of users and take it completely out of the hands of the author, surely an unacceptable result.)

Publication is also relevant to determine the 'country of origin' which is relevant to the choice of laws issues in art 5 of the Berne Convention, as well as being relevant to the term of protection. Article 5(1) gives authors of works protected under the convention, the same protection in countries other than countries of origin as the former countries' nationals would have enjoyed, as well as the minimum convention rights. (In other words, the South African author enjoys the same rights in France as a French author would have enjoyed.). In contrast to this 'foreign' protection, another subsection deals with 'domestic' protection. Article 5(3) provides namely that protection in the country of origin is to be governed by domestic law. Because of the 'simultaneous publication' provisions of art 3 (referred to above), it may be argued that publication takes place in each Berne Union member state with access to the Internet, that each such work will therefore be a domestic work in each such country

---

50 Visser op cit 271. He refers to Jane C Ginsburg *Private International Law Aspects of the Protection of Works and Objects of Related Rights Transmitted through Digital Networks* (report presented at the meeting of the Group of Consultants on the Private International Law Aspects of the Protection of Works and Objects of Related Rights Transmitted through Global Digital Networks, convened by WIPO in Geneva 16–18 December 1998) GCPIC/2 at 27–8.

51 Op cit 272.

52 This possibility is enhanced by the presence of Internet access points at most international airports now.

and enjoy mere domestic protection, without the Convention rights awarded to 'foreigners'.

As far as the term of protection is concerned, the term of protection is determined by the domestic law of the country where protection is claimed.[53] However, it also provides for a 'shorter term', namely, if the term in the country of origin is shorter than that of the country of protection, the shorter term shall apply. Article 5(4) of the Convention states that where there are multiple countries of origin, the real one shall be the one whose term is shortest. With the simultaneous publication of matter on the Internet, the country of origin will the one with the shortest term, which comes down to the fact that all the Internet-linked countries will enjoy (or suffer) the term of only the shortest of them!

(The above would seem to indicate that the nature of the Internet has not been anticipated by the legislature when using terms such 'domestic', 'country of origin' and 'simultaneous publication'.)

Visser then proceeds to analyse the choice of law as far as initial ownership and transfer of copyright is concerned. He finds the Continental approach to be that initial ownership is determined by the country in which protection is claimed. This is deduced from the phrase 'the extent of protection shall be governed exclusively by the laws of the country where protection is claimed.'[54] Visser criticizes this viewpoint for three reasons:

> 'First, it leaves the question of the initial ownership of copyright open until protection is claimed. Only then will one be able to determine according to which national system the initial ownership of copyright should be decided. Secondly, if protection is claimed in different countries, different national systems will apply, which may mean that different answers may be given to the question as to the initial ownership in a work of copyright in a work of authorship. Thirdly, the possible initial legal vacuum may entail legal uncertainty, as prospective licensees, for example, will not be able to determine from whom they should acquire the relevant exploitation rights.'[55]

He prefers the law of the country of origin to determine ownership and quotes the case of *Tass Russian News Agency v Russian Kurier Inc*[56] in this regard. However, the national law of the country in which a work of authorship is due to be exploited could 'disrupt' the normal conflict-of-laws rules in this regard.

Copyright may, of course be assigned or licensed to another.[57] According to

53 Article 7(8) of the Berne Convention.

54 Article 5(2) of the Berne Convention.

55 Op cit 274.

56 1998 WL 544189 (2d Cir 1998).

57 According to Visser, a copyright licence is basically an undertaking by the author not to sue the licensee for infringement.

Forsyth's *Private International Law*[58] and *LAWSA*,[59] an express choice of law between contracting parties will be upheld even when it excludes mandatory rules of the otherwise applicable legal system. Although more rare, even a tacit choice of law might be made. With regard to the Internet, Visser argues that when an author puts her work on the Internet, he or she by implication licences the ephemeral copies required for browsing. If this act of browsing is seen as completing the contract, then the law of the forum where that happens, the *lex loci solutionis*, would govern the implied license. For lack of any agreement, tacit or express, on the governing legal system, the courts might apply the legal system which has the 'closest and most real connection',[60] — in other words, the proper law of the contract. According to Visser, the *lex loci contractus* will apply unless the contract has to be performed (complied with) elsewhere, when the *lex loci solutionis* will apply.

As far as infringement is concerned (here the criminal law also comes into play) one could use art 5(2) of the Berne Convention which speaks of the extent of protection and the means of redress and required that these 'shall be governed exclusively by the laws of the country where protection is claimed'. I agree with Visser that this clause was meant to govern jurisdiction and also that 'the laws of the country' does not mean its rules with regard to conflict of laws too. If this were the case the claim might be shuttled to and fro depending on these often unknown and unexpected provisions. Furthermore, the phrase '*where* protection is claimed', has been interpreted by most commentators on the convention as reading '*for which* protection is claimed'.[61] However, this could lead to a multiplicity of claims, since Internet infringement especially can take place in many countries at the same time. Visser suggests the following alternatives if one has to confine jurisdiction to a single system. First, the law of the country where the copyright infringement originated, or secondly the American "root copy" approach which any further reproduction, any place in the world, of an initial unauthorized reproduction made in the United States could be tried by American law. Visser himself prefers the test of the law of the place where the harm was felt.

If one extends jurisdiction to multiple alternative systems, the following tests for choice of law could apply. The defendant's place of business might be first prize and where the defendant's use was for commercial purposes, the legal systems of all the countries of receipt of the infringing software might also be applicable. If the defendant's use had been non-commercial this would extend to the

58 C F Forsyth 3 ed (Juta 1996) 278–82.

59 W A Joubert (ed) 'Conflict of laws' *The Law of South Africa* vol 2, (Butterworths, first reissue 1993) *Private International Law* 413.

60 As applied in *Bonython v Commonwealth of Australia* [1951] AC 201 at 219.

61 The fact that these subtle distinctions are made in French in the original may make the interpretation more believable!

laws of countries where the harm to plaintiff's interest had been substantial. Another test could be the law of the country where the server hosting the alleged infringing content is located as first prize, whereas alternative systems might be the law of the country where the website operator has his residence or principal place of business or otherwise simply the law of the forum.

The preceding discussion has been based solely on copyright law where a great amount of international co-operation and harmonization of law has taken place. With other systems of law, such as e-commerce, some development has taken place but it is nowhere near as advanced yet. Perhaps some lessons might be learnt from the parallel development of copyright, particularly as far as the Internet is concerned. Hofman[62] states that a South African court would be guided in choice of law situations by the following factors:

- protection of acquired rights
- predictability and uniformily of results or legal consequences.
- convenience, simplicity, ease in the determination, and application of the law to be applied.

He also mentions that South African courts will not follow the chauvinistic tendency of United States courts to apply their own law.

(3) Jurisdiction

The question of civil jurisdiction is almost pure common law in the sense that the field of civil procedure has never been legislated as comprehensively as happened with the 'criminal procedure code'.[63]

Hofman[64] mentions that the United States courts are more aggressive in assuring jurisdiction in an international dispute and that South Africans doing business on the Internet have to keep this in mind. He adds that the United States courts would consider the following factors to determine whether they have jurisdiction:

'(1) Is there a close connection between the events that occurred and our jurisdiction?

(2) Is it fair to hear the case here?

(3) Will hearing the case w affirm the goals of fairness, judicial administration, and international country'?[65]

62 Op cit 149ff.

63 The Criminal Procedure Act, 51 of 1977 is often referred to as the 'criminal procedure code' because an attempt has been made to deal with the matter comprehensively.

64 Op cit 149.

65 Ibid, citing some American case-law.

(In the present writer's opinion these 'tests', especially the second one, are very subjective and not likely to give a court firm guidance.)

Even though his book deals mainly with international private law, Forsyth[66] has written a section on jurisdiction. He defines it as 'the power vested in the Court by law to adjudicate upon, determine and dispose of a matter'. Roman-Dutch law always tries to find a link between dispute and territory and these are called the 'jurisdictional connecting factors', also known as the *rationes jurisdictiones*. Examples of these factors are domicile, residence, commission of a delict, creation of a contract, breach of contract, submission and the situation of property. It is easy to see that the Internet could make possible trans-continental delicts and international contracts in each of which the courts will be faced with the question of jurisdiction.

The author does not believe that effectiveness is the only principle behind the rule of jurisdiction since that would be 'to confuse the sequel of a competent judgment (attachment to levy execution) with a prerequisite for its competence' — which would be to switch around cause and effect from their normal order. The author explains further that there are two possible basis for jurisdiction. The first is effectiveness, but this was not the pre-eminent principle in Roman law. The Romans distinguished between actions *in rem*, where the matter turned on a claim related to an object, and actions *in personam*, where the matter turned on a personal claim which one had against another. With the first type of action the *forum rei sitae*[67] would determine which court has jurisdiction and with the latter the *forum domicilii rei*.[68]

With the addition of a 'mixed' action, this was also the position in Roman-Dutch law and, according to Forsyth, also in South African practice, until recently at least. Pollak in his *The South African Law of Jurisdiction*[69] preferred to place the basis of jurisdiction in effectiveness, because he felt that jurisdiction had more to do with the possibility of the relief being granted than with the nature of the action: 'courts could only render an effective judgment if the relief claimed could be effectively granted.'[70] The courts have recently found a *via media* between these two viewpoints, as was explained in the Appellate Division case of *Hugo v Wessels*.[71] In his (Afrikaans) judgment, Hoexter JA explained that the question of jurisdiction entails two enquiries. The first is to check whether one of the

66 Op cit 149ff.

67 Literally 'the court of the site of the matter', or where the object in dispute was situated.

68 Literally 'the court of the domicile of the matter'.

69 W Pollak *The South African Law of Jurisdiction* 1 ed (Hortor's 1937). Cited by Forsyth in this regard.

70 Forsyth op cit 123.

71 1987 (3) SA 837 (A).

grounds of jurisdiction is present (*rationes jurisdictiones)* and, if so, then to check whether the courts' jurisdiction would be effective.

The doctrine of attachment does not come from the Roman law, but was imported into the Roman-Dutch law by a reception of Germanic custom in the Netherlands. [72] Before starting we should perhaps explain the distinction between an *incola*[73] and a *peregrinus*[74] as defined in *Civil Practice of the Supreme Court of South Africa.*[75] The *incola* is only 'inhabitant' of the area of jurisdiction of a specific High Court and not of the whole Republic: 'It follows, for example, that a person domiciled or resident in the area of jurisdiction of the Cape Provincial Division is a *peregrinus* in the area of the Transvaal Provincial Division.'[76]

The normal Roman law position had been that an *incola* plaintiff would have had to follow a *peregrinus* to the latter's jurisdiction in line with the maxim *actor sequitur forum rei.*[77] According to the doctrine of attachment, the *incola* was now permitted to sue in his local forum after attachment of either the person or the goods of the *peregrinus*. This Roman-Dutch position has been inherited by present South African law.

According to Herbstein et al[78] one should distinguish between claims sounding in money, claims which involve property and matrimonial actions. With regard to territorial jurisdiction for claims sounding in money, the following rules apply:

(1) Where the plaintiff is an *incola* and the defendant a *peregrinus* for that jurisdiction (and not an *incola* of any other part of the Republic), the court will exercise jurisdiction on the following grounds, First:

'(*aa*) That the cause of action arose within the court's area of jurisdiction and either the person of the defendant has been arrested or part of his property has been attached to confirm the jurisdiction (*ad confirmandam jurisdictionem)*.'[79]

The authors explain that the cause of action might arise out of contract (*ratione contractus*) which was either entered into or was to be performed (either wholly

72 Forsyth op cit 172.

73 Literally 'an inhabitant'. A person domiciled in a particular country or resident in the same, provided that his residence is of some permanent or settled nature.

74 A person who is neither domiciled nor resident in the required sense in the country in question.

75 Herbstein and Van Winsen *Civil Practice of the Supreme Court of South Africa (now the High Courts and the Supreme Court of Appeal)* 4 ed by the late Louis de Villiers van Winsen, Andries Charl Cillier & Cheryl Loots. Edited by Mervyn Dendy (Juta 1997).

76 Herbstein et al 58. The authors apologize in the preface for still making use of the term 'Provincial Division', which has now been changed to 'High Courts'.

77 'The actor (claimant) has to follow the forum of the matter.'

78 Op cit at 56ff.

79 Literally, 'towards confirmation of jurisdiction'. The passage is quoted fiom Herbstein et al op cit 61.

or partly) within the court's area of jurisdiction. If one applies this to electronic commerce it seems clear that most such transactions would fall within this reasonably wide idea of cause of action. (Now the *peregrinus* contractant just has to move his body to within the court's jurisdiction so that he can be arrested in order to confirm jurisdiction!). The cause of action might also arise out of delict (*ratione delicti commissi*) committed within the area. Here one could think of a libellous statement originating from an overseas server which hurts the receiver locally. (Again we need either the person or his property within the jurisdiction so that the arrest or attachment to confirm jurisdiction may take place.)

Secondly:

> '(*bb*) That, in the absence of any recognized *ratio jurisdictionis*,[80] the defendant's person has been arrested or his property attached in order to found jurisdiction (*ad fundandam jurisdictionem*).'[81]

For Herbstein et al it is important to distinguish between the two types of attachment, given legislation on this point. Attachment to found jurisdiction can only be at the instance of a plaintiff who is also an *incola,* whereas attachment to confirm jurisdiction may only be done at the request of a *peregrinus* of that court's area. The authors speculate on the basis of the attachment concept and although effectiveness of the court's order is obviously one of the justifications, some other authors have suggested other bases for the phenomenon, for instance 'fairness to litigants'.[82]

(2) In the case of a company, whether domestic or foreign, the concept of 'residence', could be tricky. A 'domestic corporation' includes all bodies directly or indirectly incorporated in the Republic and would therefore be the equivalent of a 'resident'.[83] A provincial or local division would have jurisdiction with regard to a domestic corporation in any of the following instances:[84]

> '(*aa*) the corporation has its principal place of business — sc the place where its general administration is centred — within the court's area of jurisdiction. In this connection the fact that the cause of action arose outside the court's area of jurisdiction is irrelevant.
>
> (*bb*) The corporation has its registered office within the court's area of jurisdiction.

80 Literally 'reason (ground) for jurisdiction'; ibid.

81 'Towards founding jurisdiction.'

82 eg Pollak *The South African Law of Jurisdiction* 52.

83 Deduced from the definition of 'external company' in 51(1) of the companies Act, 61 of 1973.

84 Herbstein et al 69–70.

(*cc*) The cause of action in respect of which the corporation is being sued arose within the court's area of jurisdiction.'

With regard to e-commerce, however, the South African customer is more likely to be dealing with a foreign company. Herbstein et al refer to a 'foreign corporation' as one which has been incorporated outside the Republic.[85] If the foreign corporation has its principal place of business within the jurisdictional area of the court, that court will have jurisdiction, without attachment and without the cause of action having arisen within the jurisdictional area. If the principal place of business is outside of the Republic but the respondent 'carries on business' within the Republic, the court will have jurisdiction if the cause of action arose within the jurisdictional area. Since the corporation is 'resident' within the meaning of s 28(1) of the Supreme Court Act,[86] at the place where it carries on business, attachment will be unnecessary.

This gives cause for concern, since any business carrying on e-commerce worldwide would be 'doing business' in many countries, but not in the physical sense that the legislature obviously had in mind in 1959.

Whereas the aforegoing all dealt with a claim sounding in money, claims with regard to other property[87] have also caused consternation. A second heading in Herbstein et al deals with 'claims relating to property'.[88] We shall leave out immovable property for purposes of the present discussion, since that is not likely to turn up in an e-commerce situation. With regard to movable property, Herbstein et al cite Voet[89] and Pollak[90] to show that there is uncertainty as to whether two courts (local and international) could each have jurisdiction, even though the property could obviously only be in one place at a given moment. Pollak argues that a court may have jurisdiction if the property is outside the court but inside the Republic, provided that the defendant is an *incola* of the area of the court. On the other hand, it has been held that courts do not have jurisdiction to order *incolae* defendants to deliver movable property situated outside the Republic.[91]

From this it should not be too difficult to deduce that in the e-commerce situation, where the defendant is not an *incola* and does not have any property in the Republic (trading virtually, via the Internet) the court is unlikely to have jurisdiction with regard to general property matters. In certain matters relating

85 Ibid.

86 Act 59 of 1959.

87 A side-issue is the problem that property has always been required to be tangible. Will music or a program downloaded over the Internet qualify?

88 Herbstein et al op cit 70.

89 5.1.77.

90 Op cit 102.

91 *Lenders & Co Ltd v Lourenco Marques Wharf Co Ltd* 1904 TH 176; *Minister of Agriculture v Grobler* 1918 TPD 483; *Makoti v Brodie & others* 1988 (2) SA 569 (B).

to trading in money an attachment might convey jurisdiction, but is very unlikely to occur in practice when the defendant is probably sitting pretty with his servers in some Internet 'tax shelter'.

For some real-life, Internet-related situations, the readers is referred to an article by Stuart Dutson entitled (rather long-windedly) 'The Internet, the Conflict of Laws, international litigation and intellectual property: the implications of the international scope of the Internet on intellectual property infringements'.[92] Otherwise than in Africa, where economic groupings are not yet supported by legal instruments, the United Kingdom is now part of the European grouping and subject to the 1968 Brussels and 1989 Lugano Conventions. These were made applicable to England by means of the Civil Jurisdiction and Judgments Act 1982.[93] Nevertheless, Dutson asks the question which one is also left asking after reading the South African section on jurisdiction above:

> 'If a person with no presence in the United Kingdom uses the Internet to infringe English IP rights what remedies can the injured party seek?'[94]

By using the example of China, where factors contribute to the fact that foreign copyright holders do not receive the same protection as in the United Kingdom, Dutson gloomily concludes that an infringer resident in China 'can infringe English IP rights and disseminate information on the Internet with impunity'. He suggests that one may still be able to use some of the United States 'long-arm' statutes indirectly to get at perpetrators.

(4) The enforcement of foreign judgments

Again Forsyth,[95] with his clear and lucid style, manages to make sense of the topic of recognition and enforcement of foreign judgments. He calls it 'a difficult and uncertain area' which has been complicated by the fact that 'the legislature has, with characteristic clumsiness, been attempting to swat flies in this area'.[96] Forsyth does not think that too much time should be spent on the question of why foreign judgments are recognized of enforced, since the principles are exactly the same as for applying foreign law generally:

> 'Indeed the application of foreign law is the application of a general abstract norm of the foreign system, while the enforcement of a judgment is simply the application of an individual concrete norm (*lex specialis*) of that system. Why should there be different rationales for the two processes?'[97]

92 November 1997 JBL 495ff.

93 As amended in 1991 to incorporate the Lugano Convention.

94 Op cit 509.

95 Op cit 361ff.

96 At 360.

97 Op cit 362.

The process will take place provided four conditions have been fulfilled, namely:

1. that the foreign court had international jurisdiction,
2. that the judgment was final and conclusive and had not yet lapsed,
3. that the judgment was not against public policy and that the judgment would not imply the enforcement of foreign penal and revenue law.
4. that it does not fall foul of 51 of the Protection of Business Act, 99 of 1978.[98]

The author warns against long arguments as to hypothetical jurisdiction in foreign countries in determining what 'international jurisdiction' (in the condition 1 above) really means. According to him, it is a 'term of art' which has a special meaning applicable only in this small area of law; therefore looking at its meaning in other branches of law would not be useful.[99]

In a rare example of local authority on this point, an article by P S G Leon entitled '*Roma non locuta est*: the recognition and enforcement of foreign judgments in South Africa',[100] the author poses a typical international tort and contract example. He then asks whether a judgment in this regard, properly obtained, would be enforcable in South Africa. (I leave it to the reader to apply the many scenarios of e-commerce which will end in the same question.) Unfortunately this simple question has no simple answer:

> 'One might in all innocence assume that the answer to the questions posed above and thus the criteria for recognizing and enforcing foreign judgments in South Africa could be stated without difficulty. Unfortunately for litigants this is not the case. A dearth of authority, conceptual confusion and the paralysing hand of the parliamentary draughtsman have transformed the apparently simple into the seemingly intricate.'[101]

Leon then finds four criteria for the recognition and enforcement of a foreign judgment in South Africa.[102] These are:

1. a foreign court had international competence in the matter;
2. the judgment was final and conclusive;
3. the recognition and enforcement of the judgment would not be contrary to the public policy of the *lex fori*;

98 Forsythe op cit 364.

99 Ibid.

100 In (1983) XVI *CILSA* 325ff. I presume that the Latin phrase in the title means something like 'Rome has no fixed place' in the sense that the jurisdiction of the worldwide Roman Empire was not locally confined.

101 Ibid.

102 Op cit 326.

4. the Minister of Industries, Commerce and Tourism has given his consent in terms of the Protection of Businesses Act 1978.

The first topic has already been discussed above. The second mainly turns on the question whether a right to appeal would render a judgment 'not final'. According to Leon, it appears to be settled law that the possibility, or even the actual existence, of an appeal would not destroy the finality of the judgment, especially in the light of the case of *Rosenstrauch v Korb*.[103] According to Ellison Kahn, cited in an article by Hahlo entitled 'The finality of Foreign Default Judgments',[104] a default judgment would not be considered "final" because of the possibility of rescission of that judgment.

The third topic, that of public policy, is illustrated by the case of *Lissack v Duarte*.[105] Here the court held that if the foreign court did not inform the defendant of correct procedure before giving default judgment against him was a serious breach of the rules of natural justice.

The fourth topic is the biggest bugbear. Section 1(1) of the Protection of Business Act[106] is a sweeping provision which prevents any enforcement of foreign judgments in the Republic of South Africa without the permission of the Minister of Industries, Commerce and Tourism, if it is connected with 'an act or transaction', if it:

> 'is connected with the mining, the production, importation, refinement, possession, use or sale of or ownership to any matter or material, of whatever nature, whether within, outside, into or from the Republic'.

The excuse for the grant of such draconian powers is apparently to combat the 'extra territorial reach and jurisdictional assertiveness of United States anti-trust law', but Leon sees the legislation as 'legislative overkill'.[107] He sums up this whole topic as follows:

> 'The criteria for recognizing and enforcing foreign judgments in South Africa cannot be stated with confidence. Insufficient cases and consequently insufficient experience amongst the bar and the bench, coupled with the petrifying effect of an ill-conceived statute, do not augur well for this branch of private international law.'[108]

Hofman[109] opines that 'South African courts will never assume judgement when they are not satisfied that their judgement can be enforced'. They will also not,

103 1939 GWL 103.
104 (1969) 86 *SALJ* 354.
105 1974 (4) SA 560 (N).
106 Act 99 of 1978.
107 Op cit 347.
108 Op cit 348.
109 Hofman *Cyberlaw* 151.

under any circumstances, enforce a foreign criminal or fiscal award. Hofman suggests that one should also investigate whether an enforcement agreement exists with a particular country.

7.2.3 Anton Piller orders[110]

These orders also deal with attachment and originated from the English decision of *Anton Piller KG v Manufacturing Processes Ltd and others.*[111] Consisting of a type of 'search warrant' applied for *ex parte* and usually *in camera,* it is often used in computer-related cases where the electronically stored evidence might 'disappear' at the slightest hint of trouble. Thus, instead of founding jurisdiction as with the previous sections, this order actually founds the proof of a case.

After a *bellum juridicum*[112] the Appellate Division[113] now seems to have settled that this type of order DOES have a place in the South African legal system and can be used to preserve fragile evidence (as would typically be the case with computer-based evidence). Herbstein et al point out, however, that the Anton Piller order might run into trouble with the privacy provisions of the South African Constitution, which is obviously in conflict with the drastic procedures of the former. The test case would have to decide whether the curtailment of the right to privacy is justified in the light of some greater good.

7.2.4 International public law and the *lex mercatoria*

According to *LAWSA,*[114] international law is the law governing relationships between states *inter se,*[115] and between states and international bodies. As such it is a mechanism which should be able to assist with the tremendous internationality of computer law and Internet law.

The sources of International law are as follows according to *LAWSA*[116] and as listed in art 38 of the Statute of the International Court of Justice,[117] namely:

'(a) treaties;

(b) international custom;

---

110 See in this regard especially Herbstein et al 1091ff for one of the rare complete treatments of this controversial subject.

111 [1976] 1 All ER 779 (CA).

112 Literally a 'legal war', where different courts take up mutually destructive points of view.

113 In the cases of *Shoba v Officer Commanding, Temporary Police Camp, Wagendrift Dam & another; Maphanga v Officer Commanding, SA Police Murder & Robbery Unit, Pietermaritzburg, & others* 1995 (4) SA 1 (A).

114 W A Joubert (ed) International Law *The Law of South Africa* vol 11, (Butterworths first reissue 1998) § 345.

115 'Between themselves.'

116 Op cit § 346.

117 According to P M Mtshaulana, J Dugard & N J Botha *Documents on International Law,* signed and ratified by South Africa in 1945 (Juta 1995).

(c) general principles of law; and

(d) judicial decisions and the teachings of the 'most highly qualified publicists' of the various nations making up the international community.'

To these traditional sources, one must add decisions of international organizations. As has become clear from many of the discussions in the aforegoing chapters, treaties (especially multilateral) seem to be the way to handle the international nature of computer-law problems. See, for instance, the Brussels and Lugano Conventions mentioned under the previous heading.

An even more promising development is the so-called *lex mercatoria*, which has been defined as 'the body of law governing the activities of the international merchant'.[118] With this work the author has presented the world (and South Africa) with a possible solution to many problems which domestic legal systems are unable to handle, even by means of private international law (conflict of laws) or public international law (law of nations). He prefers this (rediscovered) field of law to be known as the *lex mercatoria* rather than as 'international trade law' or 'transnational law', even though the latter two have been used by others.. Booysen feels that international trade law deals with activities between states, whereas the *lex mercatoria* deals with the activities of the international merchant as an individual.

From the fact that the international *lex mercatoria*[119] and arbitration awards based on it have been accepted by national courts, the author argues that the existence of the *lex mercatoria* has been accepted.[120]

He distinguishes between the *lex mercatoria* and conflict of laws as follows:

> 'The international *lex mercatoria* concerns itself with the law which governs an international legal relationship, ie, a legal relationship between persons from two different legal systems. The conflict of laws also aims at providing a solution to the question of which law should govern the legal relationship between individuals from two different legal orders. Of the two branches of the law, the international *lex mercatoria* is the older.'[121]

Although Booysen's distinction, as stated, seems clear and acceptable, it has been pointed out above that conflict of laws is more than just choice of law. It includes, such matters as jurisdiction and the enforcement of foreign legal judgments. Nevertheless the *lex mercatoria* might make these kind of international problems less critical, since jurisdiction might could become superfluous in an arbitration

---

118 Booysen *International Transactions and the International Law Merchant* 3.

119 This field is a child of the old *ius gentium,* where the *praetor peregrinus* had to make use of broad principles and practicality to develop a flexible legal system that would deal with citizens who were not Roman.

120 Op cit 9.

121 Booysen op cit 13.

body[122] targeting a world market. The enforcement of foreign judgments, on the other hand, might increase as a result of international arbitration awards which have to be carried out in a specific country (as would usually be the case.).

Even though the two fields he mentioned may seem to be 'competing', Booysen points out that they can easily co-exist and really need each other. The international *lex mercatoria* might be lacking in certain areas and then needs the rules of the conflict of law in order to resolve the matter efficiently.

As regards the 'law of nations' (public international law), the author shows that its treaties and agreements have actually created the framework within which the *lex mercatoria* functions. He finds that a reciprocal influence exists between these two fields.

On the one hand Booysen welcomes the close relationship between the *lex mercatoria* and arbitration tribunals. The latter possess a greater freedom than state courts in developing new law, they can have regard to international custom, something the national courts cannot do. To these factors might be added that the parties in arbitration would be able to select arbitrators (often with scarce skills such as the combination of computer and legal expertise). On the other hand, arbitration is not that well suited for developing such a new field of law. The awards are not published (or not in sufficient detail) and there is no precedent system, so that prior awards do not necessarily bear much weight. There is not much cohesion between different awards and arbitrators often do not give reasons for their decisions.[123]

7.2.5 Conclusion

The internationality of computer law has posed challenges to which the legal system has responded with varied success.

On the one hand one despairs at the clinging to hide-bound tradition with its emphasis on area-bound concepts such as 'domicile' and 'residence' which seems to make accommodation of computer law (especially the Internet) extremely unlikely. On the other hand, we have had prescient legislation, such as the Police Services Act, which understands the internationality of the interaction between man and computer. To this may be added the dusting off and refurbishing of an old but good concept such as the *lex mercatoria*, which bears the potential of solving many of the problems associated with e-commerce. It is being argued that international arbitration might be the only way to cope with

---

122 Alternative dispute resolution (ADR) is being mooted as the most competent forum to deal with all the (international) problem that the Y2K problem is likely to give rise to — see (1999) 3 *Computerrecht* 28.

123 Booysen op cit 366.

the spate of (international) litigation which is likely to follow the ravages created by the millennium bug (the Y2K problem).

It is actually ironic that the legal system developed for the 'outside world' in Roman days, the *ius gentium*, could possibly solve many of today's Worldwide Web problems too!

7.3 LEGAL INFORMATICS

7.3.1 Introduction

Computers are much more than pesky machines creating almost insoluble legal problems. They are increasingly improving the quality and the quantity of the work of law students, legal academics and legal practitioners. As mentioned in the first edition of the present work:

> 'The use of computers by lawyers, or '*Rechtsinformatica*' merits a work by itself and is of growing importance — even in South Africa some tentative steps have been taken to explore this field.'[124]

And in a footnote to the above section, the following reference is given:

> 'Theoretically by the master's thesis of A D J van Rensburg (RAU 1980) entitled *Regsinligting*, and practically by JUTALEX, a legal information service available on BELTEL.'[125]

Both Van Rensburg's thesis and Jutalex relate to computer databases which could be used by lawyers. This information retrieval function of the computer will be explored below, but we shall also have a look at litigation support, demonstrative evidence, expert systems, document drafting, billing and scheduling software as well as at e-mail. Finally, as an academic at a distance-teaching institution, I should like to see how the computer could be used to teach law students at a distance.

7.3.2 Legal information retrieval

It is with a sentimental feeling of 'things gone by' that one reads of Jutalex,[126] which was the 'hot news' at the time of writing the previous edition of the present work. Since then, Juta has shifted platforms from the initial Prestel videotext system to 'Ghostwriter' (a South African word-processing system which gave access to the legal database via an application called 'GhostAccess'), and then again to Folio VIEWS storage and retrieval software, used for publishing both on CD-ROM and on the Internet. Quite early on the firm entered into a joint

124 At vii.

125 Ibid.

126 The original Jutalex service, offered on BELTEL and now discontinued, should not be confused with the current Jutalex Provincial Legislation Service published by Jutastat in Folio VIEWS on CD-Rom and the Internet.

venture with a software developer called 'Compustat' and the service is now provided by 'Jutastat'.[127]

In the 1993 issue of 'THRHR'[128] I wrote a review of the 'Jutastat CD-ROM Database on Statutes and Law Reports'. The headings were 'What is CD-ROM?', 'How does Jutastat work?' and 'Does one really need it?'. It may seem laughable at the present time of DVD[129] disks that I had to spend some time describing 'the small silver discs'. A more perennial issue also addressed in the article turned on the battle between online databases and databases stored on CD-ROM:

> 'Abroad many legal databases were originally made available "on-line"; in other words, one could dial into a remote computer database using the telephone network, a dedicated line or even microwave and "download" relevant data from the distant database into one's own computer. Because of the practice adopted by many of these data-providers to charge users for time spent on the system, users were often overcome by the sweaty palms" syndrome and often had to pay even for relatively unsuccessful searches. Some of these information providers (eg JURIS in Germany) have recently started to provide sections of their database on CD-ROM, which the user can order by mail, for once and for all, and then spend as much time as he likes browsing through the database and following leads at his leisure. The South African publisher Juta flirted for a while with the concept of providing legal information on-line, by means of its Jutalex service. This illustrated the main advantage of "on-line" over CD-ROM, namely that updates made at the central node are immediately available to all users connected to it. On-line data-bases are therefore usually more up to date than are those on CD-ROM, whereas Juta's current practice is to send out an updated CD-ROM disc every three months. With data which are reasonably stable, such as law reports and statutes, this does not seem to be too much of a handicap, however, with the paper-based equivalents not being updated any faster. After a survey among its users, Juta decided to drop the Jutalex service, and rather concentrate on Jutastat, its service on CD-ROM.'[130]

My own experience up to that time had mostly been with online databases — Jutalex running on the BELTEL system and an in-house database that I had prepared on the University of South Africa's mainframe computer. The latter has been more fully described (for overseas consumption) in a chapter entitled 'A database on sentencing' in *Public Administration and Decision-Aiding Software*.[131] In

127 Now a wholly-owned subsidiary of Juta & Co, Ltd.

128 (1993) 56 *THRHR* 531ff.

129 'Digital video disks', which at the moment are read only, but when they become rewritable will probably spell the end of the videotape recorder.

130 (1993) *THRHR* 531 at 531.

131 Stuart Nagel (ed) *Public Administration and Decision-Aiding Software* (Greenwood Press 1990) 111ff.

that contribution I distinguished between full-text systems where information is retrieved by Boolean searches and a less automated system where human indexing at the hand of a conceptual thesaurus is involved. The latter method was used at Unisa and although a very useful thesaurus was constructed, the system proved to be too labour-intensive to keep going. In the beginning a modem and a dedicated telephone line were used for the up- and downloading of information 'although the vagaries of the latter combination have made the permanent availability of CD-ROM very tempting'.

In a reply to my Jutastat review, Simon Sephton (then general manager of Jutastat) made a strong case for the whole world going over from online to CD-ROM:

> 'Your mention of JURIS lower down on the first page sparks an observation rather than a criticism. I believe that JURIS in fact issue all their databases on CD now and use the online system primarily as an updating system. Other traditional online publishers, like West in the USA, also have combined CD/Online services, often with the CD component designed to protect their existing online investment rather than superseding the online service. Others, though, such as Context in the United Kingdom, have completely shut down their online service in favour of the CD service (for their CELEX EEC database), and I recently heard a rumour that Kluwer intend doing the same, though this is not substantiated.'

Then, along came something which none of us had foreseen: the Internet! It is possible automatically to change the existing electronic format of documents to HTML[132] so as to make them available on the Internet. Since HTML is mostly a display language, however, the creators of really large databases have used specialized storing and retrieval software, such as Folio VIEWS (used by Jutastat and Butterworths in South Africa) and OCLC (used by Sabinet and VanZylRudd). This means that all the South African Law Reports, Statutes and *Government Gazettes* are now available electronically on the Internet, still leaving the difficult choice between CD-ROM and online (in its most recent guise of the Internet). Overseas, American legal publishers such as Lexis/Nexis and Westlaw also have their product available on the Internet, although at a price! Fear of copyright infringement still keeps certain legal information providers off the Internet, as does a fear that it might eat into their hard-copy (paper) sales. On the other hand, such inertia could prove fatal, as more and more users are demanding the right to search regularly updated databases electronically.

An objective overview of the situation by a South African advocate may be found in *Consultus*,[133] in an article entitled 'The Bar on the Internet'. It describes

---

132 Acronym for 'Hypertext markup language.'

133 The journal of the advocates' profession in South Africa; November 1996 at 142ff. The article was written by advocate Leon Bekker.

how the idea developed of a legal 'hub' at WorldNet Africa. The latter has since become M-Net, one of South Africa's biggest Internet Service Providers. In its 'Experts' section a colleague and I attempt to solve legal problems under the heading of 'Cyberlawyer'. The idea of the hub is probably best represented by another Internet start-up, called 'Legal City'.[134] Bekker foresees that the Bar could use the Internet as a window on the world to propagate its services and even to render some of these via the Internet.

7.3.3 Litigation support and electronic libraries

Litigation Support Systems (LSS) are also mainly constituted by a type of database, but dedicated to, and constructed for, one specific court case. In the useful work *Advanced Information Systems for Lawyers*[135] the authors deal with the benefits of LSS. One of the authors, V Mital, is a practising lawyer and shows great insight into the practicalities of LSS. For instance, not all cases need LSS but only those which exceed a certain size:

> 'If a case involves a few hundred documents and a stable litigation team which has overseen the growth of the case file, then there may be little of relevance in the documents that the lawyers will not be able to recall. If they cannot recall it, their notes will tell them where exactly to look. Most cases are like this. Many are not.'[136]

Some examples are then quoted where the proportions of the litigation may assume gigantic proportions, for instance in the case of mergers and conglomerations where whole systems of documentation from the different arms of the constituting companies might have to be made available. Another example would be in copyright actions where the entire recorded histories of designs and developments have to be kept track of. The authors cite a study of large law firms which indicate that one of three lawyers that have become involved with computers, have done so because of the value of computers in LSS.

Even though full-text retrieval systems can yield quite good results, these will probably improve when combined with thesauri and lexicons (as explained under the previous headings). The authors also show how a degree of artificial intelligence added to the search methods can increase the power of the system. In the five or six years since *Advanced Information Systems for Lawyers* was published, some even more sophisticated systems have appeared.

Some of the latter systems specialize, not in searching purpose-built systems, but in roaming the Internet ('surfing' seems to have become the accepted term)

134 http://www.legalcity.co.za. The M-Net address is http://www.mweb.co.za/forum.

135 V Mital & L Johnson *Advanced Information Systems for Lawyers* (Chapman and Hall 1992) 167ff.

136 Op cit 170.

in search of relevant information. Because the Internet has such short lead times and everyone can be his own publisher, some gold nuggets are to be found on the Internet before even the daily press gets hold of the news.[137] Although these Internet 'robots' can hardly be termed LSS, they may turn up some information which could be relevant in litigation, depending on how well they are programmed. Some of them have been tasked, for example, with finding out when and where pirated software is being used.

Even without such sophisticated programs, the Internet forms the world's biggest library, for practitioners, academics and students alike. Quite a number of books have been published as guides to legal sites on the Internet. Examples are, for instance, the New Zealand work *Legal Resources on the Internet*[138] and *How to Use the Internet for Legal Research*.[139] Otherwise one simply enters one of the 'portal' sites such as Yahoo! or M-Web (a local site) and click on the search engine, which will then search for single words or even accommodate Boolean[140] operators. For attorneys who are too busy to search, new specialized legal sites such as Legal City provide a service called 'Assisted Research' which should shorten search times.[141]

7.3.4 Demonstrative evidence

This is something which has come to the fore in the United States, especially in the case of jury trials. Instead of trying to paint abstract pictures with words it is often better to use a blackboard or whiteboard or even scale models to indicate the exact relationship between objects or concepts relevant in the trial.

The procedure has now escalated and computers are being used to create quite sophisticated reconstructions of accident scenes, for instance.[142] By altering parameters such as speed, or visibility, the court and/or jury can work out the probabilities for themselves. One of the biggest manufacturers of precision drawing and architectural software, Autodesk, is offering a service in which such road accident scenes may be reconstructed. By again altering the parameters, both parties' view of the affair may be accommodated.

---

137 President Clinton's relationship with Monica Lewinsky, for example, was news which broke on the Internet first.

138 The Information Source 1995.

139 Josh Blackman How to Use the Internet for Legal Research (ABA 1996).

140 Named after the mathematician Boole, who introduced such logical operators as AND, OR, BUT NOT, etc which can be used to modify electronic searching, eg: find 'land AND title'; find 'constitution BUT NOT South Africa'.

141 <http://www.legalcity.co.za> — go to ALR in the alphabetic finder.

142 See (June 1999) 8 *Information & Communications Technology Law* at 151, for an article entitled 'On Using Animations in Court' by A Narayanan, G Perry, S Hibben, S K Lochun and W Milne.

In South Africa the Council for Scientific and Industrial Research has devoted a section to this kind of service, acting as expert witnesses when they have examined the crash site. The value of the service may be enhanced if policemen investigating accident scenes could be trained to use equipment which takes exact line-of-sight measurements.

7.3.5 Expert systems

In a lecture entitled *Rekenaars, Die Reg en Tersiêre Onderrig,*[143] the present writer raised the possibility that an expert system could one day act as a sentencing aid in criminal cases. An expert system is a computer program embodying artificial intelligence, which will prompt the sentencing officer to ask all the right questions and to remember all the relevant factors. The reaction from the public (via the press) was overwhelming. Comments were made about computers not being able to observe demeanour, show sympathy etc. I had to publish a letter in the local newspaper explaining that this type of expert system would ask a number of on-screen questions which the sentencing officer himself would have to fill in and that the rule based system of the program would simply make a sentencing suggestion. If this differed radically from what the sentencing officer himself had in mind, he should check whether he has not perhaps left a factor out of the reckoning which the computer has thought of.

During the 1980 such an expert sentencing system by computer was actually constructed by Richard de Mulder at the University of Rotterdam in the Netherlands, but took so many extenuating factors into consideration that the machine rarely gave offenders more than a slap on the wrist. A more sophisticated system has been built by Cyrus Tata of the Centre for Computers and Law at the University of Edinburgh, but it is still struggling to find acceptance among the Scottish sentencing officers.

In the meantime, expert systems are finding application in other fields such as loan applications with banks, medical systems for making diagnoses and even equalizing variables in such diverse processes as calculating exposure for photographs and heating rooms effectively, by making use of 'fuzzy logic'.

Of course, a legal problem[144] could arise if unexpected consequences were to flow from the use of an expert system. It might be problematical to decide which party to cite in this case — the expert whose 'expertise' has been built into the system, the 'knowledge engineer' who reduced the expertise to computer-

143 Translated as: 'Computers, the Law and Tertiary Education' inaugural lecture as Professor of Law in the University of South Africa, 1987.

144 Informatics law instead of legal informatics in this instance.

friendly form, the programmer or producer of the final program, or even the end-user who failed to follow the instructions carefully enough.[145]

These kind of problems have been fully explored in a doctoral thesis by Karin Alheit.[146] The thesis is also a useful read for its treatment of general issues of liability arising from the use of computers.

7.3.6 Document drafting

Mital & Johnson[147] devote an entire chapter to this topic. The authors explain that the simplest application occurs in ordinary word processing programs, where prefabricated templates may be used to create different types of document:

> 'More sophisticated systems allow the creation of templates where users can fill in blanks and select between options; these are useful when relatively similar legal documents are frequently drafted. By using knowledge systems and hypertext techniques the functionality is considerably enhanced.'[148]

This would enable the drafter of, say, a will to use a prefabricated 'backbone' and then to make informed choices at each juncture, before importing the apposite (previously drawn up) clause.

7.3.7 Billing, scheduling and other useful software

Recently a Pretoria firm of attorneys, were featured in an article focusing on the 'electronic law firm'.

> 'The practice operates on a 25 user Novell computer network and runs the latest versions of legal accounting, conveyancing, debt collections, time billing, foreclosures and litigation programs. The firm is also electronically linked with the Deeds Office and has a full-blown telephone management and voice mail system for round-the-clock contact.'[149]

Other examples of productivity-related software is an American system which places an electronic recording device at each photocopier, fax machine, or word processor, if required. The system generates management reports which can be used to interpret usage and cost trends, peaks and valleys, etc, which enables

145 To keep our example believable, perhaps a mother administering an incorrect dosage to the complainant, her child, after making inexpert use of an expert diagnostic system.

146 Karin Alheit 'Issues of Civil Liability Arising from the Use of Expert Systems' (unpublished doctoral thesis, Unisa 1997).

147 Mital & Johnson *Advanced Information Systems for Lawyers*.

148 Op cit 125.

149 Even though this information comes from an in-house blurb for the products featured, it gives an idea of the great range of products available for the modern office.

the attorney to justify to the client every charge for which he or she has been billed. Only with computers is this degree of fine-tuning possible!

7.3.8 E-mail

This has often been described as the 'killer application'[150] which would force many technological hold-backs onto networks or onto the Internet.

It would seem that nobody who has tasted e-mail is likely to revert to snail-mail. The ease with which one can keep up international relations; the asynchronicity — which means that people in the United States are not woken up by your missives but can reply again while you sleep; and the increasing number of people sporting an e-mail address on their business cards, would all seem to indicate that this is a service which no lawyer should be without.

Moreover an entire conference has been held (in 1994) on 'The Effects of Electronic Mail on Law Practice and Law Teaching'.The interesting part about this conference was that it was held entirely by means of e-mail over a variety of communication networks, including the Internet and Compuserve.[151] The proceedings have been published under the same title[152] for people who would like to explore further. For a local perspective, see the review by Nico Ferreira.[153]

E-mail may also have negative implications if not handled carefully (although we do not want to get too deep into the informatics law side in this section). Suffice it to say that lot of damaging evidence against Microsoft has been obtained from the corporation's internal e-mail system in the present anti-monopoly suit being waged against them by the American Department of Justice.

7.3.9 Teaching electronically

As mentioned above, using a computer to teach is something very close to the heart of a professor at a distance teaching institution such as the University of South Africa.[154]

In an essay in the *Festschrift* the present writer argued that new technology such as hypertext and multimedia, as well as the telecommunications revolution,

---

150 This is a reference to the first spreadsheet program, 'Visi-calc', which persuaded many professional people to purchase the Apple personal computer which ran it, and was therefore known as the 'killer application'.

151 Again, in the words of Marshall McLuhan, 'the medium is the message'.

152 I Trotter Hardy (ed) *The Effects of Electronic Mail on Law Practice and Law Teaching* (William S Hein & Co 1994).

153 (1995) 58 *THRHR* 354.

154 I have formulated my thoughts in a *Festschrift* for an esteemed colleague. The essay is called 'Distance teaching of law students in the new South Africa, with specific reference to possible changes at the University of South Africa (Unisa)' in J J Joubert (ed) *Essays in Honour of S A Strauss* (Unisa 1995) 267ff.

necessitated changes in Unisa's teaching methods.[155] As a model, it was suggested that we should 'reverse engineer' a successful practising lawyer to see what skills and qualities would have been useful for her to obtain during her university education. This top-down approach has also been suggested by Roshnie Maharaj.[156]

Another idea which has been brewing in the present writer's mind for a long time and which saw the light for the first time in the above contribution, is the idea that different students have different learning styles. This thought is also not terribly original — it was formulated by the American psychologist, Anthony F Gregorc,[157] who expands upon the different styles as follows:

> 'I found that human beings use two perceptual (spatial) fields for importing and exporting data. These are the concrete (physical) space and abstract (metaphysical) space. I also realised that we order events and facts in a sequential (step by step or branch like) manner and in a random (web-like, multi-tiered, spiral) manner. I further came to realize that individuals report more comfort, challenge and fulfilment when in conditions that provide a particular space and ordering environment.'[158]

In a work which made use of Gregorc's distinctions, Cynthia Tobias[159] translates these into a student's situation. One group of learners whose use of perception in a concrete way was dominant, preferred taking in information by means of their five senses, namely sight, smell, touch, taste and hearing. This group would therefore not be very happy at a distance teaching institution like Unisa, but would prefer a face-to-face situation with a lecturer. They would also prefer doing an oral exam to a written one, would prefer group work to studying alone at home, etc. A second group with abstract perception dominant, had a greater capacity to visualize in the abstract, to conceive abstract ideas and to live according to concepts and precepts which they can never really see, or feel. This group would therefore enjoy the present Unisa context, where most knowledge is conveyed abstractly in printed and mailed study guides, to be used by learners studying individually at home.

Once the knowledge has been assimilated, one might again differentiate between two groups according to the way in which each group orders or systematizes what they have been exposed to. The group which prefers sequential ordering, organizes the information in a linear, step-by-step, logical fashion. (In

---

155 It is an indication of the pace of development that I used inverted commas when using these terms in my article, only four years ago!

156 'The Role of the Law School in Practical Legal Training' (1994) 111 *SALJ* 328ff.

157 Anthony F Gregorc *Styles — Beyond the Basics* (Gabriel Systems 1985).

158 Op cit 27.

159 Cynthia Tobias *The Way They Learn* (Focus on the Family Publishing 1994).

my article I remarked that this seemed to represent our Greek and Roman heritage and the way of thinking upon which most of Western science has been built.) The second group prefers to use random ordering, which means that their minds organize in larger chunks of meaning, and out of sequence, experimenting first with one fit and then with another, without reducing the process by clinically logical elimination. (This randomness is a method more popular outside the mainstreams of European thought, and makes one more sympathetic to claims that most South African universities are too Eurocentric.)

Where do the computers come in? They should make it easier to accommodate the different learning styles, provided that the maxim 'high tech, high touch' is adhered to. A logically connected thesaurus would be an abstract sequential's dream. Browsing randomly by means of hypertext would be an abstract random's dream. Being taken through the program step by step by a human tutor would be ideal for a concrete sequential. The give and take of class debate should be ideal for a concrete random. (This would seem to indicate, by the way, that we cannot simply fire all the teachers and rely entirely upon computers.) All these different ways of communicating need to be harnessed and fielded in a planned way.[160]

7.3.10 Conclusion

I hope this part has filled some readers with enthusiasm for this field and at least whetted the appetite of the rest. It seems clear that in the Internet we have the biggest library in the world and with the computer one of the most powerful research tools ever conceived.

On the academic side it seems clear that we should encourage an appreciation of the computer, as an indispensable part of the Information Age, at primary, secondary and (especially) at tertiary levels of education. Teaching a student how to find answers is surely more useful than forcing him to memorize thousands of facts for short-term regurgitation in the examination.

On the practitioner's side it should have become clear from the headings above what a multi-faceted tool the computer and the Internet can be in practice. The computer can look after the administrative side better than humans can and can aid the court litigant in many ways, as explained above. In a major case the better research ability of a computer and electronic databases should ensure a tactical advantage over even a large legal team using conventional methods.

160 During an overseas visit in 1998 I exposed these ideas to overseas audiences and they were well received. In Chicago I addressed the CALI (computer-aided legal instruction) conference on '*Ex Africa semper aliquid novi* — trying to build the law school of the future in Africa' and in Stockholm I addressed the Subtech '98 conference on 'Pedagogics of the Internet.' Now I just need the time and money to make these projects work!

TABLE OF CASES

SELECT BIBLIOGRAPHY

Richard H Baker *Scuttle the Computer Pirates* (Tab Books 1984)

Josh Blackman *How to Use the Internet for Legal Research* (ABA 1996)

B S Bloom *Taxonomy of Education Objectives: the Classification of Educational Goals* (Longman 1984)

H Brett & L Perry (eds) *The Legal Protection of Computer Software* (ESC Publishers 1981)

Hercules Booysen *International Transactions and the International Law Merchant* (Interlegal 1995)

I Carr & K Williams (eds) *Computers and Law* (Intellect 1994)

W R Cornish *Intellectual Property* (Sweet & Maxwell 1996)

H Cornwall *Data Theft* (Mandarin 1989)

Hugo Cornwall *The Hacker's Handbook* (Century Communications 1985)

P Credo & J-P Michels *Computer Crime in South Africa* (Data Time 1985)

Current and Future Danger 3 ed (Computer Security Institute 1998)

J C de Wet & A H van Wyk *Die Suid-Afrikaanse Kontraktereg en Handelsreg* Volume I *Kontrakreg* 5 ed (Butterworths 1992)

C F Forsyth *International Private Law* 3 ed (Juta 1996)

G Gardiner *Intellectual Property & International Trade – A Guide to the Uruguay Round TRIPS Agreement* (International Chamber of Commerce 1997)

Jane C Ginsburg *Private International, Law Aspects of the Protection of Works and Objects of Related Rights Transmitted through Digital Networks* (GCPIC/2 Report, WIPO Conference, Geneva December 1998)

Werner Gitt *In the Beginning was Information* (CLV Publishers 1997)

Anthony F Gregorc *Styles – Beyond the Basics* (Gabriel Systems 1985)

Alain S Gutterman & Bentley J Anderson *Intellectual Property in Global Markets* (Kluwer 1997)

I Trotter Hardy (ed) *The Effects of Electronic Mail on Law Practice and Law Teaching* (William S Hein & Co 1994)

Herbstein & Van Winsen *Civil Practice of the Supreme Court of South Africa (now the High Courts and the Supreme Court of Appeal)* 4 ed by the late Louis de Villiers van Winsen, Andries Charl Cilliers & Cheryl Loots. Edited by Mervyn Dendy (Juta 1997)

V G Hiemstra & Johann Kriegler (eds) *Hiemstra Suid-Afrikaanse Strafproses* 5 ed (Butterworths 1993)

L H Hoffmann & D T Zeffert *The South African Law of Evidence* 4 ed by D T Zeffert (Butterworths 1988)

Julian Hofman *Cyberlaw* (Ampersand Press 1999)

P Huber *The Geodesic Network: 1987 Report on Competition in the Telephone Industry* (United Sates Department of Justice 1987)

W A Joubert (ed) *The Law of South Africa* vol 2 'Conflict of Laws' (Butterworths, first reissue 1993)

W A Joubert (ed) *The Law of South Africa* vol 11 'International Law' (Butterworths, first reissue 1998)

J J Joubert (ed) *Essays in Honour of S A Strauss* (Unisa 1995)

Ethan M Katsh *Law in a Digital World* (Oxford University Press 1995)

Alistair Kelman & Richard Sizer *The Computer in Court* (Gower 1982)

D G Kleyn & A Boraine *Silberberg and Schoeman's The Law of Property* (Butterworths 1992)

Bill Landreth *Out of the Inner Circle* (Microsoft Press 1985)

L C Lee & J S Davidson *Intellectual Property for the Internet* (Wiley Law Publications 1997)

Legal Resources on the Internet (The Information Source 1996)

Marshall McLuhan *Understanding Media* (Abacus 1964)

R P Merdes, P S Menell, M A Lemley & T M Jorde *Intellectual Property in the New Technological Age* (Aspen Law and Business Publications 1997)

Lance Michalson *South Africa & the Millennium Time Bomb: A Guide to the Legal Issues* (Francolin 1998)

Christopher J Millard *Legal Protection of Computer Programs and Data* (Sweet & Maxwell 1985)

V Mital & L Johnson *Advanced Information Systems for Lawyers* (Chapman and Hall 1992)

P M Mtshaulana, J Dugard & N J Botha *Documents on International Law* (Juta 1995)

Stuart Nagel (ed) *Public Administration and Decision-Aiding Software* (Greenwood Press 1990)

J Neethling, J M Potgieter & P J Visser *Neethling's Law of Personality* (Butterworths 1996)

Brian Niblett *Legal Protection of Computer Programs* (Oyez 1980)

Melville B Nimmer & David Nimmer *Nimmer on Copyright* (Matthew Bender and Co 1994)

D B Parker *Manager's Guide to Computer Security* (Reston Publishing 1981)

Donn B Parker *Computer Security Management* (Reston Publishing 1989)

W Pollak *The South African Law of Jurisdiction* 1 ed (Hortors 1937)

Ithiel de Sola Pool *Technologies of Freedom* (Belknap Press 1983)

Hilary E Pearson *Computer Contracts* (Financial Training 1984)

Chris Reed (ed) *ComputerLaw* 3 ed (Blackstone Press 1996)

Daniel Remer *Legal Care for your Software* (Gower 1984)

Ingeborg Schulze-Heiming *Der Strafrechtliche Schutz der Computerdaten gegen die Angriffsformen der Spionage, Sabotage und des Zeitdiebstahls* (Waxmann 1995)

P J Schwikkard, A St Q Skeens & S E van der Merwe *Principles of Evidence* (Juta 1997)

M D Scott *Computer Law* (Wiley 1984)

Ulrich Sieber *Computerkriminalität und Strafrecht* (Carl Heymanns Verlag 1980)

Ulrich Sieber (ed) *Information Technology Crime – National Legislation and International Initiatives* (Carl Heymanns Verlag 1994)

Alan Smith *Copyright Companion* (Butterworths 1995)

C R Snyman *Strafreg* 3 ed (Butterworths 1992)

James A Sprowl & Peter B Maggs *Computer Applications in the Law* (West 1987)

M Stranex (ed) *Judgements on Copyright* (The Law Publisher 1993)

Colin Tapper *Computer Law* 1 ed (Longmans 1978)

Colin Tapper *Computer Law* 4 ed (Longmans 1989)

The Chaos Computer Club & Jurgen Wieckmann *Das Chaos Computer Buch* (Wunderlich 1988)

The South African Business Guide to Internet Law (Werksmans 1997)

Cynthia Tobias *The Way They Learn* (Focus on the Family Publishing 1994)

Alvin Toffler *The Third Wave* (Pan Books 1980)

Eugen Ulmer *Der Urheberschutz wissenschaftlicher Werke unter besonderer Berücksichtigung der Programme elektronischer Rechenanlagen* (Bayerische Akademie der Wissenschaften 1967)

Guy Vandenberghe *Bescherming van Computer Software* (Kluwer 1984)

C G van der Merwe *Sakereg* 2ed (Butterworths 1989)

H J O van Heerden & J Neethling *Unlawful Competition* (Butterworths 1995)

Coenraad Visser (ed) *The New Law of Trade Marks and Designs* (Juta 1995)

E Yourdon & J Yourdon *Time Bomb 2000* (Prentice-Hall 1998)

JOURNALS

Columbia-Villanova Journal of Law and the Arts

Comparative and International Law Journal of Southern Africa (CILSA)

Computer Law and Practice

Computerrecht

Computers and Law

Computerweek

Computer World
Computing SA
De Jure
Denver University Law Review
De Rebus
European Intellectual Property Review (EIPR)
Harvard Law Review
ITEC Law Alert
Journal of Communication
Journal of Law and Information Science
New Scientist
Obiter
Patent Journal
P C and Office Automation
Rutgers Computer and Technology Law Journal
SA Mercantile Law Journal (SA Merc LJ)
South African Journal of Criminal Law and Criminology
South African Law Journal (SALJ)
Stellenbosch Law Review
The South African Institute of Intellectual Property Law Newsletter
Tydskrif vir Hedendaagse Romeins-Hollandse Reg (THRHR)

INDEX